MYRA HINDLEY

Inside the Mind of a Murderess

Jean Ritchie

ANGUS
& ROBERTSON
PUBLISHERS

Acknowledgements

I would like to thank the following for their invaluable help and assistance, without which this book would not have been possible:

Olive Baldwin, Carole Callaghan, Mike Fielder, Stuart Higgins, Dr Hugo Milne, Dick Saxty, Ian Smith, Ken Tucker, Neil Wallis and many others, ex-prisoners and prison staff, who prefer not to see their names in print.

ANGUS & ROBERTSON PUBLISHERS

16 Golden Square, London W1R 4BN,
United Kingdom

First published in the United Kingdom
by Angus & Robertson (UK) in 1988
Reprinted 1988 (twice), 1990

Copyright © Jean Ritchie 1988

ISBN 0 207 15882 7

Typeset by the Word Factory, Rossendale, Lancashire
Printed in England by Clays Ltd, St Ives plc

Contents

Introduction

Killing children is a particularly hideous crime. But Ian Brady and Myra Hindley are not the first or the last to commit such vicious acts, nor are they the only multiple murderers of children. Yet their crimes have wormed their way into the British consciousness like none before or since, and they have festered there to make Brady and Hindley the most infamous people in the country today.

Before I started work on this book I asked a group of sixteen-year-olds if they had ever heard the names of Dennis Nilsen, Graham Young or Peter Sutcliffe. The answer was no (although they had heard of the Yorkshire Ripper, without having any clear idea what his crimes were). But when asked if they had heard of Ian Brady and Myra Hindley they unanimously said they had, and could even give sketchy details of the crimes. The names, and particularly Myra Hindley's, are as familiar to these youngsters, born six years after the trial, as the name of the Prime Minister or the latest pop group. Hardly a week passes without a news story about one or the other, however trivial, appearing in one of the popular newspapers. In an unguarded moment Myra Hindley's solicitor described his client to me as 'like Royalty – everything about her is news, even what she eats for breakfast'. The analogy is not as preposterous as it sounds if considered purely in terms of press coverage.

Why has this happened? What separates Brady and Hindley from other killers who merit nothing more than a footnote in forensic history books?

The main answer has got to be Myra Hindley's gender. The fact that she is a woman, and women are rarely associated with crimes of violence against children (unless they are their own children) has made the Moors Murders case more than just a gruesome episode in British criminal history. It is an unremitting horror, fed by myths and rumours.

She is unique not only because she committed crimes that defy belief but also because as a result of those crimes she is now Britain's longest-serving woman prisoner (excluding women held in special hospitals). This year she celebrates a midpoint in her life: twenty-three years of freedom followed by twenty-three years of captivity.

This book attempts to put her life into clearer perspective by looking at how she lived before she met Ian Brady, the influence he held her under, and the astonishing way in which she has adapted to life inside prison.

Amazingly, there has been a whole range of apologists for Myra Hindley over the years of her imprisonment, ranging from public figures like Lord Longford and John Trevelyan through to a coterie of lesbian ex-prisoners; in this book I explore the fascination she holds for these people.

When I started work on *Myra Hindley* I, like most people in Britain, was unclear about the details of the Moors Murders case. But I knew that, with the renewed search of the moors and the fresh information that was coming to light, we were getting closer to the truth of the case than ever before, and it was important in view of that (and the clamour for Myra Hindley's release that will build up from her supporters in the coming years) to assess objectively just what her role in the killings was, and look at how she has arrived at the present situation of confession and what she deems repentance.

At the end of my research I conclude that she has cynically exploited every situation to her own ends, and her belated confession was prompted not by remorse but by the eventual realisation that any hope of release hinged on wiping her slate clean, assuaging the grief of the relatives of her victims as best she can, and hoping that, with patience, she will have worked her ticket to freedom.

Should she ever be freed? You can draw your own conclusion after studying her, as I did while writing this book.

1
Childhood

When Goering began his 'economic war' on Britain in November 1940 he named Manchester with its concentration of heavy industry and major docks as a prime target. The city had been heavily blitzed, and there were many derelict buildings and dangerous bombsites around the centre.

Pretty twenty-two-year-old Nellie Hindley passed among them on the bus journey that took her from her home in Gorton to Crumpsall Hospital, six miles away, on a Tuesday in July 1942.

Nellie, married two years earlier to Bob Hindley, an aircraft fitter attached to the paratroops, was feeling the twinges of early labour. It was her first baby, and she was nervous. With her on the bus journey was her mother, Mrs Ellen Maybury. Nellie, known to her family as Hettie to prevent confusion with her mother, lived with Bob at Mrs Maybury's small home at 24 Beasley Street, Gorton, although since their marriage Bob had only been there briefly on leave from his regiment, the Loyal North Lancashires.

Crumpsall Hospital is a Victorian monolith, a huge four-storey redbrick building on the site of an old workhouse. The four floors of maternity wards in use today, F Block, are the same ones that were used in Hettie's day. Despite her frail physique, Hettie Hindley did not have too much trouble with the birth of her first child. It was the early hours of the next morning, between 2.30 and

3.00 a.m. on Wednesday, 23 July 1942 that a beaming nurse said to her, 'Mrs Hindley, you've got a girl.'

Hettie had a name ready for her daughter: Myra. It means purity, and it was a popular name in the north of England in those days.

Today, it has lost its popularity: no mothers from Manchester choose Myra for their daughters' name now. This tiny baby, Myra Hindley, put paid to that twenty-three years after her birth, when she became the most notorious woman in Britain.

Four days after Myra was born, a German plane dropped a stick of bombs on Beswick, not a quarter of a mile from her mother's home. Three people were killed, but baby Myra was still safely tucked up in the maternity ward: and that was the closest the war ever came to her.

Back home again, her mother Hettie was soon ready to go back to work as a machinist. There were no childminding problems: Gran was there to take care of little Myra, an arrangement which suited everybody. When Bob returned from the war he and Hettie managed to find a home for themselves round the corner from Gran in Eaton Street, and little Myra was still taken every day to stay with Gran. It never occurred to the Hindleys to move further than round the corner: Bob's own family were less than a mile away, in Longsight, and most of Myra's aunts and uncles lived within walking distance.

When Myra's only sister Maureen was born on 21 August 1946, four-year-old Myra moved in full time with Gran. It was the normal sort of arrangement families made when a new baby was born: older children were shuttled out of the way for a few days or weeks to give the mother and new baby time to get to know each other. In this case it just grew from there. The fact that Myra was brought up away from her family home has been interpreted years later as deeply significant, a child without roots who grew up to exact a terrible revenge on the world for her rejection. It wasn't like that at all. The two houses, Gran's and Mam's, were so close that the child moved easily between them both. She wasn't rejected by her parents in favour of Maureen, she simply stayed at Gran's because Gran, a widow who was on her own since her youngest daughter Hettie moved out, wanted her to.

Bob Hindley, seven years older than his wife, didn't object. His older daughter was three when he came back from the war, and he never grew close to her. He wasn't the sort of father for cuddles or romping games. He worked on building sites as a labourer, and spent his spare time and money in the pub. He was physically strong, and from time to time earned extra money boxing in local halls, but after an accident at work he became a semi-invalid, only ever seen by neighbours limping from his front door to the nearby Steelworkers' Tavern on Gorton Lane. Although Bob Hindley was born and brought up a Catholic, and went to a Catholic school, he had no deeply held religious convictions, and his two daughters were baptised into the Church of England.

Gran's and Mam's houses were identical. Gran moved house twice in the same street – which changed its name to Bannock Street – during the first few years that Myra lived with her, but each move brought no discernible improvement. The houses were the typical two-up two-down terraced dwellings of any industrial city, thrown up in the late Victorian/Edwardian days to house the mushrooming population of factory workers. Manchester, first and biggest of the industrial revolution towns, had more than its fair share of these cramped terraces.

The front door led straight into what was known as 'the front room' or the 'parlour'. Behind that there was a 'back room', and then there was a lean-to 'scullery', the only room in the house with running water. And this was only cold water, from a single tap with a large white china sink under it. Copper boilers, called just 'coppers', were stored in outhouses for heating water on washing day –

traditionally Mondays – and bath night – traditionally Saturdays. Stairs from the front room led to two bedrooms, the back one with a view over the yard down to the outside lavatory. From the back bedroom of Mam's house you could see the back bedroom of Gran's, they were so close. Even when Gran moved a few doors away down the road you would still have been able to see the other house. Today, all trace of this tight little network of streets has gone, and where Myra Hindley's first home used to stand there is now the Bishop Greer High School.

At five, Myra started at Peacock Street Primary School, a three-minute walk away from home. Gran would take her there every day, and fetch her in the afternoon, until she graduated at seven from infants to juniors, and was considered sensible enough to walk there on her own. 'Sensible' was a word Gran and her neighbours would often use about Myra. She was mature for her years, even a bit bossy with her friends and the little sister she adored. She had plenty of friends among the local kids though she is remembered as a bit spoilt: she could twist her Gran so easily around her little finger, and was inclined to throw a tantrum if anyone tried to thwart her. But she was not one of the local toughs – the kids who played on the street corners until pub chucking-out time and who got up to no good. The Hindleys and the Mayburys were respectable folk. Myra and Maureen were always well dressed and, although Maureen was always pale and small, Myra was strong and sturdy looking.

In her last year at junior school she failed her 11-plus. School records showed her IQ as 109 – above average, but short of the 120+ normally needed for a grammar school place. With a bit more motivation and a bit more encouragement from home – she was allowed to stay away from school as company for Gran more often than helped her education – she might have scraped through the exam. As it was, she went to Ryder Brow Secondary Modern, a mixed school about three quarters of a mile from her home. She walked to it every school day for the next four years – or every school day that she chose to go, because again her attendance record was bad.

In other ways, though, she was a good pupil, in the A stream all her time at the school. One of her reports read, 'Progress and conduct: satisfactory; Personality: not very sociable; Attendance: consistently unsatisfactory'. English was her favourite subject: she loved poetry. Her own attempts at writing it were often read out as an example to the rest of the class, and when she was asked as a homework project to write an essay about the school, she filled an entire exercise book. It was such an exceptional piece of work that the headmaster, Trevor Lloyd-Jones, put it in the school library. Years later, when she had endless time on her hands to explore her own skills, she would discover once again that writing came easily to her.

As a young teenager she was not pretty, her hair was straight before it was fashionable to have straight hair, her nose was hooked and she was nicknamed 'Square Arse' by the boys at school because of her big hips. But she was popular with girls. She could play a few tunes on the mouth organ, and was always making up funny songs. Head girl at Ryder Brow at the time, Linda Maguirk, described her later as 'funny and always singing, with long, lanky hair'.

She was good at games, playing defence in netball, fielding well in rounders and enjoying field events like javelin and discus. She hated cookery and was so bad at needlework that in her final year at the school she didn't wear a dress made in needlework class, as all her friends did.

Mrs Pauline Graham, who as Pauline Clapton was one of Myra's gang of friends at school, said, 'She could run very fast and have a go at any game. She was always the best in the gym class.' And Mrs Pat Clarke, who as Pat Jepson was perhaps Myra's best childhood friend and lived just round the corner from her in Taylor Street, said,

'Myra would not let herself be pushed around by any of the boys. She was so tough she frightened some of them off. She was so much a tomboy that I sometimes thought that she wanted to be a boy. On the other hand, she was very intelligent and could hold her own on any subject.'

Despite that, she wasn't academically bright enough for anyone to consider letting her stay at school an extra year to take her GCEs. In 1957 the school leaving age was fifteen and for Myra and her friends it couldn't come quickly enough: their only ambition was to get a job, get some money and then – for most of them – get married. At fifteen Myra was no different from the others. She and Pat would go babysitting together for neighbours, one of their most regular customers being Mrs Joan Phillips.

Years later Mrs Phillips said, 'My husband used to say he liked Myra to babysit because we could go out in peace, knowing everything would be all right if she was there. My boys loved her because she would spoil them. She used to bring them chocolate and let them stay up late, and when it was light in the evenings she used to play football with them on the bit of waste land near our house. In her last year at school she and Pat Jepson used to play wag and come round to our house to hide. She was wonderful with our Denis. He was only a year old. She used to turn a kitchen chair on its side and put him in between the legs to teach him to stand up and then to walk.'

On Saturday mornings, Myra would take Mrs Phillips' older son Gordon, who was six or seven at the time, to a children's matinée at one of the local cinemas, the Essoldo or the Cosmo, to see a cowboy film. When she babysat she would help get the Phillips children ready for bed.

'She'd have Gordon all scrubbed clean and in his pyjamas – I think it was the only time he liked being washed, because she made such a game of it.'

Mrs Phillips remembers the schoolgirl Myra as 'chattering about boys and records, singing the latest tune. You never saw her depressed.' But she did have a deep and lasting depression, at the age of fifteen. It was caused by the death of thirteen-year-old Michael Higgins, a boy who was too young to be a boyfriend, but was her best friend outside school.

Michael – Myra told him they were destined to be linked because they both had MH as their initials – lived in the next street. He was small, timid and shy, and he appealed to the same maternal instinct that made Myra happy playing with Joan Phillips' little ones. They became inseparable. Michael, a Catholic, did not go to the same school as her, but out of school she shared her sweets with him and protected him from older children.

In June 1957, just a month before she was due to leave school for good, Manchester was sweltering in a heatwave. After school on Friday the 14th, Michael rushed to Myra's house and asked if she wanted to go swimming with him and some pals at the 'Rezz', the local kids' name for a disused reservoir that was supposed to be fenced off and forbidden, but was too inviting in the summer heat to be resisted. Myra, a good swimmer, chose not to go. She went out with Pat Jepson instead. Three hours later a schoolfriend called to tell her that Michael had drowned. She was devastated, crying out hysterically that it was all her fault for not going swimming with him.

She did penance by trailing around the local streets, collecting for a funeral wreath. His mother gave her Michael's rosary to keep. Her gloom was deeply set in, and did not lift for weeks. All the joy of leaving school was eclipsed by her misery at Michael's death, and his funeral had a lasting effect on her. It was held at St Francis' Monastery in Gorton Lane, the church attached to the school that Michael had attended – and which Myra's father had gone to as a boy. The Catholic ceremony with its candles, incense and deep mystery attracted her, and consoled her in her grief.

But it was not until eighteen months later that she eventually decided to convert to Roman Catholicism. In the meantime, there were other things to distract her. There was the big grown-up world of work. Her first job was as a junior clerk with an electrical engineering firm, Lawrence Scott and Electrometers, of Louisa Street – near enough for her to walk home for her midday meal. She ran errands, brewed tea, and did some typing: she'd been taught shorthand and typing at Ryder Brow. She was welcomed by the other girls, and when she told them how she lost her first week's wage packet they had a whipround for her, raising more than was in it. They weren't so generous when she told them a few weeks later that she had lost another pay packet. She was practising somewhat crudely an art that she would perfect over the years: the art of manipulating people and situations to her best advantage.

She was, just as at school, a bad attender and she spent a lot of time smoking Park Drive in the lavatories, keeping watch while other girls carried on their side businesses – buying and selling from catalogues – in there.

If 1957 was a big year for Myra, it was no less for all the teenagers in Britain. It was two years since Bill Haley and the Comets had had them jiving in the aisles of their local cinemas, and now the whole era of rock 'n' roll was really launched. In music terms, 1957 was an epoch-making year. As Myra and her friend Pat crowded round the juke-box at one of the many coffee bars with Italian names that were springing up all over the big cities, Sivori's in Hyde Road, they had the pick of some of the best hard rockers and swooning crooners to choose from. It was the year that saw Jerry Lee Lewis' 'Whole Lotta Shakin' Goin' On' and 'Great Balls of Fire' hit the charts, along with Lonnie Donegan's 'Cumberland Gap' and 'Putting on the Style', Jackie Wilson's 'Reet Petite', Little Richard's 'Long Tall Sally' and Johnnie Ray's 'Yes Tonight Josephine'. As they sipped their frothy coffee they could listen to the Everly Brothers, with 'Bye Bye

Love' and 'Wake Up Little Susie', Harry Belafonte singing 'Island in the Sun', Pat Boone crooning 'Love Letters in the Sand', or Paul Anka wailing 'Diana'. Buddy Holly and the Crickets released 'That'll Be the Day', Tommy Steele was 'Singing the Blues', and Frankie Vaughan was kicking his leg as he sang 'Green Door'.

Teenagers were suddenly, and for the first time ever, big business. 'The Six Five Special', hosted by Pete Murray and Josephine Douglas on the BBC, and 'Cool for Cats' hosted by Kent Walton on ITV, were launched – the first two programmes catering exclusively for kids. Just thirty-five miles away from Myra's home, the Cavern Club opened its doors for the first time in Matthew Street, Liverpool. But most important of all to fifteen-year-old Myra, Elvis Presley's first film, *Loving You*, reached Britain. She saw it twice a night for the whole week that it was on at the Apollo in Manchester. Fourteen years later, in Holloway, she relived some of the excitement of that week when the film was shown on television.

She told a relation that she expected the other prisoners would have 'Coronation Street' on, so she went for a bath. But when she returned to her cell she could hear Elvis singing. She ran downstairs in her dressing-gown to watch the film. 'Gosh, it took me back over fifteen years (or thereabouts),' she said. 'Wish he'd come to one of Holloway's Christmas concerts (joke)!'

She had Elvis Presley scrapbooks, Elvis Presley souvenirs, and every record he released.

Myra's looks were beginning to change, too, as she became more and more immersed in the teen culture. By that Christmas, when she was fifteen and a half, she and Pat Jepson had started experimenting with the colour of their hair. At first it was just a touch of bleach on the fringe, a do-it-yourself job, later a full-blown blonde head of hair provided for 10s 6d by Maison Laurette, just along from Pat's home in Taylor Street. With the new daring hairstyle came new daring adventures. There were

dancing classes at Stan's Dancing School off Knutsford
Road, 1s 6d a time. If she could afford it, Myra went on
Wednesdays, Thursdays and Saturdays. And there were
proper dances too, at the Alhambra Ballroom.

She and Pat wore all the rage fashions. Myra's face was
pan-sticked, her eyes blackened by spitting on to her
mascara and applying it with a small brush, her lips were
glossy red. She liked straight skirts, not the full styles with
yards of sugar-starched net petticoats that were coming in.
And under the tight skirts and buttoned cardigans were
roll-on girdles and the circle-stitched bras that gave girls
high, unnaturally pointed outlines.

'Myra liked jiving, it was the only kind of dancing she
would do. She never bothered much with boys. Of course,
she used to go out with them, but not a lot,' said Pat.
'Myra looked very grown-up, she always wore straight
skirts and blouses. You never saw her in a flared skirt or
dress. I think she thought the boys round our way were
too young for her.'

There was a real adventure for the two friends, when
they took a bus five miles to Ashton-under-Lyne for a
dance, missed the last bus home and had to stay the night
at a girlfriend's house. Both mothers were worried sick.

'I got a clout but Myra's mother batted her in the street
and she wasn't allowed out for a week,' said Pat.

Other mothers, in years to come, would be denied that
strange mixture of anger and relief that parents feel when
missing youngsters turn up. . . .

But the anger wore off soon enough, and Myra was able
to spend a week with the Jepson family in Blackpool, the
summer of her sixteenth birthday. It was one of the few
times she had ever travelled outside the Greater Manchester boundaries. She swam in the crowded sea, ate
candy floss and spent her money, scrimped together from
her pay packets, along the Golden Mile.

But back home, there was a feeling of emptiness and
dissatisfaction, a feeling that life had more to offer than

the confines of Gorton and the electronics factory. At first she saw it as a spiritual need, and turned to the Church. She'd been drawn to the Catholic Church ever since she started at the age of eleven at Ryder Brow School: friends and family remember that she often paused on the walk to look at the Church of the Sacred Heart, with three statuettes above the door: Christ, the Virgin Mary and one of the disciples. It fascinated her.

Her interest was reinforced by Michael Higgins' funeral and one of her aunts, Auntie Kath, a Catholic who was married to her mother's brother Bert Maybury, was quick to encourage her. As winter approached, Myra was taking instruction in the Catholic faith from Father Theodore at the Monastery, the church where Michael's funeral service was held. She was given a new name, Veronica, which delighted her. And after her first communion, in November 1958, Auntie Kath and Uncle Bert gave her a present: a white prayer book.

In the same church, the Higgins family paid tribute to her help and support over Michael's death, by making her godmother to Michael's nephew, a baby boy. Thirteen years later, from her cell in Holloway, Myra would look back on that time in a letter to a relative, 'I remember when I was godmother to Freda's second child, christened Anthony John. He must be about twelve or thirteen now. I often think of him. Michael [Higgins] was Anthony's age when he was drowned: a nephew he never knew. Hope I don't sound morbid.'

She had asked her cousin to describe the interior of the Monastery to her: 'I can see such a clear picture in my mind's eye but time could have blurred the memory, so when you describe it, imagine we are at the back of the church, just inside the front entrance, with the statue of St Anthony on our right.'

When the reply, with the description in it, came, she wrote back, discussing each of the statues in the church.

'Yes, the pieta is one of my favourite statues too. I

couldn't recall the inscription you quoted, so I was glad when you did quote it. When I used to pray in front of the pieta, I used to touch the hand of Our Lord, which hung from Our Lady's sorrow-wracked embrace, and although slightly scared because the church was only dimly lighted by candleglow and was empty, which awed me just a little, I used to quickly kiss His hand before leaving the church.'

She thanked her cousin again for the detailed description and added, 'I'll probably bore you to tears writing about it all in future letters, but it's something very dear to me, and part of me is there, constantly drawing my spirit into the blessed peace and tranquility [*sic*].'

So Myra's quest for a god had begun. But the Monastery of St Francis was not as satisfying at the time as it is in later recall. It was only a few months before she stopped bothering to attend Mass.

By now Pat Jepson was 'going steady' and was soon to be married. Myra, who'd been on a few 'dates' with local lads, fell in with the pattern of life for girls from her background. She found herself a steady, started 'courting' and eventually got engaged. Ronnie Sinclair, a year older than her, a tea blender at the Co-op, and born and bred in nearby Dalkeith Street, fitted the bill. They started going together at Christmas 1958, just before Myra was made redundant from her job at the electronics firm. In those heady days of near-full employment, she started work the next week as a junior typist at Clydesdale's Furniture Shop, in Ashton Old Road. Once more, less than a bus ride away from home.

She was still living with Gran, and now took over all the cleaning of the house: part of her preparation for marriage. She'd already been paying two shillings a week into a Christmas club, and she now increased that by another two shillings a week paid to a neighbour who ran a catalogue, and she started buying pots and pans for her 'bottom drawer'. She even took occasional evening jobs – like topping strawberries at a local jam factory – to earn more money.

But Ronnie wasn't so keen on saving. He liked a pint and a laugh, and a fumbling necking session with his girlfriend. That wasn't Myra's plan at all. Like all girls of her generation, she clung tight to her virginity. All respectable girls saved themselves for 'Mr Right'. She was even prudish to the point of not allowing her sister Maureen to walk into the kitchen while she was in the tin bath. And besides, she didn't get much fun out of the amateurish attempts to excite her of Ronnie or any of the other boys she dated.

She was proud enough when, on her seventeenth birthday, he gave her an engagement ring with three tiny diamond chips in it. But within months the engagement was off. Ronnie, she told her friend Pat, was too immature. She had a clear vision of life married to him: she described it later as a kitchen sink drama, never enough money to enjoy life and always tied down by children.

According to Ronnie's mother, he took it badly, and tore up all the photos and mementoes of Myra that he had. He called round at her house a few times to try to persuade her to change her mind, but to no avail. She forgot him quickly. But the old restlessness returned. She travelled to London and spent a few days in a hostel, looking for work. But she was lonely and soon returned home.

Every ten weeks she went to Maison Laurette for a 'root toning', to keep the dark roots in her bleached hair at bay. She confided to Mrs Laurette Howells, the owner, that she was thinking of going abroad to work, perhaps as a children's nanny. She said she wanted to drive a car and travel – big ambitions for a Gorton girl. The nearest she got to fulfilling them was to write away for an application form to join the Naafi, and work with the British army in Germany. She never even filled in the form.

Her wish to be different found one expression though: her hair. She was the talk of the neighbourhood when she emerged from Maison Laurette with a pink rinse, just after her seventeenth birthday.

She started judo lessons, once a week at nearby Gresham Street school. She found she was good at this sport, like all others. But she discovered something else, something more sinister. An ability to inflict pain. Soon girls were refusing to fight her because she was so slow to release her grip. One slap on the floor indicated a submission, but with Myra they might have to slap many times before she released them. She wasn't a popular partner.

She changed jobs again, this time moving to an engineering company, Bratby and Hinchliffe in Gorton Lane, even nearer to home. But this wasn't very satisfying: she was still hanging around the same places, with the same friends she had known at fifteen, when she left school, and she was still up to the same bad habits, like just not going to work when she didn't feel like it. In fact, her absenteeism became so bad at Bratby and Hinchliffe that, six months after starting there, she was sacked. Jobs for typists were plentiful, though. The *Manchester Evening News* was full of column after column of small ads, and she was able to find another one very easily.

And it was this job, her fourth, that spelled the end of normal life for eighteen-year-old Myra Hindley. Because it was this job, as a typist with 'excellent prospects' for a chemical company called Millwards Merchandising in Levenshulme Road, that brought her into contact with the man who changed her life: Ian Brady.

She was still living with Gran, but there was a close bond between her and her mother – she went home to Eaton Street at least once a week to do her mother's hair, and she was especially close to her sister Maureen, known as Mo or Moby.

Maureen, four years younger, grew up much faster than Myra. Although not as clever or as tough as her older sister, Maureen was streetwise from a much earlier age. She was one of the Gorton street gang, with beehive hairstyle, stilettoes and tight skirts while she was still a schoolgirl. She picked up smoking and swearing from her older sister – Myra's language developed harshly as soon as she left school. And big sister, with a job and a pay packet, indulged her little sister's craving for Park Drive, even though she herself had graduated on to Embassy Tipped.

But Myra did not approve of her sister Maureen's boyfriend, David Smith. David, two years younger than Maureen, was old before his years. Illegitimate, he had been brought up by an adoring Gran, believing for many years that she was his mother. Then he had moved with his father to live in Gorton, in the same tight little network of streets that housed both Maureen and Myra. It was a harsh childhood strewn with trauma: a first-class found-ation for his subsequent delinquency. He quickly became known as one of the local tearaways. Respectable families warned their sons and daughters not to play with 'that David Smith'. At school he was regarded as a troublemaker, a hard case. By the time he was eleven he had already appeared in court on a charge of assault and wounding.

So none of the Hindley clan were pleased when Maureen started to hang around with him. Any more that Amos and Joan Reade, who lived two doors away from David Smith and his father in Wiles Street, were when they discovered their daughter Pauline was hanging about with him. Pauline and her younger brother Paul were gentler, slower creatures than the sharp-witted David, and although their mother was always kind to the unruly motherless boy, she was distressed when she thought Pauline was his girlfriend. It came as a great relief to the Reades when Maureen Hindley became the main object of David Smith's attention.

2

Enter Ian Brady

Did she know, when she first met him, that Ian Brady was different? She would say, many years later, that he was the only man she ever met who had clean fingernails, but she would not have noticed that on her first day at Millwards. That first day was like the first day anywhere, with time to absorb a few names and faces, time to find your own desk and the ladies' lavatory, and what time the morning tea break comes.

How was she to know, on Monday, 16 January 1961, that she had been casually introduced to the man whose name would be linked with hers for the rest of her life? Brady and Hindley, as indissoluble as Marks and Spencer, Romeo and Juliet, Jekyll and Hyde. And yet, if she took in anything at all at that first meeting, it would not be his surname. It was Ian and Myra when Tom Craig, the genial manager of Millwards, introduced them.

Millwards was an old-established Manchester firm, born in 1810 of the heavy industry of the area. They were suppliers of chemicals, mostly to the cotton industry. There were never more than fourteen or fifteen employees.

Ian Brady, twenty-three years old on the day that Myra Hindley walked into his life, was a stock clerk who had worked there for two years. There was no reason why her eye should have lingered on him any longer than on any of the others she met that day. He was tall, with dark hair and grey eyes, quite good looking. But he was not fashionable, like her, nor was he friendly, like the others.

There was no way of knowing, at that moment, that Ian Brady was special, unique.

Just as Myra Hindley's destiny at that moment was unformed, Ian Brady's was set on a track that could not vary. If the two had never met, Myra might have done anything with her life. Perhaps she would have fulfilled her ambition to travel; perhaps she would have married and had children; perhaps she would have ended up ruling some typing pool with a rod of iron. She may never have been Pollyanna, sugar and spice and all things nice. It is likely that many of the people she came up against would refer to her as 'a hard cow', as the girls she had tried to con into collecting for another 'lost' wage packet had already dubbed her.

But, had she never met Ian Brady, she would have escaped being the most reviled woman in Britain today. She would not have killed children. For the impetus for the acts that were to follow came from Brady, who would have carried them out – in one way or another – even if he had never met his willing disciple.

He had, if we are to believe him, already killed before Myra came into his life. He had certainly already set himself on a course that would have ended in exactly the same place that he is in today: a secure mental hospital. In recent years he has bragged to a journalist that he was associated with a killing as early as the age of eight or nine. If that is true, the young boy hid his terrible secret well. But there are certainly more clues in his early life about what was to come than there are in Myra's.

Ian Brady – or Ian Duncan Stewart as he was christened – was born on Sunday, 2 January 1938, a healthy eight-pound baby, at Rotten Row Maternity Hospital in Glasgow. His mother, twenty-eight-year-old Maggie

Stewart, was a tea room waitress. She was not married, although the hospital had 'Mrs Stewart' written on her records. These were not the easygoing days of 'love children', these were times when illegitimacy was a stigma and 'bastard' was the worst epithet you could fling at someone.

Maggie told everyone that her husband was dead, that he had died three months before the birth. To this day she sticks to some of that story: Ian's father, she maintains, was a reporter on a Glasgow newspaper who did die three months before Ian was born. If he didn't, he is not going to step out of the shadows today to claim paternity.

Life was hard for Maggie, unsupported. She had to find a new place to live – she'd been sharing rooms with a girlfriend before the birth, and she couldn't go back there with a baby. Fortunately it was not difficult to find a room to rent in one of the depressing Gorbals tenements, and Maggie was lucky enough to get part-time work as a waitress. For a few months she struggled along, farming her baby out to childminders and young babysitters when she had to work in the evenings. It eventually became too difficult for her, and she advertised for a permanent childminder, somebody willing to take her son into their home full time.

Mary and John Sloan, who had two sons and two daughters of their own, accepted Ian into their warm and friendly home, poor but honest and respectable. Ian took the name of Sloan. Every Sunday his mother, now calling herself Peggy, would visit him. He called her by her Christian name, when he was old enough to speak. But there was never any lasting confusion in his mind: he knew that 'Ma' Sloan was not his real mother, and he soon worked out who was. Peggy bought him clothes and presents in that indulgent way that mothers separated from their children through circumstances do. He had a real full kilt for Sunday best, and the other mothers oohed and aahed over him appreciatively. That alone would have been enough reason for the neighbourhood kids to leave him in no doubt about his socially unacceptable origins. For even in the toughest of slum areas – and the Gorbals was just that – illegitimacy was a deep shame. But there were other reasons, too. Sloaney was not popular with his school mates, or with close neighbours. Even the Sloan family found him difficult, with his temper tantrums and head banging.

He had already developed a cruel streak, being remembered by one neighbour who lived in the flat below the Sloans for throwing a cat out of a top-floor window, to see if it really would land on its feet. On another occasion he trapped a cat in a pit to see how long it would last without food or water – it was released, close to death, by other children. There was another incident when he tied a mate to a post, piled paper around his feet and set fire to it.

Football was the only game that mattered around the streets and Ian was no good at team games. Although he was big for his age and well built, Sloaney was quickly nicknamed Big Lassie, which he didn't like. He didn't mind so much when, later on, it was changed to Dracula because of his fascination with horror films and horror comics.

When he was nine, something happened that deeply affected him. The Sloans left the dirty streets of Glasgow behind them for a day, and went for a picnic to the shores of Loch Lomond. It was a normal family outing, by bus, with shopping bags loaded with sandwiches and mackintoshes in case it rained. The four Sloan children, teenagers, and their mother and father enjoyed it as much as any family treat. But for Ian it was a day of discovery. He discovered in himself a deep affinity with the wild, rugged and empty scenery around the lake. He was moved by the grandeur of the hills, awed by the vastness of the sky.

When it was time to go home, the family found him

half-way up one of the hills, standing still and absorbing something – who knows what? – from the strange, open, inspiring scenery around him. It was an unusual Ian who came down the hill, one who babbled happily about his day out to one of his foster sisters, not like the secretive, taciturn child the family had grown to accept. Ian Stewart/ Sloan/ Brady had found his natural home, and he would relive that first moment of pleasure whenever he could, from that day on.

There was another, more permanent change of scenery in store for him that same year, when the family moved as part of a slum clearance programme to a new council house on an overspill estate at Pollok – only three miles away from the Gorbals, but light years away with its indoor bathroom and lavatory, a garden, and nearby fields. If Ian appreciated the family's upturn in fortune, he didn't show it. But just as he didn't reward those who had taken him in and succoured him with love and affection, at the same time he was no bother to them. The Sloans' own children were growing up, settling down, sorting themselves out. There was enough going on in the family for everyone to accept Ian's self-containment without question. And when he passed to go to Shawlands Academy, a school for above average pupils, they were pleased and proud of him.

His mother, Peggy, was no longer a regular part of his life, having moved to Manchester and a fresh start when Ian was twelve. She went with, and soon married, Patrick Brady, a meat porter at the city's Smithfield Market, thereby taking on the name that would be Ian's for posterity.

If either of these events affected him, he did not show it. He was already used to being a loner, an outsider. He started to revel in being different, it became important to him, perhaps it was his way of coping with the illegitimacy stigma which had eaten deep into his heart.

At primary school he had been held up as an example to

the other pupils for his neat work. At Shawlands, however, he quickly became one of the boys that no teacher would point to as a guiding light. He smoked, he collected German memorabilia – pestering friends with older brothers in the army for anything they could bring back – and he acquired a criminal record.

When he was thirteen, he came before the juvenile court, charged with housebreaking. The Sloans were deeply ashamed. The court took a lenient view: he was no better or worse than a whole procession of Glasgow schoolboys caught breaking into gas meters for small pickings. His schoolmates remember him as always having plenty of spending money, acquired from the housebreaking, which carried on. Nine months later he was before the court again, and was again bound over.

The Sloans, not knowing what to make of the cuckoo in their nest, were relieved when he left school at fifteen and found a job as a teaboy at the Harland and Wolff shipyard, but the job didn't last long. Nine months later he became a butcher's messenger boy.

From the age of thirteen to sixteen, Ian had a girlfriend of sorts in the background. He'd known her since the Sloans had moved to Pollok, when they shared the same bus journey to school. Now, older, he occasionally took Evelyn Grant to the pictures, his favourite pastime. But she never rated the relationship seriously, and was amazed when he threatened her with a flick knife after she'd gone to a dance with another boy. The affair, if affair it was, ended then.

There were to be no others, until Myra.

Perhaps because Evelyn broke off with him, or perhaps because he had never stopped, he was housebreaking again. This time the courts could not be so lenient. There were nine charges against him, and everyone expected Ian to 'be put away'. But he escaped custody. The Glasgow courts saw a way out of adding yet another youth to the hundreds who regularly appeared before them, destined to a lifetime of petty crime.

They gave him probation, with a condition attached that would change a city's history. Just three weeks before his seventeenth birthday Ian Stewart/Sloan/Brady was ordered to leave Glasgow to live with his natural mother, in Manchester.

It cannot have been an easy time for mother, son and stepfather. Peggy had had no contact with her son for nearly five years; Ian had never officially been told that she was his mother, although he'd put two and two together many years before; Pat, an Irishman, had never met his stepson.

But they welcomed him to their home in the Manchester slum area of Moss Side, into a house identical in size and shape to the one where Myra was growing up. Again, he was no bother to them. He wasn't a teddy boy, although it was only months after he arrived in England that 'Rock Around the Clock' had parents wringing their hands and despairing of the younger generation.

He felt a misfit with his thick Glaswegian accent among the flattened vowels of Lancashire. But Ian Brady liked to feel a misfit, liked to be different, never wanted to be the same as everyone else. He couldn't care less if the natives couldn't understand him. At home he spent long hours in his room. His new stepfather gave him his new name, and found him a job at the meat market. It was the fresh start that the Glasgow courts had ordered for him.

The family moved from house to house. Ian, always smartly dressed, again appeared to have more money to spend than his humble job should have afforded. Exactly a year after he caught the train south, he was in court again, this time for stealing lead seals from boxes at the market where he worked. There were no fresh starts left and this time he was sentenced to two years' borstal training.

The first year was spent at Hatfield, Yorkshire; a borstal for above average intelligence offenders with relatively light criminal records, a place where the system prided itself on reclaiming youths hovering on the brink of a lifetime on the wrong side of the law.

But the outsider refused to conform: he brewed his own alcohol and got drunk on it, which resulted in him being shipped out to another borstal at Hull, where the inmates were tougher and the regime was harsher. And this was where he prepared himself to become a big-time criminal, fantasising about bank jobs, payroll snatches and wads of banknotes.

When he left he went home again to Peggy and Pat, and another series of moves from house to house across Manchester. While in borstal he had discovered he had an aptitude for figures, and had been given some rudimentary bookkeeping training. Now he decided that, if job he had to have, it would be one where he could wear a suit and polished shoes and have a pen in his top pocket.

Such jobs are not ten a penny, especially not for youths with borstal records. He settled instead, after four months of unemployment, for a labouring job in a brewery. By this time the family had moved to 18 Westmoreland Street, Longsight. Apart from one minor brush with the law, when he was fined £1 for being drunk and disorderly, he stayed away from trouble. But the job only lasted six months, because the brewery were forced to make staff redundant and Brady was one of the first to go.

For his twenty-first birthday, his mother and stepfather, trying to do their best for him, bought him a new suit. It rekindled his ambitions to find a job where he could sit in an office all day, pushing bits of paper around on a desk. He brushed up his bookkeeping and applied for – and got – a job with the firm of Millwards Ltd.

Ian Brady didn't make much of an impression in the two years before Myra Hindley crossed the threshold of Millwards. He was punctual, neat and on the whole polite. He was known to have a temper – an attempt to set up a lunchtime bridge school was abandoned because of his fury with his partner – and it was also known that if he lost at pontoon he would be in an ill humour all day. He'd make frequent visits to the recently legalised betting shop nearby. But that didn't set him aside as unusual.

He wore a long black overcoat over his dark three-piece suit, so the local kids around Westmoreland Street called him The Undertaker. At work he wasn't sociable. Apart from joining in card games, he'd rather eat sandwiches at his desk with his nose buried in a book than join the rest of the staff in the little kitchen, brewing tea and sharing the contents of their lunchboxes. And what books: the rest of the staff were impressed when they saw him reading *Teach Yourself German* but bemused when they caught sight of *Mein Kampf* and a whole selection of books about Nazi atrocities.

Yet they were a tolerant, friendly crowd, quite prepared to live and let live. Ian Brady bothered nobody as long as you didn't get him in a temper; he even gave the cleaner a bottle of port every Christmas. Can't be all bad, they thought, but a shame he didn't join in more with the fun of the office.

At home, too, he was no trouble. The Bradys received the odd complaint from a neighbour because he played his record player too loud. But what youngster hasn't suffered from that? It was what he played on the record player that grated, though: German marching songs, records of Hitler's speeches, even some records he had paid to have made for himself, from tape recordings made off the radio.

He loved all modern new-fangled technology: tape recorders, transistor radios, record players. And he loved hire purchase – the never-never they called it in Manchester – which enabled him to live now and pay later. He loved books, too, and he became a regular member of the local library near his home in Longsight. Where the library failed to satisfy his craving for books on Hitlerian propaganda, he spent large chunks of his wages buying them (£9 a week when he joined Millwards, rising to £14 when he was arrested six and a half years later).

He saved up to put down the first payment on a motor-bike, a secondhand 250cc Tiger Cub. That was a real liberation, because now he could discover what to Ian Brady was the most significant truth about the city where fate had dumped him. It sits, this sprawling metropolis of Manchester, in the lee of the Pennines, below a windswept and bleak moor: Saddleworth Moor, 1,600 feet above sea level, as haunting and compelling a scene as the one that had first made the nine-year-old schoolboy gasp with pleasure on the shores of Loch Lomond. Square mile after square mile of black crags and lonely peaks, their slopes clothed with purple heather and yellow gorse in the summer, red with bracken in the autumn, snow-white for the long harsh winter.

The Pennine moors are in Yorkshire, but they sweep down to the Lancashire borders, almost touching the city of Manchester and its satellite towns. Emily Brontë wrote poems about them, recognising the rugged, stirring beauty that eludes many of the travellers who today can cross the moors on the transpennine motorway. The only place that the golden eagle has ever found a home in England was on these moors.

Long before Brady and Hindley defiled them for posterity, local people knew that Saddleworth Moor had a bloody history. Towards the end of the eighteenth century the children of a farmer called Robert Bradbury and his common law wife one by one disappeared, and there was talk that the farmer was seen digging on the moors at odd hours of the day and night. Eventually his wife disappeared mysteriously, too: and to this day the inhabitants of Greenfield, the nearest village and the highest, most isolated village on Saddleworth talk about a 'grey lady' ghost who walks the hillside, and tenants of the farm have handed down tales of silent, ghostly children.

There are more ghostly children haunting the area, the

ghosts of the pauper children who were taken from all over the country to work in the mills, in the nineteenth century. Their skeletons were found buried in a mass grave near to Forty Row, the row of forty tiny dwellings that the mill owners used as a dormitory for their slave labourers: children found abandoned, born in prison, or unwanted because of mental subnormality. They lived cold, hungry, miserable lives, worked literally to death in the grim cotton mills.

Saddleworth, too, was the site for a murder that is still to this day claimed to be one of the bloodiest ever, when an innkeeper and his gamekeeper son were brutally battered to death in 1832. No culprit was ever brought to book, despite several current theories as to who the killer was. The gamekeeper had been young and fit, and had put up an incredible struggle, so that the walls, floor, stairs and all the furniture in the inn were covered with blood, and the doctor first called to the scene found two and half pounds of coagulated blood in one spot by the pantry door.

It certainly wasn't love at first sight for Myra and Ian. The brassy, smart blonde, looking much older than her eighteen years, and the dour Scotsman: on that first day nobody would have picked them out as a match made in heaven – or hell.

But it wasn't too long before Myra, itching to be different, despising the boys from the backstreets of Gorton as 'too immature', aware that there was more in the big wide world than she had even started to dream of, took notice of the taciturn, bad-tempered Brady.

Her favourite singer, Elvis, was topping the charts with 'Are You Lonesome Tonight?', and it touched her. Even though she was still going on dates with local lads, none of them was the man she wanted to spend her evenings with, and she was lonely. Many years later she said that she was going out with a policeman just before she became involved with Ian Brady. If she was, that policeman must have been heartily glad to forget about his dates with the tough blonde five years later, when her name was making headline news.

But by her nineteenth birthday, six months after starting work at Millwards, she was deeply smitten with the silent stock clerk who dictated letters to her. We know this because just before that time Myra Hindley started to keep a diary, which she wrote in for seven months. Many of the entries are routine: reminders about family birthdays, hairdressing appointments for her daring pink and blue rinses, sums showing how she spent her weekly wage packet. But the rest is the stuff of women's magazine fiction, a chronicle of her blossoming love for the man who would ruin her life. It started with 'Ian looked at me today.

'July 23rd '61. Wonder if Ian is courting. Still feel the same.

'July 25th. Haven't spoken to him yet.'

Two days later she wrote that she had finally screwed up her courage to speak to him, and he had smiled in an embarrassed way. She vowed that she was going to change – although she didn't write how or why. Wistfully she noted a few days later that one of her friends at work had 'clicked' with a boy and was now courting.

As for Ian, she still wasn't sure what to make of him. One day she was writing that he didn't like girls at all, the next she detected him taking sly glances at her in the office. Every little detail of his life was manna to her: she recorded how be bet on horses, and that he drank Boddington's beer, and even that she thought their boss, Tom Craig, was afraid of Ian.

On 13 August she described him as 'Misery', but the following day she wrote: 'I love Ian all over again. He has a cold and I would love to mother him.' If he didn't speak to her for a whole day, it upset her and put her in a bad mood. On 29 August she wrote: 'I hope he loves me and will marry me some day.'

A week later she confided to her diary that she knew nothing about his parents or his background. When he wore a black shirt to the office she wrote: 'He looks smashing.'

October was a bleak month, and the diary is full of entries about how little she knew of him, how he was still ignoring her, and how much she still loved him. When, towards the end of the month, she heard him making arrangements to meet someone for a drink she was jealous, which may have spurred her into going out with another man at work, called Eddie. But Ian still dominated the diary entries, even though she was condemning him as uncouth because of his swearing and his rows with Tom Craig.

At the beginning of November she recorded plaintively that it was months since she had spoken to Ian, and a few days later she seemed remarkably unemotional when she wrote that her short fling with Eddie was over, and that Eddie had another girlfriend.

On 28 November she wrote: 'I've given up with Ian. He goes out of his way to annoy me, he insults me and deliberately walks in front of me. I have seen the other side of him and that convinces me that he is no good.'

She was still feeling the same way four days later, recording that she hated him: 'He has killed all the love I had for him.' But less than two weeks later she was writing that she was in love with him all over again.

And then came the most dramatic entry of all, one of the few remaining ones before she stopped writing down her innermost feelings:

'22nd December: Eureka! Today we have our first date. We are going to the cinema.'

Her patience had finally been rewarded. Brady, who could live well enough without female companionship, had been content to play her on the line until the hook was deeply embedded. He must have known for months that the stocky blonde fancied him, even if he could not guess how deep her romantic longings were. He waited until he was ready, and then he took her out.

Their first date was an initiation. He took 'the girl', as he was later to refer to her, to see a film that combined two of his favourite subjects: death and Nazi atrocities. The film was *Trial at Nuremburg*. She had already learned of his devotion to Germany and his interest in Nazism by glancing at the reading matter that kept him so occupied every lunchtime.

Now she would show him just how much she cared. If he agreed to let her into his secret silent world, she would become as devoted to his subjects as he was himself. She, Myra Hindley, would laugh when he laughed at the horrors of the death camps. She would be as inspired as he was by the rantings of Hitler. She, too, would become devoted to the German language, which he was struggling to learn in his lunch breaks.

It is not an uncommon syndrome. Countless thousands of girls have stood on freezing cold touchlines on Saturday afternoons, trying to convince themselves and the object of their desire that they are having a great time. Many more have struggled to look alert and fascinated by talk of gaskets and big ends and brake horse power. Some of those girls will have grown into women who genuinely enjoy watching Saturday afternoon sport with their husbands, who really get a thrill out of visiting the car showrooms to choose the next family saloon. Others will have managed to convey the message: I love you but not your hobby.

A relationship is usually a two-way traffic. In the early days, while both sides are trying to please the other, they unconsciously absorb standards and interests from each other, and these form the bedrock of the subsequent marriage or long-term involvement. Occasionally one partner is more domineering, and imposes their personality on the other, so that some women – and some men – have married lives spent scuttling about in the shadow of their partner, doing the other's bidding without even having to be bid.

And in other cases, and this is what happened to nineteen-year-old Myra Hindley, one partner is more developed than the other and becomes the stronger partner if not necessarily the stronger personality. Myra, so desperate to be grown-up and mature, above the rank and file of the Gorton girls with their horizons limited by wedding rings and nappies, was happy to go along with everything that Ian Brady suggested.

She was a young girl who had never even begun to tap her intellectual potential, a girl for whom school and education was a matter of serving time before being allowed out into the world, a girl who found 'the world' nothing but a procession of dead-end junior office jobs giving no fulfilment, no satisfaction. She didn't know what she wanted, but she knew there was more to her than the girls she grew up with who were happy to settle with the first boy who asked them to marry, or who got them pregnant. She felt innately superior. She was one of the toughest in that small network of Gorton streets: both the boys and girls were in awe of her. But she knew she was a big fish in a tiny pond. She'd had glimpses – from the women's magazines she read and from the television, of wider horizons, but they frightened her. And yet, and yet. . . .

Many young people meet one teacher in their school career who inspires them, someone who recognises their talents, whether practical or intellectual, and helps them to see their potential. Many others go home to a hearth where parents and family expect the best from them: plenty of children from mean terraces just like Bannock Street have been taught to soar above their surroundings. Others have a built-in gritty determination to make something of themselves. They need no inspiration, the drive comes from within. And countless thousands more are happy with their lot, growing up to want nothing more than a decent job, a decent home, a happy family, a bit of fun.

Myra was not one of these. But neither was she lucky enough to have the drive within herself to change her life. All her talk about jobs abroad was just that: talk. And she had never met anyone to push her, at school or at home.

The first person to inspire Myra Hindley was Ian Brady. And he was a psychopath.

It was never the sort of romance she read about in her magazines. They never went dancing at the Alhambra, or Belle Vue, or played Cliff Richard's 'The Young Ones' on the juke-box in any of the pubs with cosy corners for coupless intent on holding hands and gazing into each other's eyes. It was always the cinema – usually an 'X' film (adults only) involving torture – and then back to Granny Maybury's to share a bottle of German wine (Granny Maybury had already adopted the habit of going to bed early in the evening). This pattern was unchanged apart from the odd trip on the back of Brady's bike out to his beloved moors, where he indoctrinated his new disciple into the worship of bleak exhilarating scenery.

At work, too, the education process continued. Myra had passed the first test with flying colours: she had shown an enjoyment of the gory films he took her to. How much of it was genuine we will never know. But if she had reacted with a girlish horror, and shown herself to be squeamish, she would have lost Ian Brady. And that was the last thing she wanted. Now he moved her on to higher things. She was given books to read at home, and then they would huddle over them together in the office at lunchtimes.

She was worried, though, about his strange, macabre interests. In fact she was more than worried: in the early days of their romance she was terrified of him. At this stage, she was still normal enough to recognise that he was not normal. She even expressed her fears in a letter to one of her Gorton street corner pals, a girl she'd known all her life. She told her friend that if anything happened to her, the letter was to be shown to the police.

In this letter she described how Brady had once drugged her, and when she came round he was leering over her. She said she thought her life was in danger, and also named three other people who were under his threat. But the letter also revealed her obsession with him and a few months after sending it she asked her friend to destroy it. She was by then completely in Brady's thrall.

'She was a perfectly normal girl until she met him,' the friend who received her letter remembers. But today she is no friend of Myra's: she herself became the victim of a local hate campaign when she volunteered information about the letter before Myra's trial, and she wants nothing more to do with any attempt to rehabilitate Myra's reputation.

For her first year at Millwards Myra often walked home at lunchtime. Now she brought sandwiches every day, and sat with Ian to eat them. Although they tried to pretend to the rest of the staff that theirs was a friendship, not a relationship, the word was out. Myra had already confided in one of the other office girls at the start of the affair. Now she talked to nobody but Ian, and the more she became involved with him the more she withdrew from the day-to-day gossipy routines of the office.

She began to take on more and more of the attributes of the man she worshipped. Whereas Mrs Phillips, for whom she used to babysit, remembered her as a sunny-natured chattering girl, George Clitheroe, the foreman at Millwards, described her as 'starting to become overbearing, and wearing kinky clothes. They used to laugh and joke together over dirty books.'

The kinky clothes were high boots and short skirts and the imitation suede or leather jackets that he felt made her look more Germanic. Ian encouraged her penchant for blonde hair, too. She even started to carry a photograph of his favourite pin-up in her handbag: Irma Grese, the woman guard who became known as The Beast of Belsen.

To the rest of the staff they were a pain, but harmless. They kept their private jokes very much to themselves and they cut themselves off from the other staff at Millwards.

Tom Craig, the manager who was liked by all and was renowned for seeing the best in everybody, said afterwards, 'Myra was a good shorthand typist, always smartly dressed. She wore short skirts and boots and fancy stockings. But she would have been fired if it hadn't been difficult to get a replacement.

'With most of the girls in an office you have a bit of a lark around, you pull their legs and everyone tries to get a bit of fun out of their work. But Myra was heavy going. You got no response from her at all. She was surly at the best of times and aggressive if you spoke to her the wrong way. She didn't come in contact much with the other girls, but she still managed to have a bad effect on everybody. The pair of them were just plain surly and unsociable.'

Myra didn't care. She didn't need other people: she had Ian.

3

Murder-the 'supreme pleasure'

Myra Hindley was a virgin when she first met Ian Brady. He was, and is, the only man she has ever made love to. What was it like, her initiation? Was he gentle with her, passionate? Did it live up to her girlish expectations of someone who, only weeks earlier, had written in her red-backed diary: 'I hope he loves me and will marry me some day'? Did she enjoy 'going all the way', as the girls she grew up with called it?

Although she didn't know it, Ian Brady was not a lot more experienced than she was. He must have had the odd fumbling attempts at intercourse with willing partners in dark alleyways. But he had probably never had a lover, someone to develop a sexual relationship with. Myra Hindley was, and is, the only woman Ian Brady ever had a long-term relationship with.

It was altogether more civilised than backstreet petting, too. They soon fell into a routine. After Millwards, separate ways home: he to his mother's terraced house in Westmoreland Street, she to Granny Maybury's identical terrace in Bannock Street. Then, round to join her. Perhaps they would go out, up on to the moors on the bike, or to the cinema, or even just to the off-licence for more German wine. At any rate, Gran could always be relied upon to go to bed early: she didn't find Myra's young man sociable company.

'When Ian started visiting Myra he used to leave the house and say goodnight at the front door, but several times we heard him sneaking in later,' said Mrs Margaret Withnall who lived nearby.

It may have been the sixties, but Britain wasn't swinging yet. 'Living in sin' was regarded by the girls of Gorton as failure, and even Ian Brady, with his contempt for Christian institutions like marriage, went along with the convention of protecting Myra's reputation. But she was absorbing his views on everything, including marriage.

She told a friend, 'I'll never get engaged or marry anybody, because Ian and I have a very good understanding with one another.'

The understanding was getting better and better. She could now be heard denouncing black people, Jews, God and religion. She was becoming what she wanted to be: different from those around her. She and Ian were regulars at the library, borrowing books on philosophy as well as on crime and torture. Some of it was great literature too, which encouraged them both in their feelings of superiority. You wouldn't get any of that lot at Millwards reading Dostoevsky's *Crime and Punishment*, would you?

Then Ian discovered another writer, one who would become their favourite: the Marquis de Sade, the man who gave his name to sadism. His writings do not have the high literary content of Dostoevsky's, but both authors triggered a chord with Ian Brady. *Crime and Punishment* is the story of a poor Russian student who works out that he can solve all his problems and launch himself on a successful career if he has money, and there is one simple way to get that: by killing an old woman who has a box full of it. He dehumanises his victim in his intellectual arguments with himself: in the end, killing her is nothing more than a simple test of his ambition.

De Sade is even stronger stuff. He was a French aristocrat who was obsessed with the pleasure of inflicting pain: on one occasion he flayed off a prostitute's skin and poured heated wax into the wounds, on another he beat three teenage girls with a whip weighted with nails. He attempted to justify it all in his writings. Not only is his book *Justine* a catalogue of physical cruelty, it also contains a lot of half-baked philosophy that dove-tailed with the beliefs that Ian – and now Myra – already held. 'God is a disease that eats away a man's instincts.' 'Murder is a hobby and a supreme pleasure.' This was their everyday reading matter.

There was light relief, too. Like millions of others Ian Brady was a 'Goon Show' addict, and Myra soon joined that cult following. He'd found a nickname for her: Hess or Hessie, derived from Myra Hess, the famous pianist, and appropriate because it was also the name of Hitler's lieutenant. It pleased them both, because again it made them feel intellectually superior. Myra responded by calling Ian Neddie, after Neddie Seagoon (the character played by Harry Secombe). Her addiction to the Goons characters would survive: in Holloway she would nickname her best friend 'Eccles' (the character played by Spike Milligan).

Maureen Hindley had left school by now. She was following in her big sister's footsteps through a series of low-paid office jobs, and she was still going out with David Smith, to the consternation of their mother.

Myra's mother has never talked about her feelings, at this or any other time. But it can be conjectured that, in 1962, it was sixteen-year-old Maureen who was causing her sleepless nights, not Myra. Ian may not have been the most sociable of people, but he was respectable. He was bettering himself; he and Myra were a nice steady couple.

But Maureen noticed the sinister side of her big sister's relationship. In court, less than four years later, she said, 'She used to go to church, liked dancing, she was quite normal, she liked the normal way of life and had many girlfriends. She liked children. She also liked swimming and reading. She stopped going to church. She said she didn't believe in it. She didn't believe in marriage. She said she hated babies and children and hated people. She never used to keep things under lock and key, but she started after she met Brady. She kept books, her tape recorder, all her tape recordings and all her clothing locked up in the wardrobe.'

And what did Mrs Peggy Brady make of Myra? There can be no answer to that, for they never met. Myra never crossed the threshold of the house in Westmoreland Street. It rankled with her that Ian would not admit her to this most intimate part of his life, but she was not secure enough in their relationship to demand any justification. It cannot have been that she was not good enough for his family (Peggy and her husband would have been happy to see him settling down with a nice girl). Nor could it be that he was embarrassed by them and their humble home, as the houses in Eaton Street and Bannock Street were no palaces. It's more likely that Brady, acutely sensitive about his illegitimacy, didn't want Myra picking up clues to it. He told Peggy he had a girlfriend, and as he started to spend more and more nights away from home, she and her husband heaved a sigh of relief that he'd found someone to steady him down.

Myra, or 'Blondie' as they called her, became well known to the neighbours around Westmoreland Street, because she was always hanging around the corner, waiting for Ian. At first she waited on foot, but later, when they'd been going out together for just over a year, in a hired car that Myra rented for a day or a weekend. She wasn't legally qualified to drive, although she had had a few driving lessons. In fact it wasn't until her third attempt, late in 1963, that she finally passed her driving test.

Had Brady been able to drive, or had he ever been known to drive even though not qualified, Myra's whole role in the Moors Murders might have come more into question at the trial. As it is, whatever else she did, one thing is certain: she provided the hearse that conveyed the dead children to their burial place on Saddleworth Moor.

It is possible, if the things he has claimed in recent years are true, that Ian Brady was already hooked on the pleasure of killing; that he had already gone beyond the student in *Crime and Punishment* who killed for money, and was killing for the sheer joy of it; that the Marquis de Sade's perverted philosophies were not a seminal influence, but merely reinforced and gave intellectual credence to a way of life he had already adopted. There was certainly never any financial motivation in any of the murders Brady committed.

But there was a financial motive in the schemes that he and Myra hatched as they lay together on a blanket in the back of the car. They planned robberies: big, exciting, rewarding ones, like bank jobs or payroll snatches. They coined a phrase that became a secret joke to them: 'Money and food is all I want, all I want is money and food.' Myra had decorated the grey and cream walls of her office at Millwards with pictures of scenery, cut from old calendars. When the staff finally took them down, after her arrest, they found the slogan written on the wall.

It has been suggested that Ian Brady only introduced robbery plans as a way of initiating Myra into his killing schemes. But it is more likely that it was nothing so calculated as that: the plans were part of the fantasy world into which he retreated, and which he could now for the first time share with someone else.

When he injured his leg and foot in a minor accident on his motorbike, he wrote Myra a note explaining that he would be off work for a couple of days and would 'capitalise' on the situation by grasping 'the opportunity to view the investment establishment on Stockport Road'. In other words, he was going to case the joint for one of the bank jobs he was dreaming of pulling off. It was more than just a dream, too. Some careful preparations were thought up, and Myra was the one who carried them out. She became more and more Ian's front man. A neighbour remembers that when they travelled by bus together, she always spoke and paid for both of them when they went to the off-licence or called at a pub to buy cigarettes, he stayed outside while she went in.

So now, when Ian decided he wanted guns to carry out his fantastic plans, it was Myra's job to get them. It wasn't as difficult as it sounds for a twenty-year-old shorthand typist to buy weapons. George Clitheroe, the Millwards foreman, was also President of the Cheadle Rifle Club and captain of the club's team. In a small firm like that, everybody knew everybody else's hobbies – unless, like Myra and Ian, they kept them firmly under wraps. It was certainly no secret what George did on his Sundays off: his prowess as a marksman made him a minor celebrity. He was happy enough to introduce an enthusiastic young typist to his hobby. Myra went eight times to the indoor shooting range at Cheadle, and four times to an open-air .303 range at Crowden, near Saddleworth.

George Clitheroe was puzzled by her interest, but she certainly seemed keen enough. So he arranged for her to buy a .22 rifle from a gun merchant in Manchester. He was puzzled because she was no good at shooting. Every time she fired she asked 'Will it kick?' and closed her eyes. He was even more puzzled when she asked about joining a pistol club, and he told her that she wasn't suitable because of her temper. Staff at Millwards had been treated to outbursts of hers often enough for him to be wary. But behind George's back Myra bought two pistols from two other members of the club: a Webley .45 which cost her £8, and a Smith and Wesson .38, nickel-plated with a two-inch barrel, which cost her £5. She even asked if it was possible to get hold of Lugers.

So now they had something else to occupy them on the moors: target practice. They used the guns to shoot at oil drums, old tin cans and the occasional hapless rabbit. All the time Brady elaborated on his plans to 'pull off a big job'. He developed a habit that would later help the police crack the biggest murder inquiry of the century: he made lists, noting down all relevant details. He was determined not to be caught by overlooking some small clue: ironically it was this thoroughness that gave so much help to the police in the end.

As part of his dreams of becoming a big-time criminal, Brady had kept in touch with some of his old borstal mates. One of these was a youth called Philip Deare, from Bradford. Deare vanished from his home in November 1962, and after the trial of Myra and Brady he has often been mooted as another of their victims, killed because a criminal escapade he and Brady were involved in went wrong. In fact, he drifted away to carry on his life of petty crime in London, dying there an alcoholic.

Brady's boasts about killing Deare, made from his prison cell many years later, are probably nothing more than self-aggrandisement. But the lack of truth behind this one specific claim of murder throws a grave doubt over the other unsubstantiated killings he lays claim to. And the evidence produced to support the theory that he killed Deare (a 'confession' Myra is alleged to have made to another prisoner in which she admitted to knowing that her lover killed Deare) throws a similar shadow over other admissions she is alleged to have made in prison.

In the early part of 1963 the couple found another hobby, one for all seasons and all places: photography. Brady had owned a little box camera before, taking lots of happy snaps of Myra and her dog, Lassie. It was really Granny Maybury's dog, but Myra was devoted to it. The Hindleys had always had dogs, and Brady had developed a love for them as a lad, when one of his foster sisters owned one. At Westmoreland Street he had his own dog, Bruce (a name chosen to emphasise his Scottishness). But increasingly as he spent more time at Myra's, his mother was left to look after Bruce and he transferred his affections to Lassie. The two of them referred to her by a pet name, Ches.

Ian, with his love for gadgetry, wasn't content for long

with the box camera. He bought a much more sophisticated one, with a tripod and a timer. He also bought lighting equipment, and all the chemicals he needed to set up his own amateur darkroom over the kitchen sink. No corner shop chemist would have agreed to print the pictures he started to take.

Perhaps he took them for their own personal delectation, or perhaps they hoped to sell them and make money out of them – on some of them they both wore crude white hoods over their heads, hiding their identities, while they were recorded for posterity in the act of sex. In others, Myra posed on her own, her buttocks covered in red weals from a whip, also shown in the picture. In some she wore crotchless black knickers. And in some Brady was on his own, naked except for his vest.

Time has done nothing to ameliorate the crude pornography they were involved in. The day of the permissive society may have only just been dawning in 1963, but nothing has happened in the twenty-five years since Brady pressed the shutter to make this kind of explicit image commonplace or acceptable.

Myra, who eighteen months earlier had been too prudish to let her sister see her in the bath, was now so debauched that she would allow a permanent record to be made of her coupling with Brady. She had travelled a long way down a desperate road.

By June 1963, they were living together full time. Although it may have been before then, that is when Maureen Hindley became aware that Ian had moved completely into Granny Maybury's house in Bannock Street. Maureen, still close to her big sister despite the changes she'd noted in Myra's personality, had a month previously taken a job at Millwards, after being sworn to secrecy by Myra about the scale of the relationship between her and Brady.

Granny Maybury seems to have reacted to her new

lodger by closing her eyes and ears and retiring to her bedroom. When neighbours complained about the noise – the couple played their tape recorder and record player at full blast, and the family next door got sick of the sound of Ravel's 'Bolero' at all hours of the night – Mrs Maybury just shrugged and said she'd tell them about it. Nothing happened.

But within a month of Brady moving in, something did happen, something very big. It may not have been Brady's first killing, but it was certainly Myra's.

This first murder was much the most dangerous and difficult. If they could get away with this one, they could get away with anything – it is no wonder they became super-confident. Because with this one and only this one, they knew the victim. Or at least, Myra knew her.

Pauline Reade, aged sixteen years and five months, was one of Maureen's crowd, not Myra's. But in those tight little back streets, everyone knew everyone. Pauline Reade and her mam Joan and her dad Amos lived with her only brother Paul, next door but one to David Smith and his father. Her father was a baker, up and out at the crack of dawn every day. Her mother was as clean and respectable as they come, stoning the step of their terraced house, identical to all the others in the street, with the yellow slate that was the mark of a well-run household.

Pauline had been at school with both David and Maureen – a year younger than Maureen and a year older than David. She, like so many of the girls in that area, had been one of David Smith's girlfriends, causing her parents the same sort of anxiety that Hettie Hindley felt when Maureen took up with him. David's reputation was that of the toughest street fighter around, a kid who carried a knife or a razor blade all the time. So the Reades were pleased when that little romance ended after a couple of weeks. Pauline, who had a job in a sweet shop, was a good girl. They didn't want that rogue Smith spoiling her.

On Friday, 12 July, just eleven days before Myra's twenty-first birthday – and this was years before eighteen became the special 'growing-up' birthday – Pauline set out on her own to go to a dance at the Railway Workers' Social Club, less than half a mile from home. She was wearing a pink dress, beads and one of those fashionable 'duster' raincoats of the time, in powder blue. It was an exciting time for a teenager on the brink of womanhood. The Beatles had only just dropped down the charts after being at the top with their first number one hit, 'From Me to You', for seven consecutive weeks. Gerry and the Pacemakers were at the top spot that week, with 'I Like It'.

None of Pauline's friends were able to go to the dance with her that night, but she was sure that there would be plenty of girls she knew when she got there. And you never know, tonight might be the night she would meet that special boy. . . .

We never will know, because Pauline did not arrive at the dance. Her route passed the road where Myra lived, passed Eaton Street where Myra's mother and father lived, and passed the end of Westmoreland Street, where Ian Brady lived. It was early in the evening – she had left home at 7.30 p.m. – and the middle of summer, so it was broad daylight. Police investigating her disappearance found no one who had seen her with anyone. But it was Pauline's misfortune to meet Myra and Brady on one of the weekends when Myra had hired a van for their trips to the moors, to drink German wine and gin and whisky on their blankets in the back, to eat sandwiches and sleep up there too.

Pauline was persuaded to go with them. She was taken up on to Saddleworth Moor, sexually assaulted by Brady, and then killed. There can be no doubt that Brady had planned a killing for that weekend, because they had a spade to bury the body with. Although at a later date when they had their own car they kept a spade in it 'for digging peat for the garden', in July 1963 they had no car of their own.

Ever since the whole issue was first raised at the time of their arrest in 1965, the city of Manchester has buzzed with rumours that David Smith was more heavily involved than he has ever admitted. Involved with more murders than just the final one when he admitted being present.

Although it is only recently that Pauline Reade's death was officially one of the Moors Murders – neither Brady nor Hindley were charged with anything connected to her – her mysterious disappearance was always accepted by police and public alike to have been their doing. Of all their killings, this is the one that David Smith might have had a motive for, because of his earlier involvement with Pauline. But there is nothing to suggest that he and Pauline did not remain friends.

David Smith was only fifteen when she went missing, but that was not enough to stop the malicious gossip. He already had three criminal convictions: one for wounding with intent (at the age of eleven); one for assault causing actual bodily harm (at fourteen); and one conviction for housebreaking and larceny just the month before Pauline vanished, which carried a sentence of two years probation. So he wasn't frightened of violence.

But a knife flashed in a fight is a far cry from cold bloodedly murdering someone and disposing of the body. Myra had been schooled by Brady for eighteen months before she shared a killing with him; later Brady would attempt to school David Smith in the same way.

But when Pauline died it is doubtful that Brady and Smith had even met. The meticulous Brady told the jury at his trial – and he was trying his best to shift the blame for subsequent killings on to Smith – that they first met in October 1963, three months after Pauline's disappearance.

Now, at last, we know from both the testimony of Myra Hindley and Ian Brady (given separately and with no collusion) that Smith was not involved, and that Myra did not deliberately seek out Pauline Reade as a sacrificial victim because of her affair with her darling sister Moby's boyfriend. Pauline Reade, like all the other youngsters killed by Brady and Hindley, was unlucky: she was in the wrong place at the wrong time.

It was information given by Myra that enabled the police to find Pauline's body in a shallow grave on the moors in 1987. At least for her distraught parents, there has come the final peace of knowing that their daughter is dead, and is now buried in the spot they have chosen for her: Gorton Cemetery.

It is a peace that has come too late for Joan Reade. All those long years of waiting for news of her daughter, of leaving the back door open just in case Pauline came back, of worrying, when their terraced home was bulldozed as part of the slum clearance programme and they were rehoused not far away, that Pauline would not have their new address – all those years have taken a harsh toll.

Mrs Reade is an in-patient at Springfield Mental Hospital in Manchester, from where she attended the funeral of her only daughter on 7 August 1987 so heavily tranquillised that it is doubtful she knew where she was or what she was doing. Her husband Amos, who is a recluse and lives alone, hoped that seeing her daughter laid to rest would help mend Joan Reade's broken mind. Perhaps it will, eventually. But it will never mend her broken heart.

There are other mothers in Manchester who mourn.

John Kilbride was a sunny-natured child, known by all the neighbours in Smallshaw Lane, Ashton-under-Lyne, for his constant whistling and singing.

Ashton-under-Lyne is a town in its own right, with its own market and its own town hall. But driving out from Manchester you would be forgiven for not realising you had entered its boundaries. It is part of the vast urban sprawl that is known as Greater Manchester. It had ceased to be separated from the city by green fields and farmland long before the Kilbrides lived there.

The Kilbrides are an Irish family, one of many thousands in the Manchester area. Patrick, John's father, worked on building sites, and was laid off when the weather was bad. There was not a lot of money to go around, especially with seven children. But Sheila, John's mother, is one of that great tradition of women who never give in to adversity, work hard at stretching every penny and build a clean and comfortable home around themselves. The children all had their little jobs about the place. But John, being the eldest, was the most trusted. He went every day to his grandmother's house in nearby Rowley Street, to help the old lady around the house and keep her garden tidy. The neighbours there all knew him too: it was hard to miss the gap-toothed smiling boy who said hello to everyone.

That's how his day started on Saturday, 23 November 1963. Then he went home for lunch, and out in the afternoon for his weekly treat: 'the flicks'. He'd missed the morning matinée at the Odeon, but that was kids' stuff anyway. He was twelve now, a big boy. He set off for another local cinema, the Pavilion, which was showing *The Mongols*, a film that had an 'A' rating from the British Board of Film Censors (meaning that children were only allowed in if accompanied by an adult).

So John, and his friend John Ryan whom he met outside the cinema and was also only twelve, set about propositioning adults to take them in. What risks they were running, how horrified Sheila Kilbride would have been had she known! But the two Johns were safe enough. Someone took them in and they sat together through the film until it ended at 5 p.m.

'Then we went on the market to make some money by doing errands for the market people, 'John Ryan said two years later in the witness box at Chester Assizes, with Ian Brady and Myra Hindley in the dock.

'We went and fetched a trolley from the station for a man on the market. I got sixpence for this. John got about threepence or sixpence, I'm not sure exactly. Then we went to a man who sells carpets in the open market. There were two lads there, one from the same class as me. After I had some talk with them I decided to go home.

'When I set off to catch the bus, John Kilbride was not with me. I last saw him beside one of the big salvage bins on the open market near the carpet dealer's stall. There was no one with him.'

It was twenty-five minutes past five, not half an hour since the boys had come out of the cinema. Young John Ryan's was the last friendly face that John Kilbride would see.

When John didn't arrive home that evening, and after checking his Gran's and his aunt's, Patrick and Sheila Kilbride called the police.

A massive search was launched. Over 700 statements were taken, 500 posters of his gap-toothed smile were distributed with the legend 'Have You Seen This Boy?' under them. And eight days after he disappeared, on a bitter cold Sunday, 2000 volunteers combed every scrap of waste land, every derelict building, every bush in every park for miles around.

Unlike the parents of Pauline Reade, Mr and Mrs Kilbride would not spend half a lifetime wondering where his body was. The badly decomposed body of John Kilbride was recovered from Saddleworth Moor on Thursday, 21 October 1965. Sheila Kilbride, realistic enough to know that after two years her son must be dead, was relieved that she was able to give him the Christian burial she had always wanted for him. On 1 November, after a service at St Christopher's Church where Sheila was a regular member of the congregation,

John was buried at Hurst Cemetery. 'Rest with God' says the inscription on his well-tended grave.

Mrs Kilbride's ordeal was not over. She, a quiet, shy woman, would be forced to give evidence twice against her son's killers: at their committal and again at their trial. Hers was some of the most touching evidence in the case.

John's body was unidentifiable. But his clothes were intact enough for her to recognise. There was a grey check jacket, given to John's grandmother by a friend whose son had outgrown it, and carefully hemmed to make it shorter by Sheila Kilbride. She'd also sewn on new buttons, plastic ones in the shape of footballs. She had one left over, which she'd given to the police, to match with the ones on the jacket.

'I recognised the vest as one of John's father's,' she told the court. 'I had taken it in at the sides to make it fit. The pullover and underpants were similar to those John was wearing when he disappeared. The trousers were, too, and I recognised some odd coloured buttons which I had stitched on. I recognised a shoe as one of a pair that John had been wearing. I had recently had them mended at the Co-op.'

What happened to John Kilbride, how long it took between him leaving Ashton market and his body being buried on the moor, we don't know.

But we know the journey was made in a Ford Anglia, hired that Saturday morning by Myra Hindley, for £14 10s. She had arranged the hire the week before, from Warren's Autos in Ardwick, a bus ride from her Gorton home, perhaps to celebrate her passing her driving test a fortnight earlier.

She arrived alone to collect the car, wearing black trousers, a leather jacket and a high-necked sweater. And she returned it alone the next day. The man from the hire company remembered it specifically: it was covered in mud.

'It looked as if it had been through a ploughed field,' he said.

Today Sheila Kilbride, like Joan Reade, is another of the Moors Murderers' victims, sentenced to a lifetime of sorrow. She and her husband Patrick were divorced five years after John's death, and she bore the brunt of bringing her younger children up alone. She is a gentle peace-loving woman, never one to make a public show of her grief.

But it is no less real. Six other children and eighteen grandchildren cannot compensate her for the loss of that cheerful twelve-year-old whose grave she tends. Now with her family all grown-up, she lives alone, and she cries for her firstborn.

'I've cried more since the children left home than ever before,' she says. Probably because for years she struggled not to burden them with her grief.

One of them, though, did take on the mantle of his parents' suffering. Daniel Kilbride, next in age to John, the one who took over his brother's duties looking after their grandmother, is in his mid-thirties, married with his own four children. He leads a normal family life. Until someone mentions the names of Brady and Hindley. And then Daniel Kilbride, who shared a bedroom with his brother, becomes a hard and angry man. He has sworn that he will kill either of them if they are ever released.

4
Lesley Ann

Myra hired cars from Warren Autos twice more: on 27 November, the Wednesday after John died, and again on 21 December. They needed a vehicle for reconnaisance trips, to check that their handiwork had gone undiscovered. It was cold weather, and the back of the motorbike was no place for long treks up to the moors, even without worrying about needing a spade.

Then it was Christmas, and time for Myra to show another side of her character. Granny Maybury's dog Lassie had puppies, and Myra decided to keep one. She called him Puppet, one of a series of baby names she would always use for him, the most popular being Pekadese. Her devotion to the dog was excessive, even to people who did not know how that overt sentimentality contrasted with the barbarities of the private world she now inhabited.

Neighbours were by now calling Myra 'Miss Hoity Toity', because the bleached blonde who had known them all their lives would walk past with her nose in the air and a look of superiority on her face. But as long as she kept herself to herself, nobody minded. They even thought, in the Gorton backstreets, that 'our Myra is doing rather well for herself with her smart young man, and having passed her driving test and all. She's a bit silly about them dogs, mind, but that'll change when she settles down and has her own babies'.

Britain was in the grip of Beatlemania, with 'I Want to

Hold Your Hand' selling a million copies in three days, and the four mop-topped pop stars were mobbed wherever they went. President Kennedy had been assassinated the day before John Kilbride died. 'Dr Who' was launched on television the following month. Mods and Rockers were on a collision course that would erupt in fury at seaside resorts for the next few bank holidays.

In February 1964 Myra bought her first car, a second-hand Austin Traveller. It was a small car with plenty of space at the back, one of the forerunners of the modern estate car design. She didn't keep it for long, trading it in for a white Mini-van – just in time for another trip to the moors with a young passenger in the back.

The evening of 16 June 1964 was warm, bright, and sunny. But the week had been unsettled, and there were umbrellas and raincoats over the arms of the shirt-sleeved men and cotton-dressed women on the streets of Manchester.

For the same reason, Keith Bennett, aged twelve years and four days, wore a beige plastic rain jacket over his rainbow striped tee-shirt and jeans, as he dawdled along Eston Street, Longsight, at quarter to eight in the evening. He met a couple of girls who were schoolmates of his, and he started teasing them, threatening to thump them.

His mother Winnie, walking along the other side of the road on the way to her eight o'clock bingo session at St Aloysius School off Ardwick Green, saw her son larking about.

'I shouted to him to be careful in case he hurt them girls,' said Winnie, who had recently been married for a second time to Keith's stepfather Jimmy Johnson.

'He just give me one of them big grins of his, as much as to say don't worry, mam. And them's the last words I spoke to him.'

Winnie carried on walking in the same direction as Keith, but he was in front of her and she never caught him up.

'But I had him in my eye until he'd crossed the zebra crossing in Stockport Road. He'd broken his glasses, so I wanted to be sure he got across the busy road OK.'

Keith was on his way to stay with his grandmother, Mrs Gertrude Bennett, where he spent the night every alternate Tuesday. 'My mam would have Keith on a Tuesday one week, and his sister Sylvia the next,' said Mrs Johnson. Keith was the oldest of the four children she had at the time. Another three have been born since.

'He'd been to the school swimming gala the day before, and swum a length of the baths for the first time. He got a certificate for it. But he dropped his glasses and broke them. He'd been short-sighted since he was small. He couldn't see at all without his glasses, so I made sure he was across that road. The next morning my mam came up to our house and I said, 'Where's Keith?' because normally she brought him up with her on her way to her job. She was a cleaner at Toc H in Victoria Park in them days, so she'd bring the kiddie back early.

'She said he hadn't come to her last night. She said she'd been expecting him, but then she thought I must have made some other arrangements. We both started to panic. I was more than seven months pregnant. I went up to the school and the clinic, where I thought he might have gone about his broken glasses. But there was no sign, so I went to the police. They took his description, but said they couldn't do anything till he'd been missing forty-eight hours.'

Winnie Johnson's hell was just beginning. Rumours flew around the area. There were reports that Keith's body was in a river, that he'd run away to London. The police told Winnie that a schoolfriend of Keith's had seen him on the Wednesday morning, outside Longsight Library. The boy had asked Keith if he was going to school and Keith had apparently said, 'I'll be up later.'

Winnie's mother, sixty-five at the time, blamed herself and started on a fruitless two-year trek around the derelict buildings of the area, searching for her grandson. Winnie, due to have her fifth baby in June, went into premature labour two weeks after his disappearance and gave birth to David, one of three brothers Keith was never to see.

And then a fresh nightmare started for the family. Jimmy Johnson was taken to the local police station for questioning. He was taken in four times in the two years after Keith disappeared.

'They accused me of killing him, because I was his stepfather,' says Jimmy today, phlegmatically. 'I don't blame them, I'm glad they explored every possibility, they had a job to do. But it was terrible at the time. I was very fond of the lad, and to be accused of doing away with him was too much, what with all the other upset. Every time I spent the day at the police station I'd come home and all the neighbours would be hanging over their gates, ever so friendly like, dying to know what was happening. They'd seen me being driven off in a cop car, and I'm sure that was enough to make half of them think I was guilty.'

Detectives took up the floorboards of the Johnsons' terraced house, and finding that all the houses in the row were connected, searched underneath them all. They inspected the concrete in the backyard, checking that none of it was new. And they searched the grounds of an old people's home that butted on to the Johnsons' garden.

'The worst time,' says Winnie, 'was one Sunday morning when we was all in bed, and the police came and hauled Jimmy away. He didn't come back all day. Apparently someone had told the police that Jimmy had been drinking in the town and talking about what he'd done to Keith. They released him, of course. But Jimmy was getting really sick of it. He started blaming me. It was beginning to affect our marriage. In the end I went down to Bootle Street police station and said to the head of CID, "Do you think I'd have stayed with my husband if I thought he had anything to do with Keith? You're splitting my family up. And if that happens you'll have my death and the death of four kiddies on your conscience, because I'll kill myself and take them with me."

'Eventually the police laid off. But other people didn't. I was walking along Stockport Road one day with my mother and two of the kiddies when a woman stopped me. She said, "You're Keith's mum aren't you? Do you want to know what's happened to him? He's been chopped up and fed to pigs." I was upset for days after that.'

For the first two or three months after Keith's disappearance, Winnie clung to the hope that he was still alive.

'My senses told me he was dead, but I just couldn't believe it. And then one night when my new baby Jimmy was about three months old I was feeding him, and half falling asleep while I was doing it. And in my drowsy state I heard Keith call to me, as clearly as anything. "Mam!" he shouted. And then I knew for certain he was dead. And that was a sort of consolation, I felt happier just being certain even of that.'

The other children in the family were desperately upset, too. Jimmy's daughter Susan, from his first marriage, was the same age as Keith, and was living with the Johnsons.

'She and Keith went everywhere together. I can just see their little faces now,' said Jimmy, 'asking me if I'd give them the money for the pictures. And if they liked the film they'd stay in the cinema and see it twice. She was in a terrible state after Keith disappeared. We'd hear her crying in her sleep.

'And Margaret, she was only about three at the time, but she was devoted to Keith. Used to follow him around like a little dog. For days and weeks she was asking where he was, and not able to understand when we told her he wouldn't be coming back. The others, Alan, Sylvia and Ian, all missed him in their own ways. They'd talk about him as if he was there, and then remember.'

Winnie Johnson started on a lifetime's dependence on pills and tablets to calm her down and help her sleep. Every night before she went to bed she would open a drawer in her bedroom and look at Keith's broken spectacles. Then one day the police arrived on the doorstep of 29 Eston Street with a couple of photographs and a question: 'Have you ever seen these two people?' Winnie and Jimmy Johnson looked down at the now-familiar police mugshots of Myra Hindley and Ian Brady, and shook their heads.

'The police told us they thought they had something to do with it. Then the more we heard, the more we knew that was right. They only lived quarter of a mile from us, and it was horrifying to think we probably passed them in the street dozens of times after Keith had gone, and never knew. One day a couple of chaps from CID came and asked to speak to Jimmy on his own. They took him into the front room. When they came out, the detectives left. I asked Jimmy what it was about, but he didn't say a word. He just lifted Joey, the baby at the time, out of his pram and sat there with him on his knee, and the tears streamed down his face.

'Eventually, after an age, he said, "Winnie, I've got something to tell you. They've found a lad's body on the moors, but they think it's John Kilbride because it's quite a lot taller than Keith." I didn't say anything. The police brought the clothing they'd found, in a plastic bag, but it wasn't Keith's. The funny thing was that the tee-shirt John Kilbride had been wearing was very similar to the one Keith had on. For a moment my hopes were raised that they'd found the body, but then they were dashed again.'

Winnie didn't go to the Brady and Hindley trial.

'My mother wouldn't let me, she knew it would be too much for me. We had come so close to solving Keith's death but we still didn't know where his body was. I couldn't have faced seeing the killers in the flesh.'

But twenty years later, Winnie Johnson was prepared to meet Myra.

Two big things were about to happen to the Hindley family. The first was Maureen's marriage and the second was the move from Gorton.

Maureen had been working at Millwards as a filing clerk. But she'd had to give up when she became pregnant by David Smith. On 15 August, 'seven months gone' as the local gossips put it, she and David Smith were married. It was a hasty register office affair, not attended by any of Maureen's relatives. Mrs Hindley, too ashamed, stayed at home. Myra told her sister she didn't approve of marriage, and didn't go either.

The young couple moved in with David's father, into the dirty, neglected house in Wiles Street. There was no wedding reception, no telegrams of congratulation, no honeymoon. But the next day, a Sunday, to everyone's surprise including Myra's, Ian Brady suggested that the eighteen-year-old bride and her sixteen-year-old husband should be given a treat – a day out in the car.

They'd been introduced before but this was the first time that Brady and Smith had met properly. Now the trip to Lake Windermere was to be the start of a friendship that would have calamitous consequences for both of them. But it started well.

Brady enjoyed having a new audience. In two and a half years he had imparted to Myra the full gamut of his philosophies. The dogma that had so impressed her at first was now commonplace. She had been 'blooded' in every sense into his creed, and he could totally rely on her faithful complicity. But he no longer experienced the buzz of inculcating her, of moulding her unformed mind to his pattern, which he had so enjoyed. The loner whose life was dominated by a need to fulfil his devious cravings had found a pleasure that ran it a close second: the pleasure of sharing his obsessions with Myra.

Now he wanted to recreate the warm glow he had got from seeing a young face turned to him in admiration and devotion. He wanted another neophyte sitting at his feet. Enter David Smith.

There was a lot that was attractive about the lad. He was good-looking, cocky, arrogant. He stammered a bit, but it didn't seem to inhibit him. He'd had his pick of the Gorton girls, and he'd fought and beaten most of the Gorton boys. There was an air of menace about him that repelled and attracted at the same time.

As far as Brady was concerned, Smith had already gone a long way towards proving himself fit for the cause. He had convictions for violence, neighbours had seen him brawling with his father in the street, and at the time of the marriage he was waiting to appear in court on two more assault charges.

So the four of them set off together. Myra and Mo together, nattering almost like old times. David Smith in the back with Brady, who was bent on impressing the lad. There was one easy way to do that: money. Since Smith left school he had never held down a job for more than a few months, and the jobs he had had, as apprentices, were low paid. Now he was out of work with a pregnant wife. So an endless supply of cheap red wine and a couple of bottles of whisky was largesse unimagined, and as well as that, Brady paid for lunch and for a boat trip on Lake Windermere.

Throughout the day, the normally taciturn Brady talked. He started expounding his theories of life to David Smith in the back of that Mini-van, and he would keep it up for the next fourteen months. He started with the easy stuff, stuff he knew the sixteen-year-old would go along with: like how working for a living was a mug's game, you'd never get any real money together, that way. And headier stuff: the distribution of wealth was immoral, the poor had as much right to it as the rich. Leading up to: let's do a bank job one day, a payroll snatch, something that'll get us into the big money league.

It was drunken fantasy, and Smith was happy to go along with it. Yes, he'd love to be a big-time villain – what sixteen-year-old with no job, no qualifications and no prospects wouldn't? Just like Myra in the early days, he was bowled over by the long words and the literary references with which Brady laced his conversation. The dour Scotsman, so ill at ease with people that he preferred Myra to hand over his bus fare for him, waxed loquacious on his own ground. The drink coupled with the Scottish accent made it difficult for David Smith to understand everything he said, but the youngster wasn't worried. Drink was fuzzing his brain, too, and it was a nice feeling.

The trip to the Lakes was the start of the indoctrination of David Smith. There would be many evenings in the next year that the two couples would spend together, the wine flowing freely. There would be many trips, most of them up to Saddleworth Moor where Brady would teach Smith to use their guns, firing at the rabbits and old oil drums.

And Myra? David Smith was aware that she resented his presence, resented sharing Ian with him, knew that she recognised the attraction that bordered on physical between him and her lover. He was also aware that she was no doormat, no devoted girlfriend who did whatever she was told. Her temper was bad, and on several occasions he heard her shouting at Brady over trivial domestic things.

'He liked eating tinned macaroni cheese and she hated it. I've seen her fling a tin on the floor and scream at him that it was worse than dog food and what was he, a baby?' said Smith.

But although she wasn't happy about Smith's presence, she went along with it. David Smith wondered what hold Brady had on her. Besides, she liked having Mo around again. The two sisters were drawing nearer together, just as they had been before. When they were tired, they would go to bed together upstairs at Wiles Street, leaving Brady and David Smith playing cards and talking, talking, talking until the early hours. Brady, who'd been reticent about his borstal experiences with Myra, openly bragged about them to Smith. It all helped his 'big man of the world' image.

Then came the move. The post-war planners were systematically pulling Manchester down, and replacing the slums with redbrick council houses and massive complexes of flats, linked by walkways. That Gorton was not the worst of the city's slums by any means is witnessed in the fact that it was not reduced to rubble until 1964, quite late in the Manchester rebuilding programme which had boomed in the fifties.

But the city had run out of land. It had bought a huge chunk from Cheshire to build Europe's biggest council estate, Wythenshawe, on the south of the city. Now it was hungrily taking over more. But it could not extend the city boundaries, so satellite towns were built. Hattersley was the biggest of these, with homes for 14,000 people.

Granny Maybury and most of her neighbours were allocated houses there. Some, like Myra's mother, refused to go. Hettie's marriage was crumbling, and she was having an affair with a driver called Bill Moulton. It would not have suited her to be slum-cleared miles away.

Even if Gran had not wanted to go, it is doubtful whether she would have had much say in the matter. Myra and Ian both relished the move, and Gran did whatever her domineering granddaughter told her. So all three of them moved to 16 Wardle Brook Avenue. The planners had done their best, constrained by the need to get the maximum number of homes into the land available. The estate is the usual serried ranks of redbrick houses punctuated with high-rise flats, but there were patches of green, carefully seeded and planted with young trees. And away on the skyline there was real scenery: the moors. Ian Brady had moved ten miles nearer his spiritual home.

In front of Granny Maybury's there was quite a big expanse of grass: Wardle Brook Avenue is on the edge of the new development, the nearest newly built road to the existing main road, Mottram New Road. So there was no one to overlook them from the front. At the back it was a different matter: the houses of Wardle Brook Walk were close, and there was a path along the back.

Number 16 was the end of a terrace of four, semi-detached. The road runs in front of the houses, although as it dips they remain level, so that number 10 at one end of the terrace is on the same level as the road, but number 16 at the other end is ten feet above it. You are supposed to approach the house along the path from number 10.

Ian and Myra found that irksome, and parked their car below the house, scrambling up the slope. One day, with a heavy body to dispose of, they would find it more than irksome.

Inside number 16 there was a through living room with a window each end, a fireplace and a serving hatch. There was a kitchen, and upstairs there were two bedrooms and a bathroom. Hot and cold running water and an inside lavatory – sheer luxury for families used to washing at the kitchen sink and laboriously boiling all the hot water they used. Before they moved in, David Smith helped Brady decorate, painting the walls of the living room pink and putting wallpaper that looked like imitation bricks round the fireplace.

Myra, too, was carried away by the home-building urge. She went shopping for new fireside chairs, new curtains, a new red carpet. They put new grey lino with a red stripe on the living room floor, under the carpet. With the red moquette settee that converted into a bed, and Gran's old oak sideboard, and the chairs and table from the kitchen at Bannock Street, it was all looking very cosy. Gran's budgie Joey was moved into the new living room, and Myra put a crinoline doll lamp on top of the television, its pink skirt matching the walls.

Any neighbours who saw them working on it must have thought them a devoted couple. Why, they even started work on the garden straightaway, as soon as they had moved the furniture in. Ian Brady with a spade in the garden of number 16 was to become a familiar sight in the next few months.

In the hall they had installed a cigarette machine which held twenty packets of Embassy tipped, and dispensed them one at a time as half a crown coins were inserted. Every Sunday morning a man came to empty the money and refill the machine. They both smoked – Brady preferred cigars or strong French cigarettes like Disque Bleu, when he could afford them, and Myra smoked forty Embassy a day. Even with the machine, they occasionally ran out, which was when Myra would go into the New Inn on the main road.

'She was very ladylike and never drank. She would just say, "Twenty Embassy tipped please" in a posh voice. She didn't sound like she came from Manchester,' said one of the bar staff.

They had to get up earlier to leave home at 8.10 a.m. for the drive to work, but compared to neighbours who were isolated in Hattersley from their work in the city, and dependent on the vagaries of the bus service, a young couple with a car had no problems. The move seemed to have done them good. They almost became sociable, making friends with Mrs Elsie Masterson and her family who lived next door but one.

Of course they never did more than nod curtly at their closest neighbours, Phoenix Braithwaite and his wife Tessa and their three children. 'Of course', because the Braithwaites were West Indians, blacks. And Ian's views on that subject were well-known, along with his views on Jews. After all, when he'd finished with the Jews Hitler would have wasted no time getting rid of the blacks, as Ian was fond of pointing out to Myra.

But Myra's nickname, Miss Hoity Toity, persisted among many of their old Gorton neighbours on the new estate. One neighbour, Mrs Lily Yates, said afterwards, 'I had known Myra all her life but she never let on when she saw me. She'd walk past without speaking. She was proper ladylike, but very stuck up with it.'

A month after they moved in, Maureen Smith had her

baby: a little girl they called Angela Dawn. Both the Smiths, scarcely more than children themselves, were delighted. They were still living in Gorton, but their closeness with Myra and Ian continued – whenever the older couple chose it to. With a car at their disposal, they could visit the Smiths whenever they liked; the Smiths could not visit them.

Myra did not unbend towards the baby: she didn't become a devoted auntie overnight. But because her lover seemed to need and want the devotion of his acolyte Smith, they remained frequent visitors at the house in Wiles Street.

Both she and Brady were still visiting their mothers regularly, too. Most days after work Ian Brady would go round to Westmoreland Street, his mother and stepfather's house, and Myra would collect him from there later in the evening. Now that they lived ten miles away from Millwards, the car was used every day – and parked in a place Myra had found quite near the company offices.

Unfortunately, it was outside the window of an arthritic old lady's house. The old lady asked Myra not to park there, because she was unable to go out and one of her greatest pleasures in life was gazing out of her window – with the car there she couldn't see out. She was met with a tirade of abuse. Myra called her an 'interfering old busybody' and stormed away, leaving the car there. The old lady wrote to the police, and Myra had a visit from a constable, at Millwards. He told her to park elsewhere, as there were plenty of spaces available.

Probably out of sheer relief that that was all his visit was about, she complied.

Christmas was coming. The excitement of the move had died down, life was getting back into its normal routine. 'Routine' wasn't something that Ian Brady could tolerate for long.

Pat Hodges provided a diversion. Pat was the third of

Elsie Masterson's six children, from number 12. The eleven-year-old got to know Myra about three or four weeks after the move to Hattersley, when she called to see if her mother was at number 16. Mrs Masterson, cheerful, three times married and pregnant again, was the sort who got to know all her neighbours.

Pat found her mother was not at number 16. She and Myra got chatting, mostly about the two dogs, Lassie and Puppet. When Myra suggested giving the girl a ride in her Mini-van, down to the city to pick up Ian from his mother's, Pat was thrilled.

'I went with her in a little grey van. We both stayed in the car after it had stopped, and eventually Ian joined us. Myra said she didn't go into his house because his mother kept her talking.'

A plausible explanation for a situation that continued to irritate her: Myra had still not been invited across the threshold of the Brady home. Pat got into the habit of accompanying Myra on the trip most evenings. Myra liked having company. And Ian, too, seemed unusually warm towards their new young friend. Was it his idea or Myra's to take young Pat up to the moors, to their very own private burial ground?

It was Myra who suggested it to the girl.

'When we got there the first time it was light and we just sat there talking. We went up on the moors about once or twice a week. They took wine with them nearly every time. We went to the same spot except for a couple of times when we went further down the road.'

Those are Pat Hodges' words, the words she used to tell the jury about her outings with her new friends. If Myra and Ian were bitterly to regret getting David Smith involved in their schemes, then surely they must also have regretted taking young Pat Hodges so frequently to the same spot on Saddleworth Moor: because one day, in the not too distant future, Pat Hodges would be able to drive in the back of a police car and recognise exactly where they had parked on those evening outings.

They even took her up there late at night on Christmas Eve. Elsie Masterson remembers how her daughter begged to be allowed to go with 'Auntie' Myra and 'Uncle' Ian that night.

'I thought they were a nice couple,' she says now. 'They seemed to like Pat a lot and she often took her dolls and toys there. Pat was very insistent about going that night.'

What a strange picnic it must have been. Pat had already been given whisky and gin and wine to drink, at number 16 before they set off. In the back of the van she was given more wine, and sandwiches. They didn't get out of the van, but sat at the bleak and windswept roadside on the A635 to see Christmas morning come in, their own pagan watch night service.

'We stayed there until about 12.30 a.m.' said Pat. 'Then Myra said, "Shall we go home and get some blankets and come back for the night?" and Ian said, "All right." Myra then drove me back home. It was about 1.30 a.m. when I got in. Shortly after I got in the house I heard the van drive off.'

Perhaps they had been tempted to keep Pat up there in their private burial ground, to lay her to rest with the other children in the peaty earth where they had taken her for walks and given her sandwiches and alcohol many times. But if there was an urge, it was easy to resist. If Pat had been their victim, she would have been their last. She would easily have been traced back to them. Her mother still lies awake worrying about what nearly happened.

'Looking back now I know I should have been worried. I still have nightmares of what could have happened to Pat with those devil people. I lie awake at night thinking what might have happened if they had kept her. They must have had second thoughts or something like that.'

Pat is today grown up, married, and has three children of her own. She doesn't talk about her trips to the moors, or the help she gave the police, or the trauma of giving evidence – both at the committal proceedings and at the full trial – against her 'auntie' and 'uncle'.

But she must surely sometimes think about the girl who was driven up to the moors in the back of the white Mini-van on Boxing Day, less than forty-eight hours after her Christmas picnic. Because this little girl, just a year younger than Pat, might also have been married with children of her own today – had she lived.

Once a fortnight Myra took Gran to visit her son, Myra's Uncle Jim, in Dukinfield. They would arrive just after lunch, and then Myra would return at about 9.30 in the evening to take the old lady home. Boxing Day was a good day for Gran's Christmas visit to Jim and his wife Nellie, because it was Jim's birthday. Gran and Myra arrived, with presents, at the usual time.

But Myra did not return at 9.30 p.m. She did not turn up on Uncle Jim's doorstep until 11.30 p.m., and then she refused to take her Gran home.

'She came into the house and said, "I'm sorry Gran I can't take you back. The roads are too bad,"' said Jim. 'I started to have an argument with Myra. I'd been outside frequently to see whether Myra had come, and I knew what the roads were like. It had been snowing, but there was only a light sprinkling of snow in the street where I lived. The argument went on for about quarter of an hour and ended when Myra said, "I can't take Gran, and that's that." Then she walked out. We made a bed of cushions on the living room floor for Gran.'

Uncle Jim, furious as he was, saw nothing more sinister in Myra's actions than to suspect that she had a wild party going on back at Wardle Brook Avenue. But something more sinister was indeed going on.

Mrs Ann Downey, separated from her husband Terry, lived in the Ancoats inner city area of Manchester with her four children and with Alan West, the man who has now been her husband for many years. She was expecting another baby.

The family had the same happy Christmas as millions of others all over Britain. Up early on Christmas morning for the children to open their presents, mum and dad groaning for more sleep, wild excitement as the wrappings, so carefully sellotaped in place, were ripped off.

Ten-year-old Lesley Ann, the second child, was thrilled with Father Christmas' offerings: a nurse's outfit, a tiny electric sewing machine, a doll and the usual Christmas annuals and games that would need quieter moments to be appreciated.

Charnley Walk, where they lived, was a council house in the redeveloped part of Ancoats, an area that had come much higher up the city council's list of priorities than Gorton when the slum clearance programme started. Some of the old Ancoats remained. Not far from Lesley Ann's home there were blank-faced factory buildings with notices outside offering work to machinists, and there was the brown-tiled hospital, a Victorian building whose waiting room had provided inspiration for L. S. Lowry.

But the twinkling lights on the silver Christmas trees in the windows of the houses made it festive and cheery, and inside Lesley Ann's home there were paper streamers pinned up, and a box of crackers, and turkey for dinner.

Boxing Day, for children everywhere, can be an anti-climax. That's why parents plan visits to the circus or the pantomime. Lesley Ann's treat was a trip to a funfair, with her eight-year-old brother Tommy and her four-year-old brother Brett. Big brother Terry would go on his own, with his own friends.

There was a whole little posse of children who set out together for the ten-minute walk to Miles Platting, where the fairground was. There was Linda Clarke, Lesley's friend, and Linda's little brother and sister. They set off together at half-past four. None of them had much money to spend: Linda had 1s 1d, and Lesley had 6d. It didn't take long, at a penny a ride on the roundabouts, to run through it. By half-past five Linda and the little ones were ready to go home.

Lesley Ann, mesmerised by the bright lights, decided to stay for a while, even though she had no money left. A boy from the same school as her saw her, standing by the dodgems, on her own.

He was the last person to see her alive, except for Myra Hindley and Ian Brady. Because they went to the fair for their Boxing Day treat, too.

By ten that night, Mrs Downey and Alan West had tramped the streets around Ancoats, had combed the alleyways of the funfair, and were finally coming face to face with the grisly reality: Lesley Ann had been abducted. The police were called and over the next few days and weeks there was a frenzy of activity. Derelict buildings were searched, empty houses broken into, the canal dredged.

The fairground was ripped apart, the showmen's caravans searched. There were reported sightings of Lesley in Morecambe, Blackpool, Torquay, Bournemouth – and even Belgium. Every lead was followed up, all to no avail.

Mrs Downey called two or three times a week at Mill Street police station, only to be told 'We're sorry. . . .'

'It's a nightmare,' she said, 'I can't sleep or eat. If I close my eyes I can see her all the time.'

Lesley Ann's bedroom was kept exactly as she left it, with her two dolls, Patsy and Lynn, lying on the bed. The night she disappeared her mother had promised they would use the new toy sewing machine to make clothes for them. Neighbours collected £100 – a lot of money in those hard-up streets – as a reward for anyone who could give information about the little girl.

But Mrs Downey, who lost the baby she was expecting, would have no real news of her daughter for nearly ten months, until the arrest of Brady and Hindley; until the discovery, on Saddleworth Moor, of the body of her daughter, the first of the victims to be reclaimed from their lonely graves.

Then, in the weeks that followed, she would learn more about the last hours of her daughter's life than any of the other victims' mothers would know for quarter of a century.

Perhaps it would have been better for Ann West – she later married Alan West – not to have known. Perhaps knowing of some, but not all, of the agonies her trusting, shy little daughter endured has been worse than knowing nothing.

At any rate Ann West, like the other mothers, has become another of the Moors Murderers' victims: a woman whose life has been haunted by the death of her little girl, a woman who has lived with an obsession for so long that there is nothing else in her life.

Nobody knows how they would react to being in the situation that Ann West found herself in that Boxing Day evening, 1964, unless they have experienced it. Nobody can predict their own behaviour while in shock. Ann West has stayed in shock for over twenty years. And it has driven her to worry at her obsession, like a dog worries at a bone, for all those years.

She has given endless interviews, appeared on television, posed for countless pictures. But that does not mean that she glories in the publicity. It is a symptom of her obsessed state, one way of feeding her need to talk constantly about and dwell on the one thing that dominates her life.

Like the other victims' mothers, she, too, lives on tranquillisers. She, too, has difficulty sleeping. She, too, knows no peace.

Were they on the way to the moors to dispose of Lesley Ann's body when Myra called to say she couldn't take Gran home that night? Or was the little girl still at Wardle Brook Avenue then, as the police started their inquiries into her disappearance?

The timetable of the murder has not been revealed. But by 10.30 next morning, a Sunday, all was back in order at the Hattersley house, because that's when Myra went to Uncle Jim's to fetch Gran home.

Later, Elsie Masterson popped in to tell Myra about her new pregnancy. But there were no congratulations to be had. 'Can't you do something to shift it?' was Myra's response.

Otherwise, they behaved as normally as they ever did. Myra had given Ian another tape recorder for Christmas: there were now two in the little sitting room, so that he could mess around recording from one to the other.

On New Year's Day that's just what he was doing, playing around with the tape recorders. Pat Hodges was in number 16, reading magazines.

'Want to read the paper?' Myra asked her, handing over the *Gorton and Openshaw Reporter*. The front page was dominated by a picture of Lesley Ann Downey, and the headline read, 'Have you seen ten-year-old Lesley? Big search for lost girl'.

Pat spoke, 'You see that girl at Ancoats?'

'Yes . . . just now,' said Myra.

'She lives near my friend,' said Pat.

'And she lives near her house?' asked Myra.

'Yes.'

'Did she know her?'

'I dunno.'

A very ordinary conversation, not one that would merit tape recording, and certainly not a recording worth keeping, not unless you had a special interest in the subject under discussion.

Myra and Brady had. And so they kept the tape.

Maureen talked to her sister about Lesley Ann's disappearance, too, and she remembered the brief conversation clearly. Maureen read in the local newspaper that Mrs Downey was offering a £100 reward for information about her daughter. As she and Myra were going to bed together – David and Ian Brady were downstairs drinking and talking – Maureen remarked, 'Her mother must think a lot of the child.'

Myra laughed.

After February, Pat Hodges dropped out of life at number 16. She found friends of her own age, and her interest in Myra and Ian waned. Brady seems to have taken it personally, because a couple of weeks after she stopped joining Myra in the van to pick him up, he caught her and her friend cutting through his garden.

'He said "I'll break your back if I ever cop you in there again" and after that I didn't speak to him or Myra,' said Pat.

David Smith's education was still underway. Brady was lending him books to read, and the late-night induction course into the bizarre workings of Brady's mind was continuing. A bank job was discussed, and David was instructed to keep watch and make notes outside the premises, just like in the movies. Murder was discussed, and Smith was fed the Brady theories that people are like ants, and can be disposed of as easily. He was schooled in the Marquis de Sade's writings:

'Should murder be punished by murder? Undoubtedly not. The only punishment that a murderer should be condemned to is that which he risks from his friends or the family of the man he has killed. . . . Murder is a horror, but a horror often necessary, never criminal and essential to tolerate in a republic. Above all, it should never be punished with murder.'

Smith was given reading lists by his mentor. He was told to make notes, and questioned about them. The pupil was doing well: he had even started his own collection of macabre literature. There were more trips to the moors, more target practice with the guns.

But then something very real shattered the fantasy world that David Smith was now moving into, alongside Brady and Myra. Angela Dawn, the Smiths' baby, died on 25 April 1965. The two young parents were distraught. However fragile their own relationship, however difficult it was sharing a house with his father, the love for the baby had united them. The baby died of bronchitis, in Ancoats Hospital, just down the road from Lesley Ann Downey's home.

Myra was visibly upset. She took flowers to Wiles Street, and placed them on the tiny coffin. Ian stayed outside in the car. 'Another flower in God's garden,' she wrote on the card, as she looked down at her dead niece, tears streaming from her eyes. Mo, even in her grief, registered surprise. Myra wasn't supposed to believe in God any more.

'Don't tell Ian,' was all Myra said, as she wiped away the mascara smears. But the tenderness was short-lived.

'You should get a puppy, they're better than babies,' she told Mo.

'Our Mo was a fool for ever marrying that David Smith,' she said to Mrs Masterson.

Her own dog, Puppet, was still the centre of her life. Elsie Masterson remembers the day the dog was run over.

'Myra made a bed on the settee with pillows and sheets for Puppet. She said, "There'll be no sleep for me tonight, I'll be up all night with the dog." They worshipped those two dogs. I've been in their house and had to stand up while the dogs sat down in chairs.'

Life jogged along. The cigarette machine was removed after Myra gave up smoking. She gave it up easily after reading the first big onslaught of publicity connecting tobacco and cancer.

Then on Myra's twenty-third birthday, Dave and Maureen moved to join them in Hattersley. They too had been rehoused, after weeks of splitting their time between David's father's house, David's grandfather's house and Maureen's mother's house, staying usually until the regular inhabitants could take their presence no longer. For with Dave and Mo went a chronic lack of money, a disregard for normal sleeping hours, and a tendency to loud, drunken arguments that sometimes ended in violence.

Their new home was just two minutes' walk from Ian and Myra's. Underwood Court was a tall block of flats with entry-phone systems and number 18 was on the third floor. Now the four of them could spend every evening together if they wanted to – or, more correctly, if Ian wanted them to, because David Smith remembers calling a couple of times at the house in Wardle Brook Avenue and being told by Myra at the door that he couldn't come in because Ian was busy.

Usually though, and to Myra's annoyance, Brady had time for his young pupil. He didn't have any time for Granny Maybury, and the old lady knew it. Ever since he had moved into her home, the silent Scotsman had treated her as though she was the lodger. She had long since discovered that the best way of getting through the evenings was to retreat to her room.

Myra, the granddaughter she had idolised, was bossy with her, and laughed when Brady was downright rude. Whenever Granny Maybury asked for the record player to be turned down, Brady would deliberately turn it up, and Myra would hoot with laughter.

The old lady confided in a neighbour she had known from the old Gorton days: 'These people are no good to me now. They never speak to me. I go to bed at seven o'clock to get out of the way. They seem unfeeling.'

She told other friends to visit her only during the day, when the couple were at work, and if anyone stayed late in the afternoon they noticed her becoming more and more nervous. But the old lady got a fortnight's break, in September, when Myra and Ian went off on their holidays.

They'd been to Scotland before for Ian to show 'the girl' the scenery that had first stirred his blighted soul. But now he was to show her something different: Glasgow, his home town. And his family.

Although Myra did not know he was illegitimate, she knew he had been brought up by the Sloans, and that Pat Brady was his stepfather. So although it bothered her that she had never been introduced to the Bradys, it was a major source of consolation to find herself wheeled out as the girlfriend to meet the Sloans – the girlfriend, it was understood, whom their boy Ian would marry one day. It was the nearest Myra would get – until after the arrest – to a declaration of love and a proposal of marriage from the strange man she was already, in a much darker way, wedded to.

One evening while they were there, Brady went out alone and left Myra on her own with the Sloans. Glasgow police have dug back through their records for anyone who disappeared around that time, but found nothing that ties in. And yet it would make sense, if Brady had carried out another solitary killing, of a remark he would make to David Smith two weeks later.

They were discussing murder, a favourite topic. Brady was trying to convince Smith how easy it was. He said, 'I have killed three or four and I'll do another one, but I'm not due for one for three months. But it will be done and it won't count.'

Why wasn't he 'due' one? He'd been killing young people in a pattern that went roughly one every summer and another every winter. Pauline Reade, July 1963; John Kilbride, November 1963; Keith Bennett June 1964; Lesley Ann Downey, December 1964.

He was not only 'due' one, he was a few months overdue – unless there is one we don't know about. And if Brady was making prophetic remarks, so in a more banal way was Myra. At the launderette near work, where she went with their weekly wash, she heard about a stray dog that was dying of malnutrition.

'I don't know how people can be so cruel,' she said 'They ought to be arrested.'

Two weeks later, somebody was arrested. Myra Hindley. For a brand of cruelty that was in a different league from neglecting a dog.

5

The Last Murder

'That was the messiest yet,' said Ian Brady.

Myra Hindley was standing in the living room of the house at Wardle Brook Avenue, looking down at the bloody pulp that was all that was left of Edward Evans. Then she left the room and came back with a mop, a bucket, a bowl of soapy water and some rags, and started to clean up.

Edward Evans was a seventeen-year-old apprentice with AEI, the big electrical company on the Trafford Park industrial estate. He lived with his mother Edith and father John, a lift attendant, and his younger brother Alan in the Ardwick district of central Manchester. Edward was a Manchester United supporter, a regular at the Old Trafford ground. On Wednesday, 6 October 1965, he told his parents he was going to an evening match, a friendly between his team and Helsinki. He was supposed to meet a friend, but that rendezvous never happened. So Edward was on his own for the evening, mooching about the city centre.

He was a good-looking boy, dressed in the height of fashion. After his death there were allegations – from Brady – that he was a homosexual, that when Brady picked him up Edward believed it was for casual homosexual sex.

His family, distraught at the death of their son, had to face the double agony of hearing him publicly branded a pervert – after all, this was many years before the phrase 'gay lib' had been coined, and homosexuality was (and still is for boys of Edward's age) illegal.

They have always denied that Eddie was 'a queer'. It matters a great deal to them, another shattered family trying to cope with the long drawn-out aftermath of their son's murder.

Its only relevance to the substance of the case against Brady and Hindley is that it has helped fuel speculation about their devious and kinky practices. When Edward's body was found his trousers were unfastened, and there was forensic evidence at the trial that they had, at some stage of the evening, been pulled down.

The evening had started for Myra and Brady with a visit to Manchester Central Station, their second visit in two successive evenings. And there, bored and lonely, was Edward Evans.

This is how Ian Brady described it at his trial:

'When we got the city centre I told Myra to go to Central Station to see if the buffet was open. When we got there it was about two minutes off half-past ten. I said to Myra the buffet would probably be closed, but I would go and see if I could get some bottled beer. Evans was standing at a milk vending machine. I knew Evans; I had met him on several occasions previously. As I went to try the [buffet] door he said it was closed, but I tried the door anyway. Then we got into conversation.

'He kept saying there was no place to get a drink. I knew Evans was a homosexual because he went to one club especially, called the Rembrandt, in Manchester, which is a homosexuals' hang-out. I invited him back to the car.'

Whatever Ian Brady offered him, it was enough to persuade the lad to get into the car with them and be chauffeured back to Wardle Brook Avenue by Myra, who was introduced as Brady's sister. Once home Brady entertained him, pouring him a drink, while Myra slipped upstairs and changed out of her tight mock-leopardskin dress into what David Smith later described as 'an old jumper and a skirt with the hem hanging down. Her make-up was all smudged, her hair tousled up. And she had tartan pumps on her feet'.

Perhaps, if Eddie's parents are right about his sexual predilections, it was Myra who inveigled him back to Hattersley. We only have the evidence of her and her lover Brady to fill in the time between Eddie last being seen in a city centre bar at 7 p.m., and the arrival of David Smith at number 16.

Because the Smiths' flat was where Myra went, in her old clothes. Maureen Smith told the court that it was about 11.30 p.m. when her sister rang the entry-phone buzzer. She and David were in bed, but she got up and let Myra in.

'Myra asked if I would give a message to my mother. She'd said to tell her she would see her tomorrow night. She was just stroking the dog. I asked her why she had come round so late. She said she had forgotten to come round earlier on. She asked David if he would walk her home because all the lights were out. David said he would walk her home and would only be a couple of minutes. He took the dog's stick with him. It was something he normally did.'

David takes up the story.

'We got almost to Myra's house. I intended to leave her there, then she said, "Ian has some miniature wine bottles. Come and collect them now."

'As we got to the front door Myra stopped walking and she said, "Wait over the road, watch for the landing light to flick twice." I didn't think this was unusual because I've had to do this before, whilst she went in to see if Ian would have me in. He's a very temperamental sort of fellow.'

On this occasion, though, Ian was happy, even eager, to have David Smith in. He would tell the court at his trial that he had already decided to 'roll a queer' that evening for money to help the Smiths out of their pressing financial problems – and that Smith was party to the plan. The truth is that he had already chosen Edward Evans for the initiation of David Smith into his killing cult.

The two youths, Evans just six days older than Smith, never spoke to each other, never exchanged pleasantries about how United got on or fancy an old duffer like Ken Dodd being top of the hit parade. The story of what happened next is taken from the statement that David Smith made to the police:

'I waited across the road as Myra had told me to, and then the landing light flicked twice, so I walked up and knocked on the front door. Ian opened the door and he said in a very loud voice for him, he normally speaks soft, "Do you want those miniatures?" I nodded my head to say yes and he led me into the kitchen which is directly opposite the front door, and he gave me three miniature bottles of spirits and said: "Do you want the rest?"

'When I first walked into the house, the door to the living room, which was on my right, was closed. After he'd put the three bottles down in the kitchen, Ian went into the living room and I waited in the kitchen. I waited about a minute or two then suddenly I heard a hell of a scream; it sounded like a woman, really high-pitched. Then the screams carried on, one after another really loud. Then I heard Myra shout, "Dave, help him," very loud. When I ran in I just stood inside the living room and I saw a young lad. He was lying with his head and shoulders on the couch and his legs were on the floor. He was facing upwards. Ian was standing over him, facing him, with his legs on either side of the young lad's legs. The lad was still screaming. He didn't look injured then, but there was only a small television light on, the big light was off. Ian had a hatchet in his hand, it was his right hand, he was holding it above his head and then he hit the lad on the left side of his head with the hatchet. I heard the blow, it was a terrible hard blow, it sounded horrible.

'The young lad was still screaming and he half fell and

half wriggled off the couch on to the floor, on to his stomach. He was still screaming. Ian went after him and stood over him and kept hacking away at the young lad with the hatchet. I don't know how many times he hit the lad, but it was a lot, about the head, the neck, the shoulders and that.'

Smith said he felt his stomach turn 'and some sick came up but went down again'. He described Brady as swinging about with the hatchet, one blow grazing Myra's head.

'I was shaking, I was frightened to death of moving and my stomach was twisting. There was blood all over the place, on the walls, fireplace, everywhere.'

He told how Brady finished Edward Evans' short life by winding a piece of electrical flex round his neck and pulling tight, swearing and calling his victim a 'dirty bastard'. Strange gurgling noises, that would haunt David Smith for the rest of his life, were heard from the lifeless body. Then, job done, he turned to Myra who had been standing in the room all the time and said, 'It's done. It's the messiest yet. It normally only takes one blow.'

Then he wiped his hands, lit a cigarette, and told his faithful lieutenant to get the cleaning materials. After they'd scrubbed the walls and the floor and even the budgie cage, Ian asked Myra if she reckoned anyone had heard the screams.

'Yes, my Gran did,' she said, 'I told her I'd dropped something on my toe.'

Upstairs, Granny Maybury, in her bedroom since 8 p.m., had at last become aware of some of the strange goings-on in her own house. But she accepted the screams of a young man relinquishing life as nothing more than her granddaughter hurting her toe. The next door neighbours accepted it too. Phoenix Braithwaite would say after the trial that he never heard anything from next door except 'domestic noises'. There are, of course, plenty of what the police call 'domestics' on council estates like Hattersley, particularly when the estates are new and the tenants young. Family rows that erupt into violence in the middle of the night. Neighbours learn to keep themselves to themselves.

After the cleaning up of the room was over, Myra went out of the room, and Brady gave Smith a bottle of wine to swig out of. Myra came back with a well-prepared collection of materials to wrap a body in. There was a white blanket that was put round the corpse first, then a large sheet of polythene, and on top a grey blanket. Edward's head was concealed in a cushion cover. She lacked only one thing: string to truss it all up with. Brady solved this by taking the string that was bound around David Smith's dog stick. As they struggled to wrap the unwieldy bundle, Ian Brady made a joke, 'Eddie's a dead weight,' he said.

'Both he and Myra thought it was bloody hilarious,' Smith told the police, 'I didn't see anything to laugh about.'

Myra was sent upstairs to hold Gran's bedroom shut while Brady and Smith carried the body up and put it in Myra's room. Brady had decided they couldn't dispose of the body on the moors that night, because he had hurt his ankle in his frenzied attack on the youth. Also it was late, and the noise of them doing it might make the neighbours curious. Edward Evans was too heavy for them to take the short cut over the fence and down the slope.

Both Brady and Myra wanted to talk about what they'd just done. Brady asked Smith to feel the weight of the hatchet, and asked, 'How did he take it?' He then described how he'd used it.

Myra said, 'His eyes registered astonishment when you hit him.'

While they discussed plans to dispose of the body, Myra made tea. And according to Smith she sat with her feet – still wearing the blood-soaked tartan pumps – on the mantelpiece and reminisced with her lover, just as though they were remembering happy moments from their courting days:

'Do you remember that time we were burying a body on the moors and a policeman came up? I was in the Mini with a body in the back. It was partitioned off with a plastic sheet. Ian was digging a hole when a policeman came and asked me what the trouble was. I told him I was drying my sparking plugs and he drove off. I was praying that Ian wouldn't come back over the hill whilst he was there.'

All the time the couple included David Smith in their conversation as though he were now a fully fledged member of the killing cult. Smith has explained that it was in his interests to go along with this, because he was scared that he would be the mad axeman's next victim. It was agreed that Ian would take the next day off work, because of his sprained ankle, and that David Smith would collect from his father's house the pram that had belonged to little Angela Dawn. He would take this round to Millwards and load it into the back of Myra's car, and they would use it that night to wheel the body to the car.

Then David Smith went home. It was about three o'clock in the morning. The youth, tougher than most and accustomed to violence, was terrified.

'I ran all the way home. I let myself into the flat right away, woke Maureen up and had a wash.'

Maureen said that when she saw her husband that night, he was 'very white and shaky. He was sick.'

'I didn't tell Maureen what had happened and I got into bed. I couldn't get to sleep. I kept thinking about the lad, about the screams and the gurgling he was making. I got up after a bit, put the light on, woke Maureen and told her all about it. She was crying and upset, and we sat down and tried to decide what to do.'

Maureen knew there was only one thing to do. Myra might be her sister, David Smith might be her husband and they were both heavily involved. But that did not matter: the police had to be called. At six o'clock in the morning two very frightened teenagers crept out of the flat in Underwood Court, Smith armed with a carving knife and a screwdriver. They made their way in the dark to the telephone box on the housing estate, and dialled 999.

The call was logged by the duty policeman at 6.10 a.m. A murder? In Hattersley? At this time of the morning? On the other hand, it was a bit early for practical jokes, too. The two frightened youngsters hid in the shadows near the phone box for what seemed like an eternity, but was only five minutes.

A police car drew up, and they scuttled towards it like startled rabbits, David Smith trying to climb into the front seat in his haste. Police Constable John Antrobus took the knife and screwdriver off him, and – sure at least that it wasn't a leg-pull, but not sure what it was all about – drove them to Hyde Police Station.

An hour later Superintendent Bob Talbot, just five weeks after being promoted to superintendent rank and due to go off for a fortnight's leave that very morning, took a call at home. Ruefully, he decided that the story his detective had already heard from Smith meant only one thing: no holiday, at least not that day.

It was a decision that would leave its mark on the rest of his life. For Bob Talbot, like all the other police officers who were to become involved in the most notorious murder case Britain has ever known, would be deeply affected by what he was to see and hear in the next five months.

He wasn't sure how much of Smith's story was true. The boy was agitated and upset, he could be imagining things. At worst it was probably a bit of a domestic violence. But one thing was certain: it needed investigating. And because Smith had told them of the guns in the house, it would have to be handled with care.

It wasn't a policeman Myra Hindley saw when she opened the door of 16 Wardle Brook Avenue at twenty past eight that morning. It was a bread man.

New estates like Hattersley followed a pattern. Because the prime concern was to provide homes for people, the rule was: build houses first, worry about other things like shops, pubs and churches later. So in their infancy all these new estates were patrolled by mobile shops. Everything, not just milk, was delivered to the doorstep.

The warning about guns had registered with Bob Talbot. He didn't want to walk up to the front door of a house sporting his police uniform, in full view of any crazed gunman. So he was grateful for the inspiration provided by the bread man, who was parking his van and setting about his morning bread round. Superintendent Talbot borrowed the white coat and the basket of loaves, and approached the house from behind, knocking at the back door.

What went through Myra's mind when she answered the knock? They didn't have bread delivered at their house, there must be some mistake.

She was dressed, smart as ever, thick eye make-up applied, blonde hair back-combed into place, all ready to leave for work. Brady was still in bed: his sprained ankle was his excuse for not going in to Millwards. He was writing a note at that very moment, for Myra to deliver to Tom Craig: 'Dear Tom, Sorry I could not phone yesterday. My family are at Glasgow this week. I was crossing the road in town last night when someone on a bike came round a corner and knocked me down. Except for a few bruises I was all right until I got up this morning. I could not put my weight on my ankle. I must have weak ankles or something. If it is no better tomorrow I will see the doctor. Ian.'

'Is your husband in?' asked the bread man at the back door.

'I haven't got a husband,' Myra answered.

'I am a police superintendent and I have reason to believe there is a man in this house,' said Talbot, opening the white coat to show his uniform.

Did she panic? Try to run away? Collapse and confess? No. But she must have been flustered, because she stupidly said, 'There is no man here.'

Talbot told her he wasn't satisfied, and pushed his way into the kitchen. Myra, composure recovered, said, 'He's in the other room.'

Another detective came into the house, and they both went through into the front room. If it hadn't been for Myra's denial that there was a man in the house, it would have all seemed too normal to be true. The house was well-cared for, the woman smart, it wasn't what they had been expecting at all.

Brady was lying on the divan in the living room, naked except for a vest, his green biro still pushing across the page.

'I have received a report that an act of violence took place in this house last night and we are investigating it,' said Superintendent Talbot. It was a portentous sentence, caged in official police-ese.

Brady said nothing, just gazed at the two officers, unabashed by his nakedness.

Myra spoke. 'There was nothing wrong here.'

Under questioning, she told him that her Gran was upstairs in bed, and said she had no objection to the house being searched. It didn't look promising, to the two police officers. In the morning light, with children's voices from outside as they hurried to school, David Smith's story seemed all too implausible. Until they reached the door of the locked bedroom.

'I said to Myra, "What's in this bedroom?" and she replied, "I keep my firearms in there and I always keep this door locked,"' said Talbot.

When he asked for the key she told him it was at work. They went downstairs to the living room, where Brady was still lying on the bed. The Superintendent told Myra to get her coat, the police would take her to work by car to pick up the key.

She said, 'It's not convenient, I don't want to go.'

'I told her, "I am afraid you must get the key. I am not leaving this house until I have searched that bedroom." She then became silent and looked at Brady for some time.'

Talbot asked her again to get her coat. 'She looked at Brady again and said, "Well, you had better tell him." Brady then stood up and said, "There was a row last night. It's in the back bedroom. Give them the keys." Myra gave me a bunch of keys.'

So the lifeless battered body of seventeen-year-old Edward Evans was saved the indignity of a furtive night-time burial in a lonely moorland grave.

It could have been a very straightforward case.

Two young men, drinking, have a row, it turns violent, gets out of hand, one of them gets killed. The other panics, wraps up the body and hides it upstairs. Only one degree worse than a pub brawl. . . .

Except. . . . Except that David Smith had already told the police that Brady had talked of burying other bodies. . . . Except for the guns. . . . Except for the efficient trussing up of the corpse. . . .

Something didn't feel right about it to Bob Talbot. For some reason, David Smith, a scruffy seventeen-year-old with a record for violence, was more believable than this smart young couple with their car, their tape recorder, their smart clothes.

Ian Brady was told to get dressed and to accompany the policemen to Hyde Police Station. As he put his clothes on he said, 'Eddie and I had a row and the situation got out of hand.' Myra took her cue: that was the story and she would stick to it. She wasn't cautioned, she didn't have to go to the police station. But she wanted to, she wanted to stay with Ian. She picked up Puppet and, braving the stares of the neighbours, followed the little posse of policemen out to their cars. But she wasn't allowed to stay with him: Ian was taken to the CID room, and she was taken to the police station canteen. Brady gave a statement, a statement that implicated David Smith up to the hilt:

'Last night I met Eddie in Manchester. We were drinking and then we went home to Hattersley. We had an argument and we came to blows. After the first few blows the situation got out of control. When the argument started, Dave Smith was at the front door and Myra called him in. Eddie was on the floor near the living room door. David hit him with the stick and kicked him about three times. Eddie kicked me at the beginning on my ankle. There was a hatchet on the floor and I hit Eddie with it. After that the only noise Eddie made was gurgling. When Dave and I began cleaning up the floor the gurgling stopped. Then we tied up the body, Dave and I. Nobody else helped. Dave and I carried it upstairs. Then we sat in the house until three or four in the morning. Then we decided to get rid of the body in the morning early next day or next night.'

Nobody else helped.

Three words that put Myra in the clear. For the next five months, Ian Brady would try to do that whenever he could. Myra, in the meantime, was drinking tea and demanding dog food for Puppet. The police were obliging, the dog food came.

Detective Policewoman Margaret Campion was called back from another job to question Myra. She knew within minutes of sitting across the table from the bleached blonde that this was one of the toughest nuts she had ever had to crack. And the experienced woman detective would not crack her. It was to be more than twenty-one years before Myra would speak the truth.

Under questioning from WPC Campion Myra said the words, 'I didn't do it, Ian didn't do it. I am saying nothing. Ask Ian. Whatever Ian has done I have done.'

It was to become an all too familiar litany to the de-

Above: Myra Hindley, soon after she joined Ryder Brow Secondary Modern

Right: Myra shortly before her arrest in 1966, dressed in the 'smart secretary' style that was to become so familiar to the spectators who queued to see the trial

The loving couple – Ian and Myra in happy mood for the family album

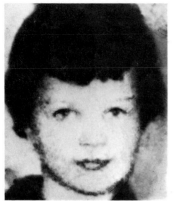
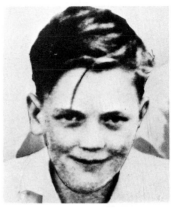

The first acknowledged victims of the Moors Murderers: *(above left)* Lesley Ann Downey, *(above right)* John Kilbride and *(left)* Edward Evans

Below left: Pauline Reade, whose family's agonising uncertainty was ended in July 1987, when her body was found on Saddleworth Moor

Below right: Keith Bennett, the victim whose mother has had the longest wait of all

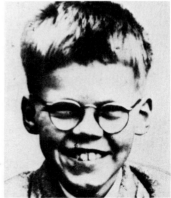

Mrs Kilbride, escorted by a detective, goes to the mortuary to identify the body of her son (Photo: Keystone)

Myra's sister, Maureen, with her first husband, David Smith, photographed shortly before they were key witnesses at the trial

Ian Brady, the only man Myra loved, on his way to a sentence of life imprisonment (Photo: Press Association)

Right: The Hindley image changes: not long after she arrived in Holloway the instantly recognisable blonde "secretary" of the courtroom scenes had become a long-haired brunette

The gates of Holloway, the forbidding aspect which Myra tried so hard not to see when she first arrived

Above: Smuggled out of Holloway: a picture of contentment that could only horrify her victims' families. Once again the smile is for a lover – prison officer Pat Cairns (Photo: Express Newspapers)

Left: Former nun Pat Cairns, the prison officer who fell under the Hindley spell (Photo: Daily Telegraph)

Dorothy Wing, the Governor of Holloway who made headlines when she took prisoner 964055 for an outing on Hampstead Heath

Janie Jones, the vice queen who became close to Myra Hindley when on the same wing in Holloway

Above: The concrete exercise yard at Durham Jail (Photo: Press Association)

Left: Michael Fisher, the lawyer who was to become so closely involved with the case of the 'Moors Murders'

tectives working on the case. They would hear those words, 'I didn't do it, Ian didn't do it' many times.

Ian Brady would tell them things, trip himself up occasionally, be provoked into speaking without thinking: but not Myra.

A lot of people passed through Hyde Police Station that day. David and Maureen Smith were there all day, carefully kept out of the way of Maureen's big sister. Edward Evans' mother came to carry out the distressing task of identifying the savaged body of her son. Then Hettie Hindley arrived, brought by the police, with Myra's Uncle Bert. Life was difficult enough for Hettie, what with having to look after Bob, who'd had a stroke, and the marriage on the rocks anyway, nothing but bickering. Money was as tight as ever. And then our Maureen was a big worry, her still with that David Smith. Now what was our Myra up to? The police had said something about a murder. . . .

It didn't seem so bad when she saw Myra. Myra was so normal, so calm. Hettie had brought clothes with her, some of her own, for Myra to change into. Myra's own clothes were needed for forensic tests.

Her car keys were taken off her, by Detective Chief Superintendent Arthur Benfield, Bob Talbot's boss. He, like Bob, was new to the promotion. He, too, had failed to get anything more out of Myra than 'I didn't do it, Ian didn't do it'.

But he got something more out of the car. Three sheets of paper, neatly folded, and equally neatly written in the stock clerk's hand: five columns on the first two sheets, each with a different heading, and notes underneath; on the third sheet, a list. At first sight it didn't make much sense. Most of the words were abbreviations. Some of them reasonably obvious: GN for gun, HAT for hatchet. Others, less easy. What did CARR mean? Or ALI? Could it be Alibi?

What the police had stumbled on was Ian Brady's

blueprint for a murder, as carefully detailed and worked out as a despatch order from Millwards. Brady would help Arthur Benfied solve a lot of the mysteries of the lists. Pro P, for instance, he would explain meant Pro Plus, a mild stimulant that could be brought over the counter at chemists' shops. But others he would deliberately mislead the police over. TICK, for instance, he said meant just that, to tick something off. And PB he said was Penistone Burn. Penistone is a village in Yorkshire, but Penistone Burn was a new one on these local policemen.

Brady stuck to the story that the lists were written after the murder, as a plan for disposing of the body. Arthur Benfield did not believe him. The three sheets of paper were the first clue the police had found to corroborate David Smith's bizarre allegations of premeditation. Perhaps the youth was telling the truth about other things, too.

He was certainly telling the truth about the guns. They turned up, fully loaded, when the police searched 16 Wardle Brook Avenue. And they searched it slowly and painstakingly all that first day of the investigation. They took away 170 photographs, a tartan-covered photograph album, some recording tapes and two tape recorders, and a photographic light bulb.

Granny Maybury, seventy-seven years old and as confused as ever about what was happening in her own home, had been taken to stay with friends. The old lady was frail and slightly deaf, but she must have heard a lot of what happened that night. Did she believe Myra's explanation of the screams, that it was because she had dropped a tape recorder on her foot? Did she bury her head under the covers while the body was dragged upstairs, Myra holding her door shut just in case she wandered out? Mrs Maybury never talked about what happened that night.

In the evening, the police told Myra that Ian Brady had been charged with the murder of Edward Evans. She took it calmly. They also told her that she could not return to

Wardle Brook Avenue, but they let her walk out of Hyde Police Station as freely as she had entered it. They had nothing on Myra, whatever they were beginning to think of her: those who were in contact with her were all beginning to form the same opinion: 'That one's a hard bitch.'

'I didn't do it, Ian didn't do it. When can I see Ian? I want to see Ian.'

It was an old exercise book, the sort of thing you could find in most homes, the sort kids use for their homework and grown-ups for shopping lists and notes for the milkman. It turned up in the wardrobe of number 16, though – a locked wardrobe. Most families don't lock their wardrobes. Most families don't keep exercise books in there. Those two facts alone were enough to make Bob Talbot look at it very closely indeed.

Some sums, some doodles. More doodles. A lot of names just scribbled all over the place: Ian Brady, John Sloan, Jim Idiot, Alec Guineas, John Kilbride, J. Thompson, John Gilbert. Wait a minute. John Kilbride. There was something familiar about that one.

It only took a few seconds and then Superintendent Talbot remembered. Have You Seen This Boy? John Kilbride, the missing kid from Ashton-under-Lyne whom Lancashire police were still looking for.

The boy's name brought another senior policeman into the story, Detective Chief Inspector Joe Mounsey from Lancashire Constabulary – the man who had taken over the John Kilbride inquiry.

Gradually, Smith's unbelievable statement was beginning to sound more and more credible. Brady had told him that there had been other murders, that there were bodies buried on the moors. It sounded like nothing more than idle bragging, perhaps exaggerated by the impressionable seventeen-year-old. But the name Kilbride, scribbled among those others, could not just be coincidence.

But one name in a notebook was nothing on its own.

Brady obviously wasn't about to crack and neither was Myra. But if this strange pair could now be tied in with the mysterious disappearance of one small boy, what about other missing children? Detective Chief Inspector John Tyrrell, from Manchester police, arrived at Hyde Police Station. He'd got Lesley Anne Downey, Keith Bennett and Pauline Reade on his mind.

One dead youth, four missing children. And three police forces involved. It was rapidly becoming a very big operation indeed.

Myra was still free. She'd moved from her mum's in Gorton to stay with her Uncle Bert and Auntie Kath, the ones who had given her a present of a prayer book to mark her first communion.

The police had already started to search the moors, taking David and Maureen Smith with them in the hope they'd recognise areas they had visited in Myra's car, and they were also trying to identify likely spots from all the photographs Brady had taken: many just of scenery, some with Myra and Puppet, one or two taken by Myra with Brady in the foreground. They found some possible sites, and policemen disguised with overalls and wellington boots had even started to dig.

Myra didn't know that when, on Monday, 11 October 1965, five days after the murder of Edward Evans, she made her daily trip to Hyde Police Station to be near Ian.

But she would not see Ian again until they met in the company of their solicitor. Because on that day, in the early afternoon, Myra Hindley was charged with being an accessory to the murder of Edward Evans. She would never be free again.

6

The Committal

Myra continued to give nothing away to the police. If Brady was a tough opponent, Myra was formidable. If the police had had to rely solely on the interrogation of the two suspects, the case would have stopped with Edward Evans. Luckily, there was some brilliant detective work going on away from the interview room, some of it by a twelve-year-old child.

Pat Hodges' mother told the police how her daughter used to go up on the moors with 'Auntie' Myra and 'Uncle' Ian, collecting peat for the garden. There was nothing unusual in that – lots of keen gardeners in the Manchester area did it. It was a long shot, but the police decided to take it. Perhaps the little girl would have a better memory for roads and scenery than David Smith.

The search had been concentrated in the Woodhead area, on the A628 Manchester to Sheffield road, largely because of the initials WH on Brady's carefully written sheet of instructions for himself, and also because it was an area David Smith remembered visiting.

But Pat, sitting in the back of a police car with a policewoman next to her and a policeman in the front, didn't want them to go that way. She took them somewhere else, a route that came back to her turn by turn, corner by corner, road sign by road sign as she retraced the journeys she had made so often only eight months before. Up through Greenfield she took them, on to the A635, the Ashton to Huddersfield Road.

'Stop here,' she said. 'This is it.'

She had found the very spot where she and Myra had shivered in the van, with the windows up and the radio on, while Ian had tramped with his spade across the bleak open land 'to get peat for the garden'. The spot where, in fine weather, they had taken her walking, insisting that she sat in certain places to eat her sandwiches and drink wine.

The little girl was sure, she had no doubts that this was the place they'd brought her to, and when the policeman with her looked closely at the map, he too began to feel they were on to something. The name of the area was marked down as Wessenden Head – the WH of the list.

Next day, a Saturday, the digging moved to the new location. By now there was an army of policemen up on Saddleworth, arriving in a column of fifteen police vehicles, and another army was forming ranks: the press and sightseers. The cars by the roadside stretched for half a mile.

News of the dig was out, and rumours were flying around. Mass burials, torture, witchcraft. The press were only allowed by law – because Brady and Hindley had been charged and were awaiting trial – to publish certain stark details: the digging was taking place, a man and a woman were helping police with their inquiries. But it was enough to fuel the fantastic speculation. The backstreets of Gorton buzzed with it. On Hattersley overspill estate, everybody had a theory about it. In the offices at Millwards Tom Craig found it hard to get anybody to concentrate on their work.

Without the photographs, it would have been like searching for a needle in a haystack, even after Pat had pinpointed the area. But with Brady's endless scenic views to work from, they were able to narrow the search down a bit. It was hard, dispiriting work, though. A blue wave of 150 police uniforms crawled slowly across the rough terrain. Each policeman carried two bamboo canes with white rags attached to them, to push into the ground at any sign of disturbed earth or a suspicious mound. Following them came men with picks and shovels to dig round each marked spot – and about 100 holes were dug. Canteens provided hot tea and thick sandwiches. A mobile police headquarters was set up. Four police forces were now involved: Cheshire, which covered Hattersley; Lancashire, with Joe Mounsey determined to find John Kilbride; Manchester, with John Tyrrell pursuing the cases of Pauline Reade, Keith Bennett and Lesley Ann Downey; and the West Riding of Yorkshire, whose area the search was taking place in.

It was the end of a long hard day when they found the first body. Detective Chief Inspector Joe Mounsey, the man who was the inspiration to all those tired, cold policemen and police cadets taking part in the search, insists it was dogged police work that made the discovery. Other policemen tell how a young rookie cop, not a week out of college, went across a hill for privacy to relieve himself – and stumbled back ashen-faced to tell his boss he'd seen a bone sticking out of the peat.

They'd already unearthed bones that day: dead sheep, a dead dog. But this bone was a human arm. They were all convinced, not least Joe Mounsey, that John Kilbride's last resting place had been found. But when they pulled from the earth a blue coat, a pink cardigan and a tartan skirt they realised it was another child: Lesley Ann Downey. The body was naked, and piled at her feet in the makeshift grave were her clothes and her brown buckled shoes. Among the clothes was a string of white beads, given to her as a Christmas present the day before she disappeared by her big brother Terry.

They threw screens around the site, mounted arc lights, called for pathologists: the whole machinery was set in motion. There was a strange feeling among the men on the moor, the policemen who had lost their Saturday afternoon's gardening or football, a mixture of elation at their achievement, at actually having something to show for their backbreaking hours of searching, and the deep sadness that comes from being close to the death of a child.

Ann Downey, Lesley's mother, had been up on the moors watching the search. But she wasn't there when the body was found. She was at her new home – she had asked the council to rehouse her after the tragedy, as Ancoats held too many painful memories. Ironically the new house she had been found was in Hattersley, just a few streets away from Wardle Brook Avenue. It was there the police car picked her up the next morning to take her to the tiny mortuary in the little village of Uppermill, where it took her just a few minutes to identify her daughter.

Ann Downey looked small, pretty and vulnerable – and much younger than her thirty-five years: a stark contrast to the other blonde, the one who had spent her first five days and nights in custody in a cell at Risley Remand Centre. One thing all the police officers who had contact with her commented on: she couldn't be just twenty-three, could she? The woman with the unflattering dark roots in her bleached blonde hair looked more like forty-three.

While Joe Mounsey was getting results on Saddleworth Moor, Detective Chief Inspector John Tyrrell was getting results elsewhere. Number 16 Wardle Brook Avenue had been thoroughly searched, as had the house in Wiles Street and Ian Brady's mother's old home in Westmoreland Street (Peggy and Pat had moved away to Heywood just a few months before). Bannock Street had already been demolished.

But John Tyrrell wouldn't let it go at that. He knew from Brady's lists that they were up against a meticulous mind. But however careful they are, most criminals slip up in some small way. . . . He went back to the house in Hattersley, and started looking again. Painstakingly and systematically, he inspected all the books on the shelves, until he came to the small white prayer book that Auntie Kath and Uncle Bert had given Myra after her first communion. There were two initials on Brady's list still unexplained: PB. Prayer Book. Rolled very tightly and slipped inside the spine of the small book he found a piece of paper. A left luggage ticket. It was a piece of meticulous detection that John Tyrrell would later be praised for in court.

The day before Edward Evans was murdered, Ian Brady had told David Smith to bring back to him all the books the youngster had borrowed: books of Nazi propaganda, pornography and the Marquis de Sade's ravings. Later Smith had seen Brady and Myra load two suitcases into the back of the van. In the awful immediacy of what happened next, he had forgotten about the cases. For two shillings they had been deposited at Manchester Central Station left luggage office that night.

Now they were deposited on Superintendent Bob Talbot's desk. They contained books, nasty stuff too: all about sexual perversions. There was a black wig, a length of rubber hose covered with lead – a home-made cosh – some bullets, a notebook containing lists of names of books and notes about perversions, and another cosh, with the words EUREKA written on it.

There were a couple of tapes, and a tin with some photographs in it. More photographs, as if there weren't enough snaps of moorland views already, the detective thought. . . . But wait a minute. Bob Talbot turned the first picture over. This wasn't a moorland view.

It was a little girl, naked except for her brown-buckled shoes and striped socks and a scarf tied across her mouth. There were nine pictures in all: Lesley Ann Downey praying, Lesley Ann Downey standing up, Lesley Ann Downey on the bed, a back view of Lesley Ann Downey with her arms spread wide, the crucifix shape.

It was such a staggering discovery that, for a moment, Superintendent Talbot forgot to play the tapes. When he remembered, he wasn't expecting them to improve on the evidence the suitcase had already yielded. And at first they didn't: there was Ian Brady's voice chanting 'Sieg Heil, Sieg Heil' – nasty but not illegal, there was some marching music, an extract from a 'Goon Show' and the voice of veteran radio commentator Freddie Grisewood talking about the rise of Hitler.

Then he came to the last track on the tape. There were lots of bumps and bangs as though the recorder had just been left on by accident, and then, quite clearly, two voices that Bob Talbot had come to know well. The voice of the woman who had opened the door of Number 16 Wardle Brook Avenue to Talbot the bread man, just ten days earlier. And the voice of the man who had been lying on the bed in the sitting room that same morning. There was another voice, too, a girl's voice. One that would be formally identified in court by Mrs Ann Downey: Lesley's voice.

Alone in his office, Superintendent Bob Talbot was the first person to listen to the tape recording that would become the most infamous exhibit ever brought before a British court of law.

It starts with Ian Brady, talking brutally to the dogs, telling them to get out of his way. Then there is the sound of a door banging, some heavy footsteps, crackling and other recording noises, the sound of someone blowing in the microphone and more footsteps.

Myra Hindley speaks, but her voice is quiet and it is impossible to tell what she says. More footsteps, more whispered conversation. The word 'upstairs' can be made out. Then there are two sets of footsteps.

A child screams.

For the next thirteen terrible minutes, Bob Talbot listened to Lesley Ann Downey pleading for her life. She begged for help from God, from 'Mum' – referring to Myra – from Brady. Myra's voice on the tape told her to 'Shut up'. As well as the little girl's pleading words, there are sounds of her screaming, crying, struggling to breathe. Myra repeatedly tells her to 'Hush' and to 'Put it in your mouth and keep it in.' At the beginning her voice sounds soothing, but she soon loses patience with the crying child.

'Shut up or I'll forget myself and hit you one. Keep it in,' she says.

Lesley Ann can be heard retching, and she asks several times what she has to put 'it' in for.

'Can I just tell you summat? I must tell you summat. Please take your hands off me a minute, please. Please – mummy – please . . . I can't tell you. [Grunting sounds] I can't tell you. I can't breathe. Oh . . . I can't – dad – will you take your hands off me?'

When she asks what they are going to do with her, Brady says: 'I want to take some photographs, that's all. . . . Put it in.'

The child begs them not to undress her, and says she wants to go because she is going out with her mother. Brady, still trying to persuade her to put something in her mouth, says: 'The longer it takes you to do this the longer it takes you to get home.'

When Lesley Ann argues, his persuasive tone evaporates and he says to her: 'Put it in. If you don't keep your hands down I'll slit your neck. . . . Put it in.'

She tells him her name and says she has to be home by eight o'clock. There is a sound of someone coming back into the room, and Myra's voice can be heard on the tape again.

The child starts crying, and complaining that her neck hurts. Myra Hindley tells her to 'shurrup crying'.

'Hush. Shut up. Now put it in. Pull that hand away and don't dally and just keep your mouth shut, please. . . . Wait a minute, I'll put this on again. D'you get me?'

The little girl continues to whimper and protest, as Myra again tells her to 'put that in your mouth . . . packed more solid'.

The voices on the tape end with Myra saying 'that's all right' and Brady making a grunting noise.

Then some music starts, a country-style tune followed by 'Jolly St Nicholas', during which various noises can be heard, then the tune 'The Little Drummer Boy', during which a voice speaks. Then there are three loud, systematic cracks, evenly timed. Followed by 'The Little Drummer Boy', fading away, and the sound of footsteps.

That tape would fill everyone who heard it with horror. It would fuel many nightmares. Grown men would weep. One top policeman would be physically sick when he heard 'The Little Drummer Boy' years later at a party. Those innocent tunes would be defiled for ever, by anyone who heard them in that macabre context.

Written down, as the court shorthand writer transcribed it, it reads horrifyingly enough. Heard, with the sounds of the child choking and crying and her desperate screams, it is heart-rending.

The full enormity of what they were dealing with began to sink into Bob Talbot's head as he sat alone in his office with the tape recorder running. Brady had made another two copies of the same track, and then he had recorded little Pat Hodges, innocently reading the reports of Lesley Ann's disappearance from the local paper.

Without that tape, it would be just possible to believe that Myra Hindley was a dupe, a fool who sheltered the man she loved despite knowing that he was a murderer. The tape put her into another league.

It put her firmly in the dock alongside Brady, an equal partner in his terrible crimes. It made her a rare creature: a woman who gloried in the torture of small children. It was that tape that made Myra Hindley the most notorious woman ever to have been held in British jails, and it is the public revulsion it caused that has kept her there.

But it was also the tape that gave the police the only chink they would ever see in Myra's armour. When Detective Chief Superintendent Arthur Benfield showed her the photographs of Lesley Ann and the little girl's clothing she held her head in her hands and clutched a handkerchief to her face. But all she would say were the familiar words, 'I'm saying nothing.'

When the tape was played to her, though, she did say something. The policeman in the room taking notes noticed a pulse throbbing at the left hand side of her throat. Her head was bowed, and she was sobbing. When the tape clicked off she whispered, 'I am ashamed.' And she wept.

But, as the detective would later tell the court: 'This lasted for a very short time. And then she said again, 'I'm saying nothing.'

The search on the moors continued, revitalised by the discovery of one body and the shocking reinforcement of disgust that the tape provided. Four days does not sound a long time. But when it is four long days of fruitless digging and prodding in that inhospitable terrain, with mile after mile of moorland stretching as far as the eye can see, even the most enthusiastic men were wishing themselves back on the beat, wishing they were dealing with traffic offences rather than taking part in the murder investigation that was making headlines all over the globe.

They were using a special probe by now, designed originally for the War Graves Commission and manufactured, coincidentally, just along from the police murder headquarters in Hyde. But Joe Mounsey was using something else. He was clutching his greatest hope under his arm as he strode about urging the men on: the photograph album with the endless pictures of moorland views.

It wasn't until he crossed to the opposite side of the road from the area where Lesley Ann's body was found that he found the skyline he was looking for, the one that identically matched a snap of Myra, crouching on one knee, holding Puppet and looking down at the ground with a half-smile on her lips. She was looking at a grave.

It could have been Pauline Reade or Keith Bennett, but it wasn't. By some sort of divine justice, it was John

Kilbride, the lad whose disappearance Joe Mounsey had on the top of his list of unsolved crimes. Mounsey, the prime mover behind the search, the man who was there to brief the searchers and rally them when their spirits were flagging, had got what he was looking for.

The body, buried face down, was fully clothed, except for shoes, which were in the ground next to it. The boy's trousers had been pulled down to the knees, and the underpants rolled down and knotted at the back of the thighs.

After nearly two years in the soft earth, what was left of the small boy was nothing much more than bones, teeth, a tuft of brown hair, the clothing and the indescribable smell of putrefaction. His mother would identify him from his shoes ('I had them mended for him at the Co-op') and the football-shaped buttons she had sewn on his jacket. Dental records would do the rest.

There were a lot of things to question the two accused about now. Myra's fingerprints had been found on the photos of Lesley Ann. The pattern on the headboard of the bed and spots on the wall had identified the scene of the photo session with the little girl as Myra's bedroom at 16 Wardle Brook Avenue. Experts had proved that the pictures had been taken with a camera Ian Brady used to own.

Yes, he said, he took the pictures. But he maintained that was all he did, that the child was brought to the house alive and left alive after a pornographic picture session. The man who brought her there and took her away, he claimed, was David Smith. Myra, as usual, said, 'Ian didn't kill her, I didn't kill her. I suggest you see Smith.'

She did say something else though. In order to date the photograph of her standing on John Kilbride's grave, the police had sent her dog Puppet to a vet to work out his age. On the photograph Puppet was tiny: it was crucial to know if he had been born before or after the death of John

Kilbride. Unknown to anyone, the dog had a kidney complaint. Under the anaesthetic the vet gave him before analysing his teeth, Puppet died.

'Murderers!' Myra screamed at the police.

The search for bodies continued. People were asked to come forward with information about any mysterious happenings or disturbances on the moors, and the sites they pinpointed were ringed with a yellow dye and later searched. Soon there were 400 bright splashes of colour on the drab, wintry moors. Every one was investigated, nothing was found. The RAF flew overhead taking photographs, more digging followed, but again nothing was found. Winter was coming in fast, and with it hopes of any new discoveries were fading. Night frosts were turning the ground rock hard and making it impossible to probe. In November the search was called off.

While the hearts of the policemen went out to the mothers whose children were still missing, they were confident now that they had a case that would put Myra and Brady away for life: that would have to be enough.

But for the police to be confident they have a case is not enough under British law. The two accused, Brady and Hindley, had been appearing regularly before a magistrates' court to be remanded in custody. Brady charged with all three murders and Myra Hindley charged with the murders of Edward Evans and Lesley Downey, and with harbouring Brady after the murder of John Kilbride.

Still both were being held at Risley Remand Centre and since both had the same solicitor, a local man, Mr C. L. Fitzpatrick, they were, for some hours of each day at least, together again. And they were together again in the dock at Hyde Magistrates' Court, when committal proceedings opened against them on 6 December 1965.

A committal is heard in a lower court to decide whether there is a case to go forward to trial. The Criminal Justice

Act of 1967 (prompted in part at least by the Moors Murders committal and subsequent trial) tidied everything up by reducing the amount of time spent on a committal, and restricted press coverage. Pre-1967 the law said that the full prosecution case had to be produced before magistrates, so they could decide whether to send a case to trial. And the press had the right to report that case, unless specifically ordered not to by the magistrates.

In the case against Brady and Hindley, that meant calling eighty prosecution witnesses to repeat the statements they had already made to the police, and that they would make again at the full trial. It was a costly and long drawn-out procedure, taking eleven working days. The evidence was heard in public, despite pleas from David Lloyd-Jones, representing Brady, and Philip Curtis, representing Myra Hindley, that it should be closed to reporters and public. The only part of the proceedings taken in camera was the prosecution's opening submission, a summary of which was later given in open court.

Quite why the magistrates decided to proceed in public we don't know, although they were probably guided by the saying that justice must not only be done, it must also be seen to be done. As it turned out, the decision guaranteed the magistrates a place in the criminal history books. As with all cases that received a lot of publicity, hearing the committal in public was prejudicial to the defence: when the case came to trial it was impossible to say that the twelve jurors sworn in had been untouched by all the publicity.

For a fortnight it was the biggest news in the country. The little town of Hyde was like a league of nations, with reporters from many different countries struggling to make sense of English court procedure. Most of them did not bother to struggle too much: untrammelled by the same restrictions the English press faced, they made up what they didn't know.

But there was no need for fiction. The stories that were told in that tiny court were strong enough meat for even the most lurid journals. The magistrates, a former Mayoress, a retired union boss and a retired master baker, became minor celebrities. When the proceedings were dull, the journalists wrote about the hats worn by Mrs Dorothy Adamson, the chairman of the bench.

Myra's hair was freshly bleached for the occasion, and she wore a black and white speckled suit and a yellow blouse. Ever the efficient secretary, she carried a notebook and pen and made notes during the proceedings. Every time she left the court she came back with freshly applied powder, lipstick and heavy eye make-up, a look that was already unfashionable.

David Smith's evidence was the lynchpin of the prosecution case. It was revealed that he would not be prosecuted for his part in the Edward Evans murder: he had, in other words, been given immunity in return for his cooperation. His story, told in his quiet stammering voice, rocked the courtroom.

But the story of Edward Evans' death was not the most compelling part of the case to unfold. Neither were the sketchy details of John Kilbride's abduction and death.

Outside the court, Christmas was fast approaching. But it was the story of Christmas Past that made court staff and reporters and the people in the public gallery alike catch their breath. Christmas just past, the Christmas a ten-year-old girl disappeared after a trip to the fair. As if to underline the poignancy of the evidence that was being heard, there were times when the panelled room fell quiet and a babble of childish voices could be heard: play-time at Greenfield Street Secondary School, just around the corner.

And the most dramatic moment came when Ann Downey, giving evidence about her dead daughter, broke down in tears and shouted, 'I'll kill you, I'll kill you.'

Detective Constable Frank Fitchett, sitting in the well

of the court beneath the witness box, turned round and grabbed the water carafe provided for witnesses just before Mrs Downey could get her hands on it.

It wasn't Ian Brady Mrs Downey was looking at when she shouted. It was Myra Hindley. Ann Downey knew, just as every other person reading the press reports the length and breadth of Britain knew, that what was special about this case, specially sinister, was that in the dock was a woman, a woman accused of killing children. It defied comprehension.

7

The Trial

SMITH WILL DIE AND MAUREEN TOO. The threat was made in code, in a letter from Ian Brady to Myra Hindley while they were both held on remand at Risley. It was a simple code: the first letter of each line, read vertically, spelled out the secret message. It was by cracking the code that police first learned of the couple's plans to apply to be married.

They even got as far as filling out official forms requesting permission from the Home Office. Why, when one of the tenets of Brady's anti-religion anti-establishment doctrine was that marriage was unnecessary and ridiculous? Myra had often said she did not believe in marriage. But now there was a good reason for it. Prisoners who are married are allowed some access to each other. They realised, as the date of their trial approached, that after sentence was passed there would be no other way of seeing each other, at least for many years. The Home Office turned their request down.

'Should a murder be punished by murder? Undoubtedly not. The only punishment which a murderer should be condemned to is that which he risks from the friends or the family of the man he has killed. . . .'

If Ian Brady and Myra Hindley could have been handed over to the friends and families of those they had killed, then the Marquis de Sade's brand of justice would have been exacted. Feelings were running very high in Manchester. Patrick Downey, uncle of little Lesley Ann, and her father Terence were arrested outside the magistrates' court at Hyde, for trying to attack a police car they believed contained the two accused. In fact, the people under blankets inside were decoys. The men were not charged, but were warned by the police that if they caused any more trouble, they would be.

Patrick Downey wasn't worried about that. He went out and bought a gun, with the sole intent of shooting Brady. But his wife persuaded him to hand it in to the police – and after the confusion over decoys he realised there was a chance he would injure an innocent person. Both he and Terence were told not to attend the main trial, which opened in Chester on Tuesday, 19 April 1966. If they did, police said, detectives would be assigned to them full time.

John Kilbride's aunt and uncle were in the court to hear the trial. Elsie and Frank Doran had organised a petition urging the return of the death penalty for child murderers, and had sent more than 10,000 signatures to the Home Secretary.

The abolition of the death penalty was a political hot potato. At the time Brady and Myra committed their crimes, the punishment was the hangman's rope. By the time they came up in court for committal, the law had been changed. The MP Sydney Silverman's 'Murder (Abolition of Death Penalty) Act' was passed in November 1965. The Moors Murder case was the first big case, the first involving multiple murders, to be heard after that date. When it became law Brady and Myra were already in custody – she confident that she would be acquitted of the main charges, he gloating that he would cheat the noose.

Many people had been opposed to the new legislation; many others who had held no strong views found themselves swayed against it by the horror of the story that unfolded, first in the magistrates' court and then at Chester Assizes. When, later that year, Patrick Downey stood as a pro-hanging candidate at the General Election – standing against Sydney Silverman – he polled a substantial 5,000 votes and did not lose his deposit.

Among opponents to the abolition of the death penalty were many senior police officers. They used the threat of hanging effectively in their dealings with murderers: a plea of insanity, if accepted, would mean a lifetime in a secure mental hospital rather than the gallows. When more killings were suspected, it was often in the murderer's interests to confess, on the grounds that he had a better chance of proving himself insane if he owned up to several murders. Without the death penalty, there was nothing for the murderer to gain by confessing.

As Chief Superintendent Arthur Benfield said, 'There was no question of capital punishment in the Moors case. Brady and Hindley were not fools, so why should they admit any more? If they did, there might be no possibility of release in the future.'

So the case went to trial, with the two accused being as unhelpful and unco-operative as they had been since the morning when Myra Hindley told the bread man that she did not have a husband.

Chester is a beautiful old walled city, a Roman fortress on the banks of the wide, shallow River Dee. It has classy, expensive shops, and twee little tea rooms, catering for American tourists and the comfortably-off retired folk who make up a substantial part of its population.

In the spring of 1966 it withstood an invasion. One hundred and fifty journalists, of many nationalities, and many more camera crews and sound technicians, booked every available hotel bed in the city. The GPO telephone lines out of the city were permanently engaged. Pub takings were up. The Trial of the Century, as it was billed in the press, was on.

The Chester Castle court room, the stage for the dramatic event, had been specially prepared, at a cost of £2,600.

Carpet had been fitted, to reduce noise, microphones had been installed to the witness box, and large press rooms with telephones were provided to cater for the two thirds of journalists who would not get a seat in court. A special bullet-proof glass screen had been erected behind the dock, between it and the public gallery – bizarre modern touches among the oak-panelling, red leather and velvet drapes of the historical setting.

From the early hours of the morning, a steady queue of raincoated women and men – but mostly women – had formed outside the court, hoping for seats in the public gallery. Each day of the trial, that queue would not diminish. Three hundred policemen had been drafted in to help with security, forming a thick blue band at either side of the roadway as the van from Risley Remand Centre arrived, its two passengers in different compartments in the back.

Ian Brady and Myra Hindley arrived in the D-shaped dock from a whitewashed corridor below, mounting stone steps to their light wood seats. They were together again: Neddie wearing a smart grey suit with a white handkerchief in the breast pocket, a white shirt and a blue tie; Hessie in an equally smart black and white speckled suit, blue blouse and white shoes – the boss and his secretary. She even carried a shorthand notebook and pen, just as she had at the committal.

Her hair had been carefully rinsed a lilac-blue before the trial. The colour would be washed out by the end of the three weeks, but her hair had been recently bleached and there was no sign of dark roots. She listened to the charges against her with blue hair and heard her sentence with bright yellow hair.

If they were the stars, there were other leading parts. The Judge was Mr Justice Fenton Atkinson, who handled the extraordinary attention focused on the court room in a low-key manner, never once playing to the gallery and discouraging others, whether counsel or witnesses, from doing so. Godfrey Heilpern QC, a Manchester man, appeared for Myra Hindley. By a terrible coincidence he learned on the first day of the trial that his sister-in-law had been murdered, and he was absent on the day that David Smith was cross-examined. His junior, Philip Curtis, who had defended her at the committal proceedings, took over.

The other three top lawyers in court were all Welshmen. The case against Brady and Hindley was conducted by the Attorney General, Sir Elwyn Jones QC. Traditionally the Attorney General only prosecutes in cases involving national security, and in the most serious murder cases. It was Sir Elwyn Jones' first case since becoming Attorney General two years earlier. He had been involved in the prosecution of Nazi war criminals at the Nuremberg trials, and ironically was probably the only man Ian Brady had ever encountered who knew more about Brady's Nazi idols than Brady did himself.

The other prosecution lawyer was William Mars-Jones QC, and Brady was defended by Emlyn Hooson QC, the Welsh-speaking Liberal MP. Each of them – with the exception of the Attorney General, who was salaried – would be paid in excess of £1,500 for the fourteen-day trial, considerably more than the average man earned in a year at that time.

At the committal, both Brady and Hindley had been charged with murdering Edward Evans and Lesley Ann Downey, Brady had been charged with murdering John Kilbride and Hindley with harbouring him. Now the charges against her were increased: she, too, was charged with the murder of John Kilbride, although the secondary charge of harbouring Brady remained.

Before the trial started, the judge had to decide whether the two accused should be tried together. Both defence counsels submitted that they should not, but Mr Justice Fenton Atkinson said that he had given the matter a great deal of consideration and felt that it was in the interests both of the accused and justice that they be tried together. When the jury was sworn in, Brady and Hindley's lawyers each objected to two of the four women, making it an all-male jury. Then it began.

The Attorney General opened the proceedings, and spent the first day and half of the next outlining the crimes and the circumstances leading up to them. He warned the jury that they were going to have to examine harrowing exhibits and listen to a distressing recording. And he ended his opening speech by presenting them with the most distressing exhibits they would face: the pictures of Lesley Ann Downey taken in Myra's bedroom.

The most dramatic day of the whole trial would come exactly a week after it opened, on the day that the tape recording of the last few minutes of Lesley Ann Downey's short life would stun everyone present. At the committal, the court had been cleared when the magistrates listened to it. At the trial, press and public alike heard it. Three women in the public gallery covered their ears with their hands. Two of them bent forward, dropping their heads on to their chests. There was no escape from the sixteen minutes of relentless anguish: the judge had ordered that no one leave their place while it was played.

Both Hindley and Brady stared ahead throughout, although at one point Myra Hindley sighed and pulled a handkerchief from the breast pocket of her blue-striped blouse.

A BBC sound engineer had worked hard at eliminating background noise from the tape, so that it could be heard clearly. Before being seconded to help the police, he had been working on a 'Pinky and Perky' radio programme. It would be many years before he, and many of the others involved on the periphery of the trial, would be prepared to let their own children go out unescorted.

But the evidence against Brady and Hindley started with Maureen Smith, small, frightened-looking and heavily pregnant. She was taken out of turn because her baby was due the day the trial opened and there was a fear that the case would have to be interrupted if she was in hospital. The police had made arrangements to whisk her away from the court and to hospital should it become necessary. Perhaps the most startling part of her evidence, a part that had not been heard either at the committal or in the Attorney General's opening speech, was her revelation that her husband was in the pay of a newspaper, and was receiving £10, £15 or even £20 a week. For a young couple whose combined wages had been £12 10s a week six months earlier, before the death of Edward Evans, this was big money.

It also transpired when David Smith himself gave evidence that he had been promised £1,000 for his story after the trial, that his hotel bill during the trial was being met and that he and Maureen had been to France on holiday, again all paid for by the newspaper. Smith refused repeatedly to identify the newspaper involved, which was the *News of the World*. Unwittingly the journalists involved in the decision to 'buy up' Smith had given the defence what the judge describes as 'a stick with which to beat' the chief prosecution witness and his wife.

David Smith's own background of violence and petty crime did not make him the most credible witness. His obvious involvement in Brady's sadism and pornography cult – he admitted in court that he enjoyed reading the books Brady lent him – and his part in planning criminal activities with Brady made him even less salubrious. That, coupled with his vested financial interest in seeing the two people in the dock convicted, diminished his value as an independent witness even further.

'I love having money, it is gorgeous stuff,' he told the court, when talking about his arrangement with the newspaper.

But the Attorney General, whose case rested very heavily on Smith's testimony, disposed of the defence objections easily.

If Smith's evidence was suspect because he was in the pay of the *News of the World*, the prosecution would simply ask for Smith's original statement to the police, made within hours of him leaving 16 Wardle Brook Avenue after the death of Edward Evans, to be read out to the court. The statement was made long before any newspaper had even heard of David Smith or the Moors Murders – nobody could argue that the lad had any vested financial interest when he gave it.

That statement was the last thing the defence wanted to hear in court because, although David Smith in the intervening months had picked up a lot of journalese (he was now referring to Ian Brady as 'the butcher' and likening the battered body of Edward Evans to 'a rag doll') there was a stark ferocity about that earlier statement, stammered out at Hyde Police Station and written down by a numbly disbelieving policeman, that was lacking in his court performance. He was cool in court, although his low voice, his stammer, and his habit of playing with the microphone did not help his delivery.

Myra Hindley, especially, was more deeply implicated in the Evans killing according to that original statement. In it Smith was unequivocal about her position during the killing of Evans: she was, he said, in the room where it was happening. In court he said he was not sure whether she was in the room or not. So it was not in her interests to have it read out, and her interests were of paramount importance to the defence. Ian Brady has said since, and it was apparent at the time, that the main purpose of his testimony – both to the police before they came to trial and at the trial itself – was to get 'the girl' off.

He may never have been able to declare his love for her in any conventional way. But he declared his own bizarre loyalty at a trial where he knew, from the beginning, there was no hope for him.

'Myra wasn't in the room,' he said about the Evans killing. 'I told Myra Evans was dead and she became overwrought, hysterical. . . .'

He told the court that Lesley Ann Downey was brought to the house by David Smith for pornographic photographs but that Myra did not know about the arrangement for the pictures until the child arrived. He said she did not want to witness the pictures being taken, but that he insisted. He said that when he played the tape to her she wanted it to be destroyed. He said that she was not involved in any robbery plans he and David Smith hatched. When he was asked by Myra's counsel, 'Supposing you and she were having a discussion about going anywhere or doing anything, and you had different views about it, whose view would prevail?'

He answered, 'Mine. She was my typist in the office. I dictated to her in the office, and this tended to wrap over.'

Yet if this was the defence they had jointly decided on for Myra, that she was the innocent dupe of a much more powerful man, her whole demeanour in the court room gave it the lie.

She remained impassive and stony-faced almost throughout, only once or twice sharing secret smiles with Brady when something was said that amused them. They shared mint sweets, and occasionally inclined their heads together to whisper. Just once, as she was led out of the court at the end of a day, she was provoked by the curiosity of the onlookers into putting her tongue out at one of the reporters. She wrote copious notes, and pushed them forward to her solicitor, for him to pass on to the barrister.

One that arrived in front of Godfrey Heilpern said, 'I told you, no cross-examination that damages Ian.' Its peremptory tone suggests she was something more than an overawed young typist, under the spell of a wicked Svengali. But it does confirm the strength of their alliance at the time of the trial. While Brady was fighting to get her off, she was worried about her defence lawyers damaging him. And when he was giving evidence she only once or twice took her eyes off him, and that was when she leaned forward and rested her forehead on the wall of the dock.

Was it love?

On the eleventh day of the trial, when she went into the witness box, Myra Hindley told the court and the world that it was. She was asked what her feelings for Ian Brady were.

'I became very fond of him. I loved him. I still – I love him.'

When she went into the witness box she did not take the oath on the Bible, choosing instead to affirm that she was telling the truth. The reason, she said, was because she had no religious beliefs. Myra the once devout Catholic publicly denounced her faith.

She was in the witness box for nearly six hours – Brady had been there for eight and a half. Her voice, husky and low when she started speaking, grew stronger the more she said. Her 'Coronation Street' vowels were overlaid with a slight Scottish burr, picked up from Brady whose Glasgow accent had survived nearly ten years living in Manchester. While she was speaking, Brady never glanced at her. He remained as he sat throughout the trial, his chin cradled in his left hand, gazing absently around the courtroom.

Myra described her attitude to Lesley Ann Downey, as revealed on the tape, as 'brusque and cruel' but said it was because she was worried about anyone hearing the child screaming and crying while Brady was trying to take pictures of her. Myra said she had drawn the curtains in the room, and was standing the other side of the curtains, looking out through the open window.

'I was embarrassed at what was going on. I didn't want to be there in the first place, but Ian asked me to. She started getting undressed and I went in there. I didn't want anything to do with it. I was embarrassed and ashamed.

The radio was on and I was really listening to the radio. I switched it on to ease the tension in the room. There's no defence for what I did. I think it was cruel, criminal and I am ashamed.'

She said she didn't remember saying 'Shut up or I'll hit you one' but that if it was on the tape, she must have said it. 'I was desperate that no one should hear. The doors and windows were open. I was panic struck.'

She said that although she was heard threatening to hit the child on the tape 'I would not have hit her much. I never touched her. I never harmed her. . . . When she started crying and shouting and screaming I just wanted her to be quiet.'

When she was questioned about the part of the tape on which she said, 'Pull that hand away and don't dally, and just keep your mouth shut please,' Myra winced visibly. The old-fashioned Northern expression 'don't dally' was not one she normally used, she told the court.

Brady had made a significant slip when he had talked from the witness box about the photo session with Lesley Ann Downey. He had said that when it was over 'We all got dressed and went downstairs,' perhaps giving the greatest clue of all as to what really went on in Myra's bedroom that Boxing Day.

Myra denied that anyone was undressed, except the child. She was asked by the Attorney General, 'Did you indulge in any pleasures while these things were happening to the child?'

'No,' she said.

She answered a barrage of questions about the moorland views photographs, flatly denying that she knew any of them had been taken on or near the graves of young children. It was a relentless cross-examination by an excellent lawyer: she never cracked. Just as Joe Mounsey and all the other good detectives who had spoken to her had failed to find a way through her armour, so Sir Elwyn Jones also failed.

But her strength was part of her undoing. Her toughness under such unremitting questioning confirmed the impression everyone in that court rom had already formed: Myra Hindley was a very hard case indeed. A few tears, a bit of confusion, a look of genuine embarrassment and shame might have served her own cause better. But she was not interested in impressing the court, only Ian. She didn't let him down: her performance was better than his.

The case lasted fourteen days, until the Friday of the third week. Sixty-seven prosecution witnesses were called, ranging in importance from David Smith to a borough engineer who explained where the street lights were positioned in the area of Hattersley where the Smiths and Brady and Hindley lived. There were only three defence witnesses: Ian Brady, Myra Hindley and Myra's mother, summoned under her real name Nellie, who told the court that her daughter Maureen was frightened of her husband, David Smith, and that her other daughter Myra was not in the habit of shopping at Ashton market (from where John Kilbride vanished).

Outside the courtroom there was a freak heatwave, although it stayed cool within the stone ramparts of Chester Castle. The Queen visited Chester races, the first Royal visit to the city since her great-grandfather Edward VII was there sixty years before. Speculation that the court would take a day off was unfounded, and the Royal visit didn't reduce the numbers queueing for seats at the greatest show in town.

Summing up for the prosecution, the Attorney General said Brady and Hindley had formed 'an evil partnership together and co-operated together in all they did'. He described Myra Hindley as 'a calculated pretty cool co-operator' in the murder of Edward Evans, and said that after the 'uttermost indignities' that the pair subjected Lesley Ann Downey to, they could not afford to allow the child to live.

'My submission is that the same pairs of hands killed all three of these victims, Evans, Downey and Kilbride, and these are the pairs of hands of the two accused in this dock.'

Godfrey Heilpern, in his closing speech on behalf of Myra Hindley, described the evidence against her as flimsy. He said that she was not involved in Brady's plans, and that because she lived with him it did not mean she knew what was going on. He said their relationship was one of master and servant who at work were 'dictator and dictatee, which spilled over into their private affairs.

'No one, least of all those appearing for the defence in this case, could listen to that tape recording, that transcript that was read out, without the most intense feelings of abhorrence and revulsion. You must not allow your natural feelings of indignation and horror to cloud your judgement about the real issues in this case,' he said.

And then it was the turn of the judge, Mr Justice Fenton Atkinson, to sum up the case for the jury. It took him five hours, carefully summarising the evidence and weighing the pros and cons of the prosecution and the defence. He described it as a 'truly horrible case', and said that the very nature of it inevitably produced strong emotions and reactions. Few human beings could listen to the tape without some strong feelings being aroused.

'From first to last there has not been the smallest suggestion that either of these two was in any way mentally abnormal or not fully responsible for his or her actions. That leads on to this – that if the prosecution is right you are dealing here with two killers of the utmost depravity.'

He suggested that the doodling of the name John Kilbride by Brady on the exercise book was not significant. But Brady's slip, when he said that after photographing Lesley Downey 'we all got dressed' was important.

'It possibly casts a flood of light on the nature of the activities that were going on.'

About Myra Hindley's role he said, 'You have a picture of her being very closely in Brady's confidence. . . . Brady was quite dependent on her for transport. That must lead to this: that if you were to conclude, for example in the Downey case, that Brady had buried Downey's body on the moors, the prosecution can say that he could not have done that without motor transport available, and nobody has suggested that he had anyone with whom he could have shared such an operation other than Hindley.

'You may take the view that the really crucial case from her point of view is the Downey case. There the prosecution have a strong case against her, because you heard her voice speaking on that recording and you know so much of what was going on on that occasion, and if you are satisfied that she was guilty there and has really told a lying story to try to put the blame on to Smith, that may throw light in your minds on the Kilbride case, because of the marked similarity between those two cases.

'If you think she was a party to both of those, it may colour your view as to the Evans case – as to whether she was in on that with Brady as a willing participant or whether it was a complete surprise to her and she was in the kitchen when it all happened, covering her ears, with no sort of advanced knowledge what was being planned by Brady and by Smith.'

He warned the jury of the dangers of convicting on the strength of David Smith's evidence alone.

'The first thing to remember in considering Hindley is this: that a great deal of the evidence against Brady is not evidence against her; and in particular Brady's statement to Smith about killing people and burying them on the moors. That is something said behind her back, and that is not evidence against her. Anything that Brady may have said to the police by way of an apparent admission is not evidence against her. The plan to dispose of Evans' body is only evidence against her if you think that from the whole of the evidence she must have seen it and known its contents.'

It was twenty minutes to three on the afternoon of Friday, 6 May that the jury of twelve sober-suited men retired to consider their verdict on Brady and Hindley. It took them two hours and fourteen minutes. The prisoners in the dock were standing, eyes straight ahead. The clerk of the court asked the foreman of the jury for their verdicts: Brady, guilty of all three murders; Hindley, guilty of the murder of Edward Evans, guilty of the murder of Lesley Ann Downey, not guilty of the murder of John Kilbride but guilty of the charge that she 'well knowing that Ian Brady had murdered John Kilbride did receive, comfort, harbour, assist and maintain the said Ian Brady'.

She looked up as the verdicts were read out, her hands holding the edge of the dock. They were asked if they had anything to say before sentence was passed. Ian Brady, the meticulous stock clerk, corrected one tiny piece of evidence about the date that the guns were bought. Myra Hindley shook her head.

The Judge spoke, 'Ian Brady, these were three calculated, cruel, cold-blooded murders. In your case I pass the only sentence the law now allows, which is three concurrent sentences of life imprisonment. Put him down.'

Brady, emotionless, was led from the dock. He did not turn and look at Myra. Then it was her turn.

'In your case, Hindley, you have been found guilty of two equally horrible murders, and in the third as an accessory after the fact. On the two murders the sentence is two concurrent sentences of life imprisonment, and on the charge of being an accessory after the fact to the death of Kilbride, a concurrent sentence of seven years' imprisonment. Put her down.'

Myra Hindley swayed forward, and her arm was caught

by the woman prison officer sitting behind her. She was led down the stone steps and out of the courtroom.

The Judge praised the police detection work, particularly that of Detective Chief Superintendent John Tyrrell, who found the left luggage ticket in the prayer book. He thanked the jury.

It was not long after five o'clock. Nobody would be late home that night. The jurors and the lawyers and the people in the public gallery and the press and the policemen could all go about their normal business, resume the rest of their lives. But there would not be one among them who would ever forget those three weeks at Chester Assizes.

About 250 people gathered outside the court, to jeer and boo at the police van that took Ian Brady and Myra Hindley on the last journey they would ever make together, back to Risley Remand Centre for the night.

Could it have gone differently for Myra Hindley? If the Brady and Hindley alliance had dissolved the minute the police took Ian Brady into custody, she might have been able to present a stronger defence, a defence that made far more of his domination over her, of her weakness and compliance with all his wishes. She might have been encouraged to appear more weak and compliant in court.

There was no evidence that she was actually physically involved in the killings: it is possible that she could have worked for a defence that said she simply harboured him after all the deaths, although the evidence against her on the tape was formidably damning. But the strategy for the defence was Brady's. He has said so. Her note to her counsel underlines it. She was either still very much in his thrall – or there were compelling reasons for her going along with him.

Now that it is known the pair were guilty of at least two more murders – Pauline Reade and Keith Bennett – her willingness to toe Brady's line in her defence becomes clear. (The names of Pauline Reade and Keith Bennett were mentioned only once during the trial, and then by Brady. He told the court he had been questioned about them by the police.)

Each of them had a lot on the other, a lot that neither of them wanted revealing. Their shared secrets gave their relationship a sinister strength. In later years those secrets would become pawns in a game of chess played out between them, Britain's two most notorious prisoners, but at the time of the trial their precious confederacy was sustained by their secret jubilation at having 'got away' with two more murders.

If hanging had still existed, and if they had not been able to prove they were criminally insane, the Brady–Hindley story would have drawn to a close after the trial.

In Manchester it would have been re-examined periodically, focusing attention on the unresolved grief of the mothers whose children had been found. The six books written about the case at the time of the trial would have been published, and one (Emlyn Williams' bestseller, *Beyond Belief*) would probably have been made into a film, which would have been shown every few years on late-night TV. But by now the case would have been relegated to a footnote in legal history, the odd chapter in books about the greatest murder cases ever.

But there was no hanging. Ian Brady and Myra Hindley lived. For Brady, prison was to become a death-in-life. But for Myra life meant just that: the chance to live, albeit only within prison walls. She would make the most of it.

8

What Makes Myra Run?

'From first to last in this case there has not been the smallest suggestion that either of these two was in any way mentally abnormal or not fully responsible for his or her actions,' said the Judge in his summing up. It was true, there had been no such suggestion. But that does not mean that the two defendants were sane and normal, it simply means that neither prosecution nor defence wanted to use evidence about their mental state.

British law is an adversarial system, with evidence only presented by either side when it suits their case. There is no independent evidence – independent to the court. It is always allied to either prosecution or defence.

Many forensic experts would like to see the system changed, so that experts are not set against each other, but are called in by the court. In cases of a guilty plea, for instance, it can constitute a threat to the public if no psychiatric evidence is heard.

If a man or woman pleads guilty to a murder, the case can be over in as little as fifteen minutes. A life sentence, if imposed, can mean a mere seven or eight years in prison if the prisoner obeys the rules and gets full remission.

So a killer with a serious psychiatric disorder that may prompt him to kill again can be released on to the streets, whereas psychiatric evidence presented in the first case would have ensured that he was treated for his condition if possible, and if not possible at least he would not have been released without doctors being asked for their opinions on the likelihood of him ever repeating his crimes.

It has been known for some defence lawyers deliberately to choose not to use psychiatric evidence because they know that their client will probably be out of custody more quickly by pleading guilty than by pleading not guilty on the grounds of diminished responsibility. Of course, there have been several celebrated cases where the psychiatrists have got it wrong: where they have agreed to the release of a prisoner who has proved their diagnosis wrong by killing or committing some other violent crime again. But by and large, a court has a better chance of making the right decision about a prisoner if it is presented with all the medical evidence.

In the case of Ian Brady and Myra Hindley, no psychiatric reports were called in evidence. As the judge said, there was not the smallest suggestion that they were mentally abnormal. Yet the calculated and cold-blooded murder of children and young people can never be construed as normal, or a temporary lapse from 'normality'. It had to be the product of some deep-seated sickness.

When Myra and Brady were held on remand at Risley they were seen automatically by the psychiatrist attached to the remand home. They were also seen by a psychiatrist provided by the defence, Dr Neustatter, who said later that he got remarkably little information out of them.

He said that he did not believe that Brady acted out of diminished responsibility.

'The psychiatrist must interpret the law of diminished responsibility, and some people feel that anyone who behaved as Brady behaved must exhibit some abnormality of mind. But from the information I received from him, abnormality could not be assumed. Obviously he behaved extremely abnormally, but there was more than one possible interpretation of that. Some people argue that if there is abnormality of mind, then diminished responsibility must be assumed. But I do not agree that because Brady behaved abnormally over a long period the law of diminished responsibility must hold good in his case.'

Even if Dr Neustatter argued differently it is unlikely the defence would have been substantially altered. It was Ian Brady's decision to run the defence the way it was run, for both himself and Myra. To have pleaded guilty would have required him to surrender the feelings of superiority and control that he had been nurturing for years. One of the few interesting sidelights on his personality that Dr Neustatter elicited was a fear of ever being put in a position of inferiority. Brady told him that he was afraid of doing anything that made him feel inferior. He said that if you were short-changed on a bus and you did not make a fuss about it you felt weak. The psychiatrist also observed that Brady's illegitimacy triggered feelings of weakness. He noted that Brady was embarrassed when asked for the names of his parents.

To plead guilty to three murders would have been a much greater admission of weakness in Brady's eyes: not the weakness of having a need to commit murder (the ability to commit murder was, to him, a strength), but the weakness of having failed to get away with it. As they went to trial, Brady was confident that he would only be found guilty of the Edward Evans murder, and that Myra would walk out of the court with nothing worse than probation. She shared his delusions. In fact, had diminished responsibility been entered as a plea Brady would have been exactly where he is today: in a secure mental hospital. And Myra would have been freed years ago.

The case would have been dealt with quickly, instead of becoming the most sensational murder trial of the century. Her role as a woman who was dominated by a much stronger man, and who did nothing more than shelter him after he committed unspeakable crimes, would have been accepted. The tape would never have been heard in open court: the British public would not have had a focus for their hatred. Today, her name would be all but forgotten.

Although Dr Neustatter did not accept the argument, medical evidence to support a plea of diminished responsibility could have been found. As he said himself, 'It was a case for argument.' Ian Brady was, and is, a psychopath. Just over twenty years after his arrest, in November 1985, he was transferred from prison to secure hospital, diagnosed as suffering from acute paranoia (he was convinced that his food was poisoned and that prison authorities were trying to brainwash him) and schizophrenia.

Had he been given hospital treatment in the first place, he might have confessed to the Pauline Reade and Keith Bennett murders years earlier, putting the minds of two mothers at rest. But there is no cure for psychopathy: it is untreatable. He would never have been released. And almost all of the thirty to forty true aggressive psychopaths in custody in Britain today are held in prisons, not hospitals.

Dr Hugo Milne, who is one of Britain's most eminent forensic psychiatrists and has in the last twenty years been involved with the diagnosis and treatment of over 300 killers, including the Yorkshire Ripper, the Black Panther and the arsonist Bruce Lee, says that the label 'psychopath' is used too readily by the courts and the medical profession.

'When youngsters land in trouble for the first time the diagnosis is "immature, neurotic, lacking support". The next time they come before the court they are said to be "possibly schizophrenic", and the third time, when they are convicted of an aggressive crime, the label is "psychopathic". Probably the only true diagnosis was the first one. There are, thankfully, very few true aggressive psychopaths.'

Ian Brady is one of them. He may be suffering from schizophrenia now, after over twenty years in custody, most of it alone. But there was little evidence of it at the time of the trial, although Dr Neustatter said he found 'the slight irrelevance one finds in a schizophrenic' but he decided that this was caused by Brady watching his words so closely in order to avoid giving anything away. Schizophrenia is 'easy' as far as psychiatrists in criminal cases are concerned: it is easy to diagnose and they know how to handle and treat it after the diagnosis. The Yorkshire Ripper is the classic example of a schizophrenic killer, impelled by voices in his head to carry out his crusade of killing.

But what of Myra Hindley? Her behaviour was just as abnormal as Brady's. Is she, too, a psychopath? The definition of psychopathy varies according to the age of the psychiatrist and where he trained. One of the oldest and best definitions is 'coldness of the heart and insanity of altruistic feeling'. If that were the only criterion, Myra would certainly have qualified in the years between 1963 and 1966. But there is no such thing as a temporary psychopath, and the difference between the years before she met Brady and the years after she met Brady defies that diagnosis.

According to Dr Milne, psychopaths are usually intelligent, their crimes are bizarre and sensational, they are articulate and they do not mind talking about their crimes. Their ability and willingness to talk make them popular with psychiatrists, but there is no evidence that their condition is anything other than immutable.

'Because they are articulate, extremely convincing, plausible and manipulative, it is possible to believe they will change. But they don't. A psychopath does not change in twenty, thirty years. Their personalities do not break down,' said Dr Milne.

A psychopath's behaviour is not simply anti-social, it is asocial. It is amoral and by and large egocentric. Sir David Henderson pioneered the definition of psychopathy, and delineated three different types: inadequate, creative and aggressive. Inadequate psychopaths are incompetent people who get themselves into hopeless social and marital situations, are on the fringes of petty crime, and always blame everyone else for their misfortunes.

Creative psychopaths can be very successful people whose personal behaviour is destructive. They can be great artists, composers, successful businessmen, but they are unable to deal with relationships. They damage quite remorselessly people with whom they come into contact, and any philanthropic behaviour they indulge in is for the ulterior motive of personal gain.

Aggressive psychopaths are the ones who commit violent acts, often so violent that they result in death. They show a lack of emotional response, they enjoy killing and feel no remorse. In wartime they may be translated into great heroes. As a subdivision of the aggressive category comes sexual-aggressive. These are people who commit perverted sexual acts of mutilation and sadism, usually culminating in death for the victim.

All psychopaths have in common an inability to live with other people and a tendency to destroy relationships; they never see themselves in the wrong and can always find an excuse for their behaviour.

Yet Ian Brady and Myra Hindley did sustain a relationship for four years. But it was not a relationship that Brady sought: he was a loner and would have stayed that way if Myra had not persisted in wooing him. He was prepared to abandon the relationship at any point in their early days together. Myra confided to a workmate that when they had an argument one evening he roared off on his motorbike, leaving her stranded by the roadside miles from anywhere. Many girls would have ended the liaison there and then. But she persevered with it.

Even when he drugged her and she was terrified enough to write to her friend, saying that she feared for several people's lives, including her own, she persevered with the relationship. It was not Ian Brady who kept the relationship together: it was his mesmeric hold over Myra Hindley.

He had, prior to Myra, shown classic signs of being unable to live with other people in more than just a lodging capacity. He was rootless. He had some lingering affection for the Sloan family in Glasgow, and he managed to co-exist with his mother and stepfather. But these were not deep ties.

Myra, on the other hand, was close to her mother and sister. Six months after the trial prosecuting counsel William Mars-Jones described Myra in a lecture to the Medico-Legal Society as 'a normally happy girl, a bit of a tomboy, who got on well with friends and relatives. It was not until Brady came into her life that she suddenly began to become withdrawn and secretive and changed her whole attitude to life'. She has established and maintained long friendships and sexual relations (as long as the prison system allowed) in her years in jail.

But there are two characteristics that might contribute to a case that Myra Hindley is a psychopath. First, according to Dr Milne, when psychopaths like Brady get involved in relationships it is often with other psychopaths. One psychopath chooses another psychopath. And, secondly, psychopaths show a pronounced ability to manipulate other people, an ability which Myra demonstrated by twisting her grandmother and mother around her finger as a child, and continues to exhibit in large measure today, within the prison system. But every human being is manipulative to a greater or lesser extent, and some highly manipulative people are not psycopaths.

The fact that Myra was a virgin until she met Brady reinforces the view that she is not a psychopath. Young women with psychopathic tendencies are, according to Dr Milne, almost always promiscuous. They are as casually disregarding of their own bodies as they are of the feelings of others.

So, if Myra Hindley is not a psychopath, was it some other form of mental illness that led her to commit the crimes? It has been suggested that she may have been the victim of a condition known as *folie à deux*, wherein the madness of one person temporarily infects another, or even of several members of a group or family. When the mad one is removed, the others regain their sanity.

In a way that is what happened to Myra. But it is unlikely to have been caused by the *folie à deux* syndrome. It usually happens in terms of persecution complexes: a sick wife imagines that the neighbours are plotting against her and persecuting her, and in time her husband and children assume the same paranoia, and they too believe they are the victims of a local hate campaign. If the wife is taken away for treatment the rest of the family quickly return to normal.

'It is a rare condition and the crimes associated with it tend to be very petty,' said Dr Milne, 'I do not believe it could be responsible for crimes as extensive as those committed by Ian Brady and Myra Hindley.'

So it would seem that there is no easy medical diagnosis to explain what possessed Myra Hindley in the three years that she and Brady went on their killing spree – except her devotion to him. The original impetus to kill came from him, without doubt. Perhaps she learned to enjoy it, too. If she was repelled initially, it was not enough to make her break with Brady. She was in the same position as the wife who, persuaded into swapping partners by a husband who believes their sex life needs spicing up, finds herself enjoying it – and wanting to do it again.

She certainly enjoyed the feeling of power, the feeling of being different, that the killing confederacy gave them. It was a feeling sustained throughout the six months that they were held on remand awaiting trial at Risley, months during which they were able to meet regularly to talk with their solicitor and to reinforce the peculiar intimacy that bound them both.

Police and lawyers alike who had dealings with them at that stage believed that Myra Hindley was the tougher of the two. It was a toughness that had been spotted before: in her childhood when she played with boys and bossed her friends about, in her adolescence when she took up judo and played to win. And she would exhibit it many times in the prison years that stretched ahead of her.

In years to come a prison psychiatrist would describe her personality as 'hysterical', one characteristic being her ability to induce other people to engage with her emotions – a characteristic she would display throughout her prison years. The hysterical personality also selects aspects of other personalities and reflects them as its own.

Thus on a simple level she would give back to others what they gave to her: to Catholics like Lord Longford she would be a devout Catholic, to Quaker friends she would write in simple, homespun Quaker imagery, to family people she would present herself as a devoted daughter who loved children.

It is preposterous, but none the less possible, that she got involved in a warped creed that culminated in killing children simply because she perceived that that was what Ian Brady wanted from her.

9

Holloway

Myra spent one more night at Risley Remand Centre. The day after her sentence, Saturday, 7 May 1966, she was taken in a prison van to Her Majesty's Prison, Holloway – the biggest and most famous prison for women in Britain. The move was made in the early hours of the morning. At the same time, Ian Brady was taken to Durham Jail.

She wrote later that the journey passed in a trance. 'My first impression of London was of trees. I looked and looked and looked and mercifully didn't see the yawning gates of Holloway until we were locked inside them.'

Myra's reception at Holloway shook her. If Risley had lacked refinement, this was much worse. Of the 950 women in prison in Britain on that date, half were in the gaunt, stone Victorian prison in North London, nearly twice as many as it had been designed to house when it was built in 1852. Holloway was and still is the main allocation centre for female prisoners: many of the prisoners who pass through its gates are on the move again within a week, en route for one of the other eight prisons that hold women. But Prisoner 964055 Hindley would not leave for another eleven years.

On arrival she handed in her own clothes, the smart check suit and blue and yellow blouses that she had worn throughout the trial. She was issued with the grey skirt, blue shirt and heavy black shoes that were the prison uniform. She was told to strip and have a bath in just a few inches of tepid water. The girl who had refused to let her sister into the room when she bathed had no option but to allow a prison officer to watch her washing. She was then 'topped and tailed' – the hair on her head and her pubic hair were inspected for lice. She said later she was 'appalled and affronted' at having to go through the ritual again, after enduring it once at Risley.

But her 'sensibilities' were further offended when she had to submit to a VD test. She said she hadn't known that 'there was such a thing'. When she got to the hospital clinic she was told by the elderly woman doctor to 'Take your drawers off dear, and hang them on the nail.' She burst into floods of tears and protested that she'd only ever made love to one man, and surely she would have known before then if she'd had VD? Years later she was able to laugh about the whole incident, and in the next few months, the doctor would become a valued friend.

After the clinic, she was given bedding, a small tin of green tooth powder (instead of toothpaste) and a bar of medicated soap. She was then taken to her cell.

Her first few months in Holloway were hard. In prison terminology she was a 'nonce', a sex offender. That alone was enough to guarantee her a lot of 'aggro'. But her case was so famous, and there were so many women in there who had children of their own, that she came in for more vicious treatment.

To avoid trouble she was held at first on the hospital wing, C Wing, where there were extra staff and where most of the prisoners were heavily sedated and would have no idea who the celebrity in their midst was. But as soon as she was moved from the hospital to D Wing, the whispering began. She was expecting it, and walked with her head held high, looking neither to the left or right.

'Suffer little children to come unto me' was what the other prisoners whispered as she walked past. A prisoner cleaning the stairs between landings lashed out at her with a broom. Another group of prisoners feigned friendship with her, persuaded her to join them in a game of cards, and then savagely beat her up. About ten of them leapt on her and pummelled her to the ground. Then they threw her on to the mesh, the wire mesh stretched between each landing in the prison to prevent women committing suicide by hurling themselves from the top landing.

The alarm was raised, prison officers rushed to the scene of the fight. All the women in the wing were locked into their cells before any attempt was made to bring Myra off the mesh, because they feared there would be more trouble. She was badly bruised and shocked, but had no broken bones. Nobody admitted doing it, no prisoners admitted seeing anything, and Myra knew better than to name her tormentors.

After that, Myra asked to be 'put on Rule 43' – solitary confinement. Ian Brady was already on Rule 43 in Durham, after another prisoner poured scalding tea over him. Male sex offenders were automatically advised by the prison authorities that they would need the protection of solitary confinement, and Brady was quick to ask for it.

But an assistant governor and the prison doctor, the same one who had carried out the VD test, persuaded Myra that with many years stretching in front of her, Rule 43 would not help. One day she would have to learn to live with the other prisoners, or go mad in solitary. Her only hope for survival was to face the other prisoners, and wait till their interest in her died down. In the meantime, an officer was assigned to escort her everywhere.

This in itself isolated her from the other prisoners, and she became reclusive, talking to only a few women, and waiting desperately for her letter from Ian Brady, which arrived each Saturday. She wrote bitter, tough letters by return, or schmaltzy nostalgic love letters peppered with intimate nicknames and private jokes, depending on her mood. On one occasion she joked about the epithet 'Moors Murderers'.

'I didn't murder any moors, did you?' she wrote. Brady wrote back rebuking her for her flippancy.

'Dearest Ian, hello my little hairy Girklechin. It was with profound relief I received your letter today. . . . It was a lovely smoothing nostalgic letter which comforted me almost as if you were here yourself. I had a beautifully tender dream about you last night and awoke feeling safe and secure, thinking I was in the harbour of your arms. . . . I pictured your face and said your name to myself over and over again and imagined the arms of the chair I was clenching to be your hands, lovely strong "insurance" hands (remember?).

'Freedom without you means nothing. I've got one interest in life, and that's you.

'We had six short but precious years together, six years of memories to sustain us until we're together again, to make dreams realities.'

They agreed by letter to start studying 'O' level GCE German, as an act of togetherness. On her cell door she had a white card, that denoted she had no religion and did not want to be visited by any of the spiritual advisors who are available to counsel prisoners.

Then George Blake came to her rescue. Blake was the master spy who was sentenced to forty-two years at the Old Bailey in 1961. He escaped from Wormwood Scrubs in October 1966, six months after Myra Hindley arrived in Holloway. The escape made the Home Office sit up and take notice: they became very concerned that other spies in British jails should not be 'rescued' by their Communist mentors. Helen Kroger, one of the Portland spy ring, was promptly moved from an open prison to Holloway, where E Wing was made into a special maximum security wing to accommodate her. Ethel Gee, another but less important member of the Portland ring, was also housed there.

But they couldn't have an entire wing to themselves, so eleven other long-term prisoners who might be security risks were allocated to E Wing. Myra Hindley was one of them. Compared with other wings, with fifty-odd prisoners on them, E Wing became a soft billet, an easy place to watch the years tick by. Because the prisoners on the wing were not allowed to mix with the rest of the jail's inmates, they cooked their own food in their own kitchen. They had their own garden to work in, exercise in, or sunbathe in. And because there were so few of them, the atmosphere was more relaxed than on other wings.

It was also much safer for Myra. There was a higher rate of staff to prisoners, and because the others on the wing were also serving long sentences, they were less likely to risk losing their remission by attacking her.

Her cell, number 11, was identical to all the others in Holloway: ten feet by six feet in area, with a bed, a wooden wash stand, a bucket, a plastic jug and bowl, a cupboard, a chair and a table. When the maximum security wing was first opened, no work was provided for its inmates, so after being woken up at 7 a.m. to the strains of Tony Blackburn's Radio One programme they would spend their time bathing, doing their own or each other's hair, reading, cooking their meals, and enjoying the sunshine in the wing garden.

Myra had very quickly learned that homosexuality was rife in the jail. If she really was naive enough, as she claimed, not to know that VD tests existed, how did she react to the open lesbianism around her? If she was shocked, she didn't show it. In fact, within a few months of arriving in Holloway, with a weekly letter still coming from Ian Brady and with his photograph adorning her cell, her love for him was waning, and she was embarking on her first affair with another woman.

Lesbian activities – LA as it is called by prisoners – is regarded by most of them to be a prison offence. In fact, there is no prison rule that specifically forbids LA, although the general rule 47(2) bans anything 'that in any way offends against good order and discipline,' and is used as a catch-all to limit overtly sexual behaviour.

Some prisons are tougher on lesbians than others, with rules about not sitting on each other's beds, putting arms around each other or walking arm in arm, and some officers are more inclined to turn a blind eye than others. As one officer who worked in Holloway when Myra was there explained, 'We were always overworked. There were always fights and trouble. If two women were getting on well we chose to ignore just how well. It was better than having them screaming and tearing each other's hair out.'

In women's prisons much of the homosexuality is emotional rather than physical – although there is plenty of physical love, too. In the old Holloway, the buildings that existed when Myra was in there, the prisoners would call love messages to each other from the windows of their cells after they were locked in at night. Those who shared cells would engineer swaps until they were with their lovers. Officers, checking on them through the night, would be grateful for peace.

'We would shine a torch in and if they were both there and quiet, we wouldn't worry too much if they were in the same bed,' said the officer. But the lesbian relationships could themselves be the cause of a lot of friction between prisoners.

Myra Hindley's first female lover was a girl called Rita, a pretty bespectacled teenager with short blonde hair, whom she met on D Wing. Prison lesbians fall into two groups: the 'dykes' who are confirmed lesbians, and who choose homosexuality as a way of life outside prison; and the 'kicksters', the heterosexuals who outside prison prefer relationships with men, but indulge in lesbianism to pass the time and ease them emotionally through their sentence. A third group of women do not get involved in any sexual liaisons in prison.

Rita was a dyke, with her hair cut short like a boy's. But she was small and pretty, not as formidable as some of the older, mannish dykes. Her relationship with Myra was short-lived: it was soon after they had declared their love for each other that Myra was moved to the maximum security wing. But a prisoner who was on D Wing in 1966 with Myra remembers her as 'very quiet. All she ever said to anyone was "Where's Rita?"'

On E Wing Helen Kroger was the star, and she made sure everybody knew it. She was in her late fifties, short and stocky with a pronounced American accent. She and her husband Peter had been running a sophisticated electronic spy centre from their unprepossessing bungalow in Middlesex. She spent a lot of her time in her cell, learning Russian from tapes, reading *The Times* and writing to her husband, who was also serving twenty years for spying.

But when she was not in her cell, she was causing trouble. She hated Ethel Gee, known as Bunty to the other prisoners, and accused her of causing the discovery of the Portland Spy Ring. She would verbally attack Gee whenever their paths crossed, berating her for being ideologically unsound. Gee, seduced into spying in middle age by her lover Harry Houghton and not by political conviction, would not retaliate but would sulk in her cell for days. It was the cell next door to Myra Hindley's, number 12. Myra felt sorry for her and perhaps even empathy, describing her as someone who had become involved in crime for the love of a man. When Gee was being morose, rude and petty with the other prisoners, Myra would defend her. Most of the time, Ethel Gee would stay out of everyone's way, sitting in her cell following the fortunes of her stocks and shares in the *Financial Times*. She was prudish, and would irritate the others by letting her disapproval of them show.

Myra had learned, in her few months on an open wing, the value of keeping quiet and waiting for the others to come to her. In such a relatively small group she soon made friends: a common dislike of Kroger, who was constantly complaining about the others, helped to unite the rest. Myra had one dramatic run-in with Kroger, when the spy hit her over the head with a teapot. At the time Myra was working in the wing kitchen, and one of her jobs was to hand out the 'dry rations' that were issued to all the prisoners on the wing: tea, sugar, soap powder etc. Kroger complained that she was being served short rations. After being hit with the teapot, Myra staggered, and Kroger pushed her to the ground and started to kick her before she was pulled off, screaming and spitting.

Myra had a short flirtatious relatonship with the wife of a gangster, a very attractive woman in her thirties who was a 'kickster' while in jail. But it was not a deep involvement, and it broke up when a dyke in her forties, Norma, was transferred to E Wing. She was tall and slim, with her grey hair cut like a man's, and she wore prison-issue dungarees for her job in the garden. She was serving a life sentence for stabbing her girlfriend to death with a pair of scissors. She and Myra began an affair that would last for several months.

Their behaviour was not outrageous: they were not seen holding hands or cuddling, as many women in Holloway are. But they spent as much time as possible together, locked in deep conversations. And when they were together in Myra's cell the door was kept closed.

One person was convinced it was more than just a platonic relationship, and that was an ex-lover of Norma's, a girl called Bernadette who worked with Myra in the kitchen. She was very jealous, and the situation exploded into a fight with Bernadette rampaging around the wing offering to take on the combined forces of the staff and the prisoners.

After that, they were both taken off the kitchen job. But Bernadette, who was mentally unstable, continued the feud in typical Holloway fashion: she threw urine over Myra Hindley's clothes and put excrement into her bed.

In February 1968, Myra was transferred to Risley Remand Centre for one week. It was a special privilege granted by the Home Office on compassionate grounds. Her grandmother, who had brought her up, was very sick and could not make the journey to Holloway to see her. She was able to visit Myra twice in Risley, only thirty miles from her home, that week. The following month, Mrs Nellie Maybury died.

But the 200-mile journey north did more than give Myra the opportunity to see Gran again. Word that she was at Risley reached Fleet Street, and a *Daily Express* photographer scooped a picture of her being driven back to Holloway down the M1 at 70 m.p.h., sandwiched between two prison officers in the back of a police car. There was an outcry about public money being spent transporting Myra Hindley around the country, and as a result the Home Office decided to make her a Category A prisoner.

All prisoners are divided into categories: A, B, C and D, ranked by the degree of security they need while serving their sentence. Category A are those 'whose escape would be highly dangerous to the public, the police or the security of the state'. They are deemed to need escorts of officers when they move around their prisons, and their visitors are more keenly vetted. Myra was told that all her visitors – including her mother, who had been travelling to Holloway regularly since her sentence – would have to be photographed by the police and have their identities corroborated. She was furious.

'Every gateman knew my mother and greeted her by name,' she said later. She wrote to her lawyer immediately, and he arranged for the police to meet her mother at his office (her mother had used the same solicitor when she was divorced by Myra's father, six months after Myra went to jail).

'I didn't want any Manchester policeman near my mother's house – she'd had more than enough hassles as it was,' she said.

On the maximum security wing, being Category A made little or no difference to Myra's everyday life. She had adapted to life in prison very quickly: unlike most long-term prisoners she was not on permanent medication. She had trouble sleeping – she always slept with her light on – and occasionally asked for sleeping tablets. But she did not take tranquillisers during the day.

She was popular with prison visitors, the philanthropists who have special Home Office clearance to visit prisoners outside the normal arrangements for families and friends to visit. Myra's most famous and controversial visitor over the years has been Lord Longford. He first met her in 1969, three years after her sentence. He was a leading campaigner for penal reform, and she wrote to him asking him to help her case with the Home Office for visits from Ian Brady, who was, she argued, her common law husband. Lord Longford replied, and later visited her.

Myra's feelings about Lord Longford were then, and have remained, ambivalent. The first time she met him Lord Longford was surprised by her intelligence, her demure demeanour, and her devotion to Catholicism.

Within minutes of his leaving she was shrieking with laughter about him to her best friend. 'That hair!' she giggled.

Later she would tell fellow prisoners he was a drag, a bore, a stupid old moron. When she was in the thrall of an intense lesbian affair his visits irritated her, especially if they coincided with her playing table tennis with her lover.

Perhaps in her ridiculing of him there was a braggadocio element: she did not want her friends among the prisoners to see her in the light she presented herself to him. But her true feelings about him were probably revealed when she talked cynically to her closest friend about how useful he – and her reconversion to Catholicism – would be to her in her pursuit of freedom.

As, over the years, Lord Longford became increasingly a figure of ridicule in the press, painted as a bumbling do-gooder who was duped by those whose causes he espoused, so Myra began openly to question his effectiveness as her advocate, and despite the fact that he remains her most dedicated supporter she has said in recent years that she would be better off without him.

When she gave three of the books he has written – all personally inscribed to her – to a friend recently she invited her to 'have a good laugh'. Myra described the books as 'vanity publishing', because Lord Longford's publisher is his family firm, Sidgwick and Jackson.

But he was only one of many who took an interest in her. Within a few months of reaching Holloway she met Lord Stonham, who described her to a meeting of prison visitors as 'calm and collected. She was wearing a neat dress. She was studying for her "O" levels. She was more concerned about the fact that she was not recognised as Brady's common law wife than anything else.'

He told the meeting that he was worried that a person like this could be in prison. He was the first of many visitors, male and female, who would be won over by her. Throughout her adolescence Myra Hindley had wanted to be different from her peer group: in Holloway she achieved that distinction, and she quickly learned to capitalise on it. She became a 'fashionable' prisoner, one whom the distinguished visitors wanted to see. Her articulate conversation and her ability to present herself, chameleon-like, the way she thought they wanted to see her was already winning her allies.

Soon after Lord Longford started visiting her, he put her in touch with a former secretary of his, a blind lady called Mottie who was in her late seventies when she and Myra started to correspond. A couple of years later he introduced her to an old schoolfriend of his, John Trevelyan, the former film censor. They all became her allies. And in the early Holloway years she was visited by a clutch of titled ladies. Other long-term prisoners got no visits at all.

In 1968 she had another regular visitor, a woman who was a magistrate and who organised discussion groups for the prisoners on E Wing. Myra and her lover Norma were regulars at these meetings, and Myra was the magistrate's favourite.

'She seemed to be under Myra's spell,' said another inmate.

It was at one of these meetings that Myra met a prisoner who would play a big role in the rest of her life: Carole Callaghan. Carole arrived in Holloway serving six years for demanding money with menaces: she and her husband were armed when they were caught attempting to extort money from a Cardiff motor trader.

Carole was allocated to maximum security in April 1968, a troublesome and intelligent prisoner. She was twenty-two, beautiful and rebellious. The prison authorities thought that the extra resources of maximum security might channel some of her energies away from trouble. They were right. As a start to the process, the principal officer on the wing suggested that Carole attend the group meeting.

'I walked in and they were all sitting in a circle. Myra stood up and told me it was a private group. I swore and said, "Who's going to throw me out then?" She said, "I'm Myra Hindley," as though I was supposed to kowtow to that. So I said, "Let's see how hard you are with me, I'm not a little kid." I attacked her, and the magistrate grabbed me and pulled me off.'

That was the inauspicious start to one of Myra Hindley's greatest prison friendships. Not long after Carole arrived, Norma was moved to Styal – probably because prison authorities had become aware of the relationship. Carole Callaghan enrolled for English classes, and found that she and Myra were the only two there.

'We soon discovered that we'd got the same sense of humour. When you're in prison you don't worry about what other people are in there for, you just care about whether you can get on with them. On that wing, with only thirteen prisoners, it was especially important that you found some you could be friendly with. Myra and I

were soon good friends. She told me that she had felt
very threatened by me at first, because I was so self-
confident and seemed to her glamorous.'

Carole and Myra were never lovers. Carole outside
prison is firmly heterosexual: inside she was a 'kickster'
who had a series of very short lesbian affairs. Her relationship with Myra was based on their shared Goonish
humour – Carole was dubbed 'Eccles' (the character
created by Spike Milligan) by Myra – on the bond of
their mutual love of English literature (they both got A
grades in their 'O' levels, and can both quote extensively
from the authors they studied) and on proximity: they
had adjoining cells.

'Mine was number 10 and hers was 11, so I called her
my Chancellor. We could see the main road, and buses
going past, and the Holloway Castle pub. We used to
stand at the windows of our cells when we were locked in
at night, talking for hours and dreaming of what we
would do when we got out. She was confident then that
she'd be out after seven years.'

They blossomed together under the prison education
system, adding French to their studies. Their conversations covered music (Myra had started to develop a
taste for classical music while with Ian Brady), literature,
philosophy and religion. With the aid of the prison
library and helpful visitors, they became well read. They
refused to watch television with the others on the wing,
largely because the choice of programmes did not suit
them, and they decided not to read newspapers as news
of the outside world would exacerbate their yearnings for
freedom. With time on their hands, they wrote poetry. In
the three years that they served together, Carole
Callaghan became closer to Myra than perhaps anyone
else ever had. Myra has referred to her many times since
as 'my alter ego'.

There was fun, too: Myra singing 'Swanee River' as
she came down the stairs, balancing a dish on each hand;

Carole defying the maximum security of the wing by squeezing out through a bathroom window and ringing the bell to be allowed back in; Carole locking the needlework tutor in her room for several hours. There were raids on the kitchen for extra tea and coffee, and on one occasion Carole stole a bottle of sherry from the officers' room. They were girls' boarding school japes, but they relieved the boredom and tension.

'At first Myra wouldn't lower herself to nicking things. I said to her, "You know how to murder, now learn how to steal." I convinced her that the only way to survive was to beat the system. But when she got caught stealing coffee, she blamed me!' said Carole.

Carole taught her to speak in the prison 'language', a means of communicating without officers knowing what they were saying. It consists of putting the sound 'ag' before any vowel sound in a word (so, for instance, 'trees' becomes 'tragees' and 'running' becomes 'ragunnaging'). Practice makes them very fluent at it, and it is incomprehensible to listeners.

The atmosphere on the wing was relaxed. A pool was built in their garden, and when it was near completion, a group of prisoners including Myra were sunbathing on the lawns nearby. When two of the officers came out, they picked Carole Callaghan up and threw her into the water. The prisoners grabbed hold of one of the officers and threw her in, too. It was another adolescent lark.

All the inmates of E Wing were fascinated by a room just along the corridor from Myra and Carole's cells. E Wing was where prison executions were carried out before hanging was abolished, and cell 18 was where the hangman pulled the lever. From that cell you could look down at the drop, although the scaffold had been removed. Ruth Ellis, sentenced to death for shooting her lover, had been hanged there fourteen years earlier.

'One of the prison officers had a crush on me, so I was able to persuade her to open the door and let us look,' said

Carole, 'Myra was as fascinated as the rest of us, but she went very quiet afterwards.'

In June 1968 the government decided to carry out an experiment in Holloway allowing women to wear their own clothes. Two years later prison uniform was abolished in all women's jails. All prisoners serving more than six months were eligible for a grant of £25 a year to buy clothes for themselves (the amount today is £125). Myra, who prided herself on her smart appearance, felt disadvantaged among prisoners who had recently come into Holloway, and who had fashionable clothes sent in by their families, or others who had wealthy relations to buy what they needed. At least two of the thirteen women in E Wing had mink coats sent in. Myra, stretching the grant as best she could, ended up with two pairs of polyester trousers, a skirt and a couple of blouses and jumpers. From that day on, the quest for good clothes would become almost an obsession: she would pester visitors, and try to persuade other prisoners to leave part of their wardrobe behind when they left.

'After all, I'm in here for life and you're going home,' she would wheedle, in what she and Carole called her 'Baby Jane' voice. She became expert at using the severity of her sentence to elicit sympathy. But she had put on a lot of weight since arriving in Holloway – she weighed twelve stone at this time, had 44-inch hips and was a size sixteen – so not everybody's clothes would fit her.

In her early years in Holloway she was gluttonous, spending all her wages on sweets. Because she did not smoke, she was in a better position to indulge her taste for sweet things than most prisoners, who spent all their wages on tobacco. At Christmas, all prisoners were given three cigarettes, a bar of freesia soap and three Cadbury's creme eggs by the authorities. One year Myra traded her cigarettes for an extra three chocolate eggs with one of the prisoners, and her bar of soap for another three. After eating nine eggs she was sick – and demanded her soap

back as a consequence. The prisoner who had swapped
with her allowed her to have half of it back.

In the summer of 1968, a tapestry room was opened on
B Wing, under the auspices of a tutor from the Royal
College of Needlework. Despite her lack of ability at
sewing whilst at school. Myra proved to be a very gifted
tapestry worker. She and two other prisoners worked on
an elaborate carpet, a copy of a Polish design, which they
were told had been commissioned by the Polish Embassy.
It was an exquisite piece of work, worth thousands of
pounds. In the hem they tucked a cigarette paper with the
words 'Myra Hindley made this carpet' written on it.

Another distraction was the psychiatrist, Dr Gerald
Wolfson, who visited the prison regularly. Myra was the
first in the queue from E Wing to start seeing him
voluntarily, for two hours at a time. She spent the first six
months telling him her version of why she was in prison,
and the next eighteen months repeating it. In the end she
stopped seeing him because she felt he was not interested
enough in her. On one occasion when she was recounting
the latest in the saga of her feud with Bernadette, he told
her that she should avoid being provoked by the other
women. 'The Wolf', as she nicknamed him, pointed out
that she was more intelligent, and should not allow herself
to be dragged down into petty rows. It was an answer that
irritated her: she had been seeking sympathy.

After Norma left, Myra was not long without another
sexual partner. A girl called Alice, a big, pretty girl from
Rochdale, was transferred to E Wing from Styal Prison.
At the same time a friend of Alice's called May – later
nicknamed Blossom by Myra – also arrived in E Wing.
Because both girls came from the Manchester area they
knew the full story of the murders, and were determined
to have nothing to do with Myra. She won them over with
the technique she had already honed to perfection: she
would say nothing to them, but smile and look mildly

embarrassed when they looked at her. Because of the small size of the wing, it was impossible for them not to talk to her soon, and within hours she had converted them to her cause.

Alice fell madly in love with her. She told May, who told Carole, who told Myra. Girls' boarding school routines again. Myra said she had already guessed from the way that Alice looked at her.

'Tell her: OK,' she told Carole.

She and Alice met later that day in the record room, and a wild affair started. Alice became devoted to Myra, who used her as a slave: Alice did her washing and ironing, cleaned her cell, cooked her breakfast and carried it to her in bed.

There was so much freedom on E Wing that they could make love several times a day. They would climb under Myra's bed, which was propped up on four jam tins to make it higher. Carole or May would stand outside on guard. Myra was an inventive lover. She would save fruit, usually bananas, for their lovemaking sessions, and secrete it in her body for Alice to find. On one occasion she gave herself cystitis by using a piece of orange.

She was still writing to Ian Brady, and his letters were arriving regularly. He went on hunger strike to further their case to be allowed to meet, but by 1969 Myra had lost any desire to see him again.

'I don't give a monkey's . . . for him any more,' she said, swearing. Her language was as tough and as peppered with swearwords as it had been when she first started work. But whatever sentiments she expressed to her fellow prisoners, her letters to him gave no clue of her estrangement from him.

They united to fight a plan to turn Emlyn Williams' bestselling book, *Beyond Belief*, into a film. They were sent release contracts by the film company, but refused to sign them: even though by doing that Myra could have provided her mother with enough money to live comfortably for the rest of her life.

'Part of the contract I was sent by solicitors representing the film company asked for permission to portray, impersonate, use my likeness, biography, etc for a sum of money, the amount of which was left blank for my insertion, and of course I absolutely refused,' she wrote later to Lord Longford.

She loathes Emlyn Williams' 'faction' account of the crimes and the years leading up to them, and made Carole promise that she would never read the book.

Because the book is part fiction it contains many inaccuracies. She and the literal-minded Brady (who had used his statutory right to speak on his own behalf from the dock at the time of sentence to correct a tiny fact given in evidence) objected to any fact that was wrong. But Myra also objected to the overall portrayal of her character – for two schizophrenic reasons. One was that it made her seem 'a real hard cow', as she told Carole. But the other was the opposite: where Williams had painted a picture of her as a normal, happy child she said, 'Can you imagine me skipping along the street like that, saying good morning to the things I passed, like bloody Pollyanna?'

Her hatred of the book has become obsessional. She still refers to it with vitriol. Yet, if she could be objective about it and forget the small inaccuracies, it is sympathetic towards her in that it paints Brady as the dominant partner who inspired the crime trail. Other books published after the trial put forward the thesis that Myra could have been the dominant force, or at least an equal partner.

In October 1969 the spies Helen and Peter Kroger were exchanged for Gerald Brooke, and flown out of London to Warsaw. There was no longer a need for a maximum security wing in Holloway, and E Wing was opened up.

But it never became as big as the other wings – the number of prisoners on it only rose to about twenty. And it never lost the feeling of comparative cosiness.

Myra was terrified at the prospect of having to mix with the rest of the prisoners again, but because she still continued to work in the tapestry room on E Wing and because she was allowed to collect her meals and take them back to her cell while the others were locked in, she managed to avoid any nasty incidents.

She had two diverse reactions to her notoriety. On the one hand she abhorred it, because she knew it would always limit her prospect of freedom. And she was still able to convince herself and others that it was unjustified. But on the other hand she enjoyed the celebrity it gave her. She knew that practically every new prisoner to arrive at Holloway would within the first couple of days nudge their neighbour and ask which one was Myra Hindley.

When a BBC camera crew arrived in the prison to make a 'Man Alive' documentary about Holloway they reacted the same way. Although Myra was not going to be included in the film, they wanted to know who she was. Carole Callaghan *was* selected to be interviewed for the film – and pretty quickly offered to introduce anyone who wanted to her friend Myra. At first Myra shrank from the idea, but she warmed to it when Carole explained that the price of an introduction would be half a bottle of vodka, a box of Dairy Box (Myra's favourite) and some tobacco (Carole smoked and Myra could use it for bartering).

When the authorities realised that Alice was excessively close to Myra, they 'deported' her back to Styal. Alice was distraught, and left protesting undying devotion to Myra. But Myra had been growing bored with her anyway, and quickly embarked on another relationship.

The object of her affections this time was an older woman, another lifer, called Mary. She had been moved from Styal for attacking another prisoner with a knife. She latched on to Myra as soon as she arrived on E Wing and

Myra was flattered. But the affair was disastrous. Mary was given to throwing tantrums if she didn't get her own way, and would kick and bite and scratch and scream on the days when she didn't feel the affair was progressing to her satisfaction. Myra would be alternately covered in love bites and scratches. In the end, she broke with Mary 'for the sake of my sanity'.

But there was trouble with Mary for years. 'I had to threaten to shove her head down the lavvie pan to get rid of her,' said Carole, who by now was acting as Myra's minder. After Mary came a succession of short-term affairs, mostly with women who looked like men and had adopted masculine names: Joe, Steve, Sandy. One of them had even had an operation to remove her breasts to make her look even less feminine. But none of them lasted for more than a week or two. Myra enjoyed having them fighting over her: it amused her and flattered her.

For many women inside, their relationships are primarily a matter of emotional release. But for Myra it was sexual. 'She is a very strongly sexual person. She needs it, and she feels physically frustrated if she isn't getting it,' said Carole.

By now it was the summer of 1970, and with no girlfriend Myra was bored. She had been in prison for more than four years, and even in her wildest dreams she knew there was no prospect of release in the foreseeable future. She was coming up for her twenty-ninth birthday. Prison was starting to get her down.

She was even wallowing in nostalgia, taking trips down memory lane by playing over and over again the hit songs that she and Brady had liked: 'Massachusetts', 'San Francisco' and 'Tambourine Man' (she said that was Brady's favourite). She played Scott Walker's 'The Lights of Cincinnati' and talked sentimentally about her memories of sitting in a parked car on a high road on the moors overlooking Manchester, and looking down on the lights of the city. She even persuaded one friend, a lifer called Gail who also came from Manchester, to get her parents to take a photograph of 16 Wardle Brook Avenue – and when she saw it, complained that her flowers had been dug up.

She told her confidante Carole that she wanted another lover. For seven weeks that summer, the top of the hit parade was 'In the Summer Time', sung by Mungo Jerry. It became Myra's theme. She would look out of her cell window at night and sing the line 'I've got women, I've got women on my mind.'

Myra told Carole to, in the words of the song, 'Go out and see what you can find'. She was still nervous about venturing too far from the sanctuary of E Wing.

'I came back and told her there was a new officer just arrived, and that all the girls in the prison were mad for her. I said I thought she was just Myra's type – and when I pointed her out, Myra agreed. She fell madly in love without even knowing the officer's name.'

The name was Pat Cairns. She was smaller than most officers, with thick, shiny, dark hair cut into an urchin style, and was butch without being too masculine. She had been brought up less than a mile away from Myra's home in Gorton, Manchester, and had been a Carmelite nun for some years. It was medical problems that had forced her to leave the convent – she had had an operation on her goitre. After joining the prison service she worked at Bulwood Hall borstal, where she met and began an affair with another officer.

When this officer transferred to Holloway, so did Pat. They lived together in a flat in Earls Court, paid for by the prison service because there was insufficient accommodation at Holloway.

But Myra knew none of this when she drafted her first love letter to Pat Cairns. Without knowing her name, she and Carole decided to call her 'Dawn' because they thought she had a misty, ethereal quality that reminded them of the morning light. With Carole's help Myra penned the note, sitting on her bed one Sunday afternoon. Carole remembers it as saying: 'I've been looking at you from a distance. . . . Is it too much to hope that one day we may sit in the sunshine together enjoying a glass of wine . . . it gives me hope just being able to see you, and when you are not on duty the day drags by. . . .'

Carole promised to pass the 'flyer' – prison slang for a note that is passed within the jail or smuggled out. It wasn't easy. She carried it around for eleven days until an opportunity presented itself. It happened on the night of 22 July, the day before Myra's birthday.

'Pat Cairns didn't work on our wing, but that night she was the duty officer and was checking us. She opened my spyhole. I wasn't in bed, I was working. So I asked who it was and when she said Pat Cairns I asked her to open me up because I had a letter for her. She asked who it was from and I told her it was Myra. She unlocked my door, took it, and bolted me in again.

'When I told Myra next day she was very worried and very excited. She kept saying, "She'll take it to the Governor and we'll be cased [slang for on a charge]." But she kept asking when I thought she'd get a reply.'

Myra didn't have to wait too long. The next day, Pat Cairns made contact with her.

10

The Love of Her Life

The following morning Pat Cairns appeared outside the tapestry room where Myra and Carole were working. She caught Carole's eye. Carole slipped out and was hurriedly handed a note, to be given to Myra.

The affair between the prison officer and Myra Hindley was on.

The first direct contact between them came later the same day, when Pat Cairns came over to E Wing with a Rachmaninov record, borrowed from Islington library, to lend to Myra. It became the first simple front for the relationship: a shared love of music.

Myra was still working in the tapestry room, but as her love for Pat Cairns – she called her Tricia – developed into an obsession, she engineered a job in the prison library, cataloguing books. It meant that she had to leave E Wing and have more contact with other prisoners, but she was prepared to risk that because the main prison library was on B Wing, where Pat worked. For a few days after she took up the job the library was extra busy, as prisoners from other wings queued to borrow books in order to gawp at Myra Hindley.

To have even more contact with her lover, Myra and Carole devised a table tennis tournament. The prisoners on E Wing challenged the officers to a tournament, to be held on E Wing with its comparatively lavish recreational facilities which had been installed when it was a maximum security wing.

Pat Cairns was an inexperienced table tennis player, but she flung herself enthusiastically into the preparations for the tournament. She and the officer she lived with were both going to take part, and they went after work to the Michael Sobell Sports Centre in North London to get more practice in. Pat needed it, because the sessions when she was supposed to be practising on E Wing were spent with Myra in the records room, next door to the punishment cells on the ground floor of the wing. Carole would go in with them, put a record on and hold the door while the two lovers kissed and fumbled with each other's clothing. Myra's favourite record at that time was a Carpenters hit 'We've Only Just Begun.' Later she would play another Carpenters song for Pat, 'They Long to Be Close to You', to warn her lover that she knew how popular the officer was with other prisoners.

It was dangerous: they both knew the risks they were running. But for both of them it was a grand passion, probably the biggest love affair that Myra has ever had. They grew reckless, meeting in Carole's cell for all-out love sessions. Carole would be the lookout, and the signal that anyone was coming would be her singing 'To Be a Pilgrim'.

An inter-wing postal service was set up, with one or two trusted prisoners being bribed with tobacco to carry notes between them. Myra for the first time was having to spend her prison wages on tobacco and not sweets or toiletries, which irked her, but no sacrifice was too great.

She and Carole were still writing poetry, and Myra was sending her best efforts to Pat. She was also passing off some of Carole's as her own. One of them started:

> 'My own beloved who hast lifted me from
> This drear flat earth where I was thrown,
> Who came to me when all the world was gone
> And I who looked only for God found thee.'

There were many more written with the same heavy religious symbolism and emotional imagery. Myra had gone back to the Catholic faith a few months before she met Pat Cairns. The German priest who visited Holloway, Father William Kahle, played table tennis with the prisoners on the wing, and she had found him easy to talk to. Lord Longford, too, had been pushing her back towards her faith, and in her first letter to him in November 1969 she wrote, 'I'm still desperately trying to make my peace with God and to prove myself worthy of being a Christian. . . .'

The Governor of Holloway, Mrs Dorothy Wing, encouraged her in her quest to rediscover her religion, too. Mrs Wing took a personal interest in her famous prisoner, and as usual Myra sought ways subtly to capitalise on the situation. She discussed becoming a Catholic again with Carole, who advised her cynically that finding God would help her parole chances.

So early in 1970 Myra went to Mass. All the other Catholics who were her friends from E Wing went with her for support. She took confession.

'It is a terrifyingly beautiful thing – terrifying because I have taken a step which has taken me on to the threshold of a completely new way of life which demands much more from me than my previous one, and beautiful because I feel spiritually reborn. I made such a mess of my old life and I thank God for this second chance,' she wrote to Lord Longford.

What exactly she told the priest in the confessional will never be known, but it is doubtful that it was anything nearer to the truth about her crimes than the litany she had been reciting to psychiatrists, prison visitors, family and friends: a garbled version of the facts more or less following the defence put forward at the trial, and majoring heavily on her role as an infatuated underling to Brady.

One psychologist who talked to her during her early years in Holloway described her as reciting her story in a flat, unmodulated voice: a stage which he recognised as transitional between simply speaking her denials and actually believing them herself. There can be no doubt that by 1970 Myra Hindley had convinced herself almost as effectively as she convinced those around her of her own limited role in the savage events that led up to her arrest. Her reacceptance by the Church confirmed the new image she had created for herself, as a wronged and suffering woman.

Now her infatuation with Pat Cairns added impetus to her reconversion. Cairns as an ex-nun had an air of otherworldly mysticism about her, which was attractive not just to Myra but to a lot of the other women in the closed confines of the prison. When Myra discovered where her lover was from, and how she, too, had worshipped at the Monastery of St Francis in Gorton, the bond between them became a religious one. Her poems and her letters to Pat were suffused with cloying religious imagery.

By this time Myra had become completely disillusioned about her relationship with Brady, but she was reluctant to end it. She said it was because she was worried about the effect on his health: it is more likely she was worried about the effect on her parole chances if he decided in revenge to confess to the other two murders.

Whilst protesting her innocence, Myra seemed to worry a great deal about the other crimes hanging over her head. Other prisoners noticed how depressed she became whenever they heard of a gate arrest – a prisoner being arrested as she left the gates of the prison, for crimes that she could have asked to be taken into consideration when she was before the courts.

But although she was worried about Brady, she couldn't be bothered to write to him. So her best friend Carole did it for her. For six months, from the start of the affair with Pat until the postal strike in January 1971, Carole drafted and dictated to Myra letters for Ian. They had never corresponded intimately – he still addressed her as Hessie but she wrote back to him as Ian – so it was easy enough for an outsider to take over. He had been attacking her reversion to the Church with scathing comments about the Catholic vision of Heaven: 'Is it just full of Catholics? What happened to all the millions of Chinese souls?' But while Carole wrote the letters the correspondence was mostly centred on French literature and philosophy. They discussed Rimbaud, Baudelaire, Voltaire: and if Brady noticed any change of style, he never commented on it.

Towards the end of 1970, another friend came into Myra's life. They met for only a few days, but the friendship has lasted ever since, and given Myra one of her most devoted champions.

Dr Rachel Pinney was and is an oddball. Sixty-one years old when she first went into Holloway, she was serving a nine months' sentence for kidnapping. She was a retired doctor of medicine, divorced with three grown-up children, from a well-connected family, who had been leading a hippie-style existence in a commune described by one of the policemen investigating her case as 'an abode of educated filth'. The commune was the centre for Dr Pinney's 'Creative Listening' campaign. As a prominent member of the Peace Movement, the Quaker doctor had pioneered a technique which she hoped would improve communications between politicians of different countries and different ideological viewpoints. She had given up medicine to promote her theories, which eventually she had adapted and put to use – with some success – in the treatment of disturbed children.

The child she kidnapped was a fourteen-year-old boy who had been living with her for some months while his mother was in a mental hospital. When the mother came out Dr Pinney decided that for the boy's good he should not go back to live with his mother and she arranged for a friend to take him to Canada.

It was a bizarre case, made even more bizarre by the fact that Rachel Pinney had taken a vow of silence for one

day a week on the sixteenth anniversary of the bombing of
Nagasaki, in 1961. To this day, she observes her
Wednesday silence. It must have made her reception into
Holloway difficult, as her first day there was a
Wednesday.

She was initially only in Holloway for a couple of days,
before being allocated to Moor Court Prison, in
Staffordshire. She saw Myra Hindley, but they did not
speak to each other. It was only when Dr Pinney was
transferred back to Holloway for ten days that the two
made contact.

'Myra was sitting in the corridor with her head in her
hands. I went up to her and said, "I'm your friend, do you
mind if I talk to you?" She said, "No of course not. I wish
you had approached me last time you were here. I never
speak to people first in case they spit at me." So then we
sat and talked for half an hour.'

Rachel Pinney wrote in her diary that night, 'Something
has happened to me – I don't know what it is but it is
something special.' The next day she was invited to tea
with Myra, Carole and another of Myra's friends, Joan
Kleinert. Over the next few days Myra and Rachel talked
frequently. Myra again expounded her theories of innocence and victimisation, and Rachel Pinney believed
her. When she left prison – after serving six months of her
sentence – she set about trying to prove Myra's story true.

'I spent a year in Manchester talking to everybody,
researching a book. At the time I wasn't allowed to write
directly to Myra, because ex-prisoners were not allowed to
communicate with prisoners. But I found a way round
that. Then Myra got word to me that she didn't want me to
write a book, so I stopped.'

The way that Rachel found to communicate with Myra
was through a friend of hers, another Quaker called
Honor Butlin. Honor, a comfortably well-off and
eminently respectable widow, gentle and unassuming to
the point of naivety, started to visit Myra and write to her

regularly, and send her flowers. She and Rachel are just two of the coterie of supporters that Myra has collected outside prison.

While she was in Manchester, Rachel tracked down and talked to Myra's other grandmother: her father's mother. This old lady said she would like to see Myra again, so it was arranged that she would be driven to Honor Butlin's home in the Midlands, spend a night there, and then go on to Holloway with Honor.

'She and Myra greeted each other so beautifully,' said Honor. 'They had not seen each other since before the court case. Myra said, "Do you remember how we both thought I'd be out on probation in no time?" They hugged each other and they both cried.'

'M has been a unique relationship in my life,' says Rachel Pinney. 'It looks at first glance as though it was a sexual relationship, but it wasn't. I am a lesbian, but at the time I was in Holloway I was busy having an unrequited passion for a prison officer. Myra was involved elsewhere: our relationship was platonic. She has a very fine mind, and I was privileged to spend a few days getting to know it.'

The cheerful Carole Callaghan did not get on so well with the eccentric old doctor. 'She spent all her time on the exercise bike. Nobody else got a look in!' The two have continued to squabble through the years that, outside prison, they remained loyal friends to Myra.

In February 1971, Carole Callaghan left prison. She was excited to be on her way out, but at first her life still revolved around the friends she had left inside. She had divorced her husband while in prison, and as his sentence was twelve years he was still in jail. She lived at first with another ex-inmate. At lunchtimes on Saturdays they would go to the Holloway Castle pub and wave to Myra.

'Sometimes we stood inside the prison gates. We called to her and she called back – then we'd get chased away by the screws.'

Myra at first replaced her close friend with Joan Kleinert, an American serving a two-and-a-half-year sentence for importing 250 lb of marijuana, which she claimed was a one-off deal to finance a house purchase. Joan was distraught about being separated from her two young daughters, and Myra comforted her.

'She was a very caring person,' said Joan Kleinert. 'She was very sensitive and very attractive in a subtle way. We talked about absolutely everything and we shared on a very emotional everyday level for over a year.'

Joan, as an American, knew nothing about the Moors Murders case. But Myra told her side of the story, and she became convinced of Myra's innocence.

'The person I knew simply could not have done it,' she said, reiterating Rachel Pinney's views. Neither Pinney nor Kleinert would pass muster as a reliable character witness, but probably their devotion to Myra says nothing more sinister about them than that they were naive and easily manipulated. Rachel Pinney was also starstruck, dazzled by Myra's notoriety.

Again, as with Carole, the relationship was not sexual. But Joan Kleinert did become embroiled in the lesbian atmosphere of the prison, and when she returned to America she became a lesbian, changed her name to Sage Mountainfire, and for a time lived in a women's commune where men were forbidden.

'Myra always chose as friends the more interesting, more glamorous prisoners. She went for those with good backgrounds, or money, or education,' said one of the prison officers. 'Holloway was full of the dregs of the world, but we always used to say: Myra chooses la crème de la crap.'

Her relationship with Pat Cairns continued, although they had to be more circumspect after one of their messengers, a prisoner called Pat Ali, made a complaint about them which was heard by a board of visiting magistrates. But the letter Mrs Ali handed in as evidence was in code and was not produced to the magistrates, who dismissed her story. Pat Ali lost six months remission for making 'malicious allegations'.

'I suppose I was the perfect go-between, as I can't read or write. I carried letters between them on most days,' she said.

The code had been devised for the lovers by Carole Callaghan, and it was to her flat in North London that Pat Cairns came to decode the letters. She was still living with her prison officer lover in Earls Court, so couldn't take them home with her. The code was simple but time-consuming: numbers were used to represent letters. Coded notes from Myra to Pat were brought out of Holloway by released prisoners, who delivered them to Carole's flat. More were still being secretly exchanged within the jail.

But because of the difficulty of writing them and de-livering them, they were short. When Myra wanted to write longer letters to Pat she devised a system whereby she sent them to her cousin, Glenys, in Manchester. Glenys posted them on to Carole's address, where Pat received them. In return, Glenys would send in replies from Pat.

These letters had to go through the censor, so their contents are innocent, and ostensibly aimed at Glenys and her family. They were sent to Myra's mother's address, and when they were for Pat the initial was left out of the name. They are heavily religious, as all Myra Hindley's correspondence at this time was:

'Ever since God has given me back my faith, and some-thing infinitively precious which has made all that has happened in the past bearable [a reference to her affair with Pat Cairns] I have made a 9 weekly Novena to different saints, and the current one is St Therese.'

She writes about the books she is reading, the music she is enjoying listening to, and a cosy account of a cat that lived in the prison and had come into her cell to sleep on her bed.

She also writes about Ian Brady. Earlier in 1971 – after Carole left and stopped providing letters to him – she decided to break with him. 'The decision was an agonising one which cost me dearly,' she wrote to Lord Longford. 'It shattered me because previously I had deemed it impossible that my feelings for him could ever change.'

But although she broke off the relationship, she still corresponded with him sporadically. After a seventy-day hunger strike Brady was transferred to Albany Prison on the Isle of Wight, where he continued his fast. She professed to be very concerned about his welfare, although she said she was very hurt that he regarded her reconversion to Catholicism cynically as a means of 'working my ticket'.

Although there is no doubt that both Myra and Pat Cairns were deeply in love, neither was faithful to the other. Pat Cairns' relationship with the other officer foundered, and by the time officers' quarters were available at Holloway (rebuilding of the old prison was gradually taking place) they were no longer living together. They moved into separate flats. But 'Cairnsie' – as the prisoners called her – was still very popular with the gay women in Holloway. A prisoner called Debbie worshipped Pat Cairns, and they embarked on an affair that continued when Debbie was released.

Debbie knew about Pat's relationship with Myra. But she was so anxious to please the officer that she helped smuggle a letter from Myra out, and she 'kited' a beautiful suede suit for Myra. (Kiting is prison slang for cashing stolen cheques.) Myra was extremely pleased with the suit. From the start of her affair with her beloved 'Tricia', Myra lost weight. She dropped from a thundering twelve stone down to under eight stone – a very low weight for her big bone structure. One reason was that she was buying tobacco to bribe messengers, and had no wages left over for sweets. Another was that, since she was on an open wing, she had to eat food prepared in the central kitchens, like the rest of the prisoners. This was not as good as the freshly prepared food the maximum security prisoners had become used to. And food continued to be an easy way for other prisoners to attack Myra (most frequently by urinating in it). So she began to eat less and less.

As the weight fell off, her vanity grew. She became very choosy about what she would eat, and the change in her appearance was so dramatic that she was assigned an extra bottle of milk a day to try to build her up. Her mother, visiting, became very worried about her weight loss.

Myra, too, was having other affairs. There was not much opportunity for her and Pat Cairns to make love, although they took every chance they could, even meeting in the prison chapel for sex sessions. But Myra, who has a highly developed need for sex, was physically frustrated. She and Pat Cairns communed with each other from a distance every evening: at a certain agreed time they would each masturbate while thinking of the other.

But that wasn't enough, and Myra continued to have brief affairs with other girls. She made Pat Cairns jealous over one relationship, with a black girl nicknamed Bibby.

Bibby's friend, another black girl, acted as lookout. 'Myra told me she wanted to try it with a black girl. She said she'd always fancied it. She and Bibby made love whenever they could. It was wild, erotic stuff, I could see it all. One day Pat Cairns arrived and caught them together and there was a nasty jealous scene, but it ended up with Pat and Myra making up. Myra's affair with Bibby lasted nine months, until Bibby was released. Sometimes they would have another girl in with them, three in a bed – under the bed, actually.

'Bibby used to plait Myra's hair for her into Afro plaits: whenever Pat saw her with her hair like that she went mad. I was glad of them: all their little dramas made my sentence go quicker, and that's what you want when you're inside.

'Once I was in on it, Myra used to tell me how much she loved Pat. She often said how much she wished they could just be allowed to live quietly together. Often she'd have love bites on her neck and we used to joke with her, "Were there mice in your cell last night Myra?"

'Pat was a good officer. She would always smuggle twenty Benson in for you if she could. She was very popular. Myra certainly loved her, worshipped her. She would do anything to be near her "Tricia".'

They used to have long whispered conversations through a hole in the wall between the tapestry room, where Myra was working, and an officer's room next door.

Myra got on well with the Governor of the prison, Mrs Dorothy Wing. Her intelligence and her polite manners always commended her to the staff, and when she deemed it would be advantageous to her she would woo their support. Her chameleon-like ability to be all things to all women meant that she would find some link between her and them, and play on its importance to her.

Mrs Wing liked English nineteenth-century poetry, to which Myra's 'O' level English literature had introduced her. In one of her frequent trips to see the Governor ('She was in and out of there like a yo-yo once she discovered Mrs Wing would listen to her,' said an officer) they discovered this mutual interest.

Mrs Wing was a humanitarian who had softened the regime in Holloway by her avowed mission to give the prisoners 'as much freedom and dignity as possible'. She had come to Holloway in 1966 – the same year as Myra, which Myra later concluded to be divine intervention on her behalf – and had been made Governor the following year. Prior to joining the prison service in 1956 she had served in the army, and referred to the prisoners as 'troops'. She had fought for the abolition of prison uniform, installed an aviary of budgerigars in the prison, and allowed long-term prisoners to have their own curtains, bedspreads and ornaments in their cells.

When she took charge of Holloway she said, 'Very few women are real criminals, in the sense that men are. Most women prisoners are just weak, stupid or inadequate. We must help them out, so that when they go out from here they have at least a chance of defeating the circumstances that once defeated them.'

Mrs Wing took to inviting Myra to her house inside the prison perimeter for fireside poetry readings. 'Matthew Arnold was her favourite,' Myra wrote later. 'She used to say that many a night, when the traffic outside her window kept her awake, she thought of his "Dover Beach" and the soothing surge of the tide washing away the shingle lulled her to sleep.'

The poetry readings were an unusual privilege. An even bigger one was to come. Myra had recently petitioned to have her Category A status taken off, and had succeeded. It meant that she did not have to walk around the prison with an escort.

'After they took that ridiculous, farcical Cat A tag off me I had almost the run of the prison – took myself to work, education, library and even worked a couple of afternoons in the garden,' she wrote later.

Losing the Category A status also meant that Mrs Wing had the discretion to take her outside the prison. It was normal, but not necessary, to get Home Office approval for taking a Category B prisoner out, but Mrs Wing took the decision herself without consultation.

On 10 September 1972 she and Myra climbed into a car, with a male friend of Mrs Wing's and her pet cairn terrier, Piper. They drove to Hampstead Heath where, for one and a half hours, they walked. Myra said on many occasions afterwards that it was the happiest time she had had since her arrest, and how it allayed all her fears that she would be recognised. She recalled later her feelings of panic when one man they passed seemed to stare at them.

A prisoner who was working in the garden saw them return. She told one of the prison staff, who leaked the story to Fleet Street. It made massive headlines, and there followed a storm of public protest. Questions were asked in the House of Commons. Police chiefs joined with the mothers of the dead children to express their horror. Home Secretary Robert Carr publicly rebuked Mrs Wing for her 'error of judgment' and ordered that there should be no more outings for Myra, and that there should be a review of the procedures enabling Category B prisoners to go out.

An on-the-spot inquiry was held at Holloway, headed by the regional director of women's prisons. The Home Office put out a statement to stop speculation that the outing was a preparation for Myra being released on parole in the near future:

'Myra Hindley is not being prepared for release on licence. Her security classification has recently been changed from Category A to Category B and yesterday the Governor of the prison, in her own discretion and for the first time, took the prisoner out for about one and a half hours.

'The Home Secretary considers this was an error of judgment. He has given instructions that this arrangement is not to be repeated.'

Mrs Wing, who was sixty-two and planning to retire three months after the incident, was very shaken.

'The outing was a perfectly simple thing I would do for any prisoner. I took Myra out because I thought it would do her some good to see some grass and trees and have a breath of fresh air. Bless her heart, she enjoyed it very much. She said "Doesn't the grass smell beautiful?" She is reasonably happy, but I am afraid that the reaction from the press and television has rather taken the edge off what was meant to be an outing. In my judgment, it seemed to be a good thing to do at the time. I now realise that it was an error of judgment because Mr Carr has said that it was.'

She said she was on leave on the day that she took Myra for the walk.

'I go out with prisoners half a dozen times a year. It is usually when I am on leave or have the weekend off. At other times I am too busy. There are a variety of reasons why women are taken out of prison at the Governor's discretion. A number of the women have children in the care of the local authorities, and children's officers think children are frightened of being taken to prison to see their mothers. We arrange for them to meet at a hostel.

'Sometimes a prison visitor takes a prisoner out at the Governor's discretion. Another occason for prisoners to be taken out is the exhibition in Piccadilly of entries in an annual artistic competition for prisoners. If any of our prisoners win a prize and have their work exhibited we take them to the exhibition. We don't just let them out. They always go with someone reliable.

'Taking prisoners out is a way of rehabilitating them. Sometimes they are taken out to give them a breath of fresh air. In the case of Hindley, because she is a life sentence prisoner, I took her out myself.

'I am not a sentimentalist or a do-gooder. I am what could be described as a liberal Governor. I don't believe in grinding prisoners' faces into the ground. And I have never done so.'

She told later how she had taken another woman, a murderess, for a day to Cruft's dog show, and how she'd taken other prisoners to the Royal Tournament, Madame Tussaud's and the Tate Gallery.

Lord Longford joined in the debate, stating that he believed that Myra's walk was a good idea. 'She is no longer the person she used to be. She has changed. She is now very religious and full of remorse,' he said. But Father Kahle, who had left the post he had occupied for ten years as prison chaplain two months earlier because of health problems, disagreed. When asked if, in the six years he had known her, her personality and attitudes had changed, he flung out his arms and said, 'I don't think so. Has your personality changed in ten years? Has mine?'

Father Kahle, a naturalised Briton whose parents were persecuted by the Nazis, said he had first been asked to talk to Myra because the prison authorities feared that if she didn't find her way back to religion she would become either suicidal or very, very hard.

'I was asked to see her because I was Roman Catholic and a German with a lot of knowledge of a cruel people. Lord Longford said to me, "Hasn't she changed a great deal? Hasn't her personality changed?" I told him I did not think so.'

At the time of the furore, Myra had been in jail for six and a half years. Any long-term prisoner is entitled to apply for parole after serving a third of their sentence: and for parole purposes life is deemed to be twenty-one years. So she was within six months of being able to apply. She had been writing to Lord Longford about her 'rampant gate fever' for some time: 'I've always lived with both feet well and truly inside the prison gates. But now, not only have I got one foot outside but, which is much worse, my spirit has left me and is hovering restlessly on the other side of the wall.'

Although the Home Office pointed out that she was still at liberty to apply for parole the following year, the public outcry about her walk gave her the first real warning that she would be unlikely to get it. The strength of public anger about her case spelled out the unlikelihood of any Home Secretary agreeing to her walking free.

After the wait she wrote to Lord Longford that she had spent the two 'happiest and quickest hours of my life' on the Heath. She told him she was mortified by the media's treatment of Mrs Wing, whom she described as 'kind, humane and sensitive'. She said she accepted the public hatred of her which was 'more or less justified by my convictions and the myths that have sprung up around me' but was distressed that it should be deflected on to Mrs Wing.

Within Holloway, her reaction was less Christian. She threatened the woman who had shopped her, and it has gone down into prison mythology that she told her she would die in prison. The prisoners who make this claim are quick to point out that that woman was released but is now back inside, serving a life sentence.

At the end of the year Mrs Wing left Holloway, and retired to live with her sister in a cottage in Herefordshire. She asked Myra to write to her. Myra paid another of her glowing, emotional tributes: 'I shall miss her very much. She has been a constant source of support and encouragement and I grew to love and respect her very much. . . . Something solid and dependable has gone out of my life. Mrs Wing occupies a particular space in my heart and always will.'

She did not establish the same rapport with Holloway's next Governor, Dr Megan Bull. But there were other staff who were happy to put themselves out for her. In one letter to a relative she wrote glowingly about Fauré's Requiem, an extract from which she had heard on the radio programme 'Your 100 Best Tunes'. The day after her letter went through the censor, an officer brought her a copy of the record, to borrow.

'She liked talking to officers and lots were prepared to talk to her,' said a former officer. 'They got some sort of buzz out of saying they were friends with Myra Hindley. A lot of them began to believe her stories about how innocent she was. It was the younger, less experienced ones usually, and the lesbians.'

And another member of staff, a welfare worker, said, 'I was never starry-eyed about Myra. She was a very unusual woman, naive in many ways, but with tremendous strength and influence. I always had to make a conscious effort to work out what was right for her and what was right for me.'

But some officers were starry-eyed about her. 'We all liked to believe we had a special relationship with Myra,' said one who admitted being 'intrigued by the Myra enigma'.

And of course there was one who did have a very special relationship with her. Pat Cairns.

11

Escape Plot

With seven years served and no prospect of parole, Myra became depressed. She missed the fun that Carole had brought into prison routine, she missed a close companion after Joan Kleinert left, and she longed for freedom.

She and Pat Cairns fantasised about the life they would lead together when she was released. They dreamed of going to Brazil to work as missionaries (a total fantasy because even had Myra been granted parole, she would not have been allowed to leave the country). And gradually the dream acquired substance: if Myra was not going to be released, they would break her out of Holloway.

Pat was still using the flat that Carole shared with another girl to decode her letters from Myra. She knew Carole had underworld connections, and she asked her if she could find a gang to bust Myra out.

'She told me she had £4,000 saved. I told her that any of the lads I knew would want at least £20,000 – and then they'd only bust Myra out to bump her off, not save her. She told me about their plans to go to Brazil and I told her, "You must be mental. There's nothing in Brazil except an awful lot of coffee, and you haven't got a cat in hell's chance of getting Myra out." I never thought they'd really try to do it. But after I said that, Pat didn't come round so much. I still saw her, off and on, for a drink. But I didn't take her talk of escape seriously.'

Pat and Myra took it seriously, though. They enlisted the help of a twenty-two-year-old girl on the same wing as

Myra. Maxine Croft, a pretty girl who had become involved in petty crime and was eventually sentenced to prison for three years for passing dud fivers, was a 'green band', a 'trustie' who was allowed more freedom than most prisoners. One of her jobs was to make tea for visitors to the prison, another was to clean the officers' sitting room. This made her useful, so Myra turned the full beam of her friendship on to the young impressionable Maxine. She invited her to tea, took her into her confidence, made a fuss of her.

When Maxine asked Myra about the rumours concerning her and Pat Cairns, Myra denied them. But one day when both Maxine and Myra were working together preparing a meeting room, Pat Cairns came in and she and Myra slipped away together. When Myra returned she was still fastening her shirt and straightening her skirt, and she took Maxine into her confidence.

From then on, Maxine carried letters for the lovers. The first time an escape plot was mentioned to her was when Pat Cairns asked her if she had any underworld contacts who could provide forged passports. Then she asked her to smuggle a camera to Myra, as she wanted some photographs of her. Myra was already carrying photographs of Pat Cairns with her everywhere, in a little leather pouch which she concealed in her knickers. Maxine picked up the camera which Pat left in a broken clock in a cupboard in the officers' sitting room. The clock was the usual place for Pat to leave gifts for Myra – apples or the occasional Mars bar. The inner workings of the clock had been removed, so it was a convenient place to hide contraband.

Maxine put the camera in her bra and the flashbulbs in her kneesocks, under her trousers. She took about twenty photographs, but Pat found later that the camera wasn't working and the whole charade had to be repeated. Myra changed clothes several times for the pictures, wearing a nightdress on some of them and on the others wearing the suede suit that, unknown to her, had been acquired for her by Pat's other lover, Debbie.

Next Pat Cairns asked Maxine to make impressions of keys. She bought her three bars of soap to make moulds with. Maxine Croft said later that she was very tempted to go to the prison authorities at this stage, but the knowledge that Mrs Pat Ali had not been believed and had lost remission for making allegations against Pat Cairns and Myra deterred her. She was also afraid of both Pat Cairns – an officer who could make life difficult for her – and Myra who, despite the sweetness-and-light face she turned on for her visitors, was by now quite able to handle herself with other prisoners. One woman who threatened her was told by Myra that she would be 'squeezed through the mesh and come out like chips'.

Pat Cairns brought keys to Maxine's cell to make the impressions, but they did not work very well. So she smuggled into the prison a bag of hospital plaster, but that did not work either. The conspirators were getting reckless now, and Pat Cairns was nearly caught by another officer with the plaster on her. But she did not give up: modelling plaster that she brought in made adequate moulds, which Maxine hid in the clock for Pat to pick up and take home with her.

But Officer Cairns was worried about the moulds being stored in her flat. Maxine was due a day's parole, as she was only twelve days away from release. She left Holloway with a probation officer to go shopping. She was allowed some free time on her own, and met Pat Cairns at Speakers Corner in Hyde Park. They went for a drink at the Cumberland Hotel, and over vodka and lime Pat told her the full escape plan and the dreams of going to South America to work as missionaries.

The two women planned to take the moulds to the left luggage department of Paddington Station, a convenient place to hide evidence, as Myra and Ian Brady had discovered. But 1973 was the height of the London bomb scares and the left luggage offices at main line stations had been closed. So Maxine gave Pat Cairns the address of a friend who she thought would store the moulds until Pat needed them.

The package was sent to the friend, at his car workshop in Ilford. But because of the bomb scares he was suspicious of the parcel, and did not open it. Later that day, by chance, a detective inspector called to talk about having his car repaired. Maxine's friend told him about the strange package, which the CID man took and carefully opened. Inside he found the moulds, and a note from Maxine. When he was told that Maxine was in Holloway he realised the significance of the find, and contacted the Home Office.

At the end of her day's parole, Maxine arrived back at Holloway late and very distressed. The full impact of what she was involved in had hit her, and she told officials, 'I am frightened. Pat is going to break Myra out.'

As soon as Myra got wind that an inquiry was starting, she set about systematically destroying her cache of letters from Pat, and her photographs of the officer. They were ripped into small pieces and flushed down the lavatory. But there was plenty of other evidence against the conspirators. Myra gave Maxine Croft a story to tell the police: about how a former Assistant Governor, now retired, used to leave her keys in a certain spot and she had made impressions of them in the hope of selling them when she got out. Maxine was told that if she didn't stick to this story, she would have no protection while she was in jail.

But the young girl, terrified by now, told the truth. Myra and Pat Cairns initially lied about the escape plot, despite the police finding a driving licence in the name of Myra Spencer at Pat's flat, and continued to lie about their relationship, which they claimed was emotional and not physical.

Worried about the inquiry, Pat Cairns asked for

permission to talk to the Governor privately. The Governor, Dr Bull, said that she could not speak to an officer in confidence about a matter that was the subject of a police investigation.

News of the attempted breakout was quickly leaked. Two days after the plot was discovered it was front page news. Pat Cairns was suspended without pay, but allowed to remain in her prison flat. Carole Callaghan, running her own business by then, gave her typing work to do. 'She refused to accept money without working for it. And when I told her she should leave the country before the trial and start a new life elsewhere, she wouldn't hear of it. She was still crazy about Myra.'

Two months later Myra and the other two women were formally charged, and in April 1974 the case came to trial at the Old Bailey: eight years to the month after Myra had left the dock at Chester Assizes. They stood in the dock together: Maxine Croft, pretty and timid-looking; Pat Cairns, smartly dressed and looking as though she belonged behind the counter in a bank or a building society; and Myra Hindley, staggeringly different from the police mugshot that had been printed so often since the Moors trial. None of the reporters crammed into the press benches would have recognised her.

'She looked softer, prettier and feminine. Pat Cairns was fresh-faced and pretty, not at all masculine-looking,' said one of them.

The story of the escape plot was told in court, and the three pleaded guilty to a charge of conspiring between January and November 1973 to effect the escape of Myra Hindley from lawful custody in Holloway Prison. Maxine Croft's defence was that she was in the weakest position of the three, and had a fear of offending anyone in authority at the prison in case it affected her parole. The court was told how Pat Ali lost remission for making a complaint against Myra and Pat.

Maxine had told police that Pat Cairns said to her after

she started carrying letters, 'You are in it now and if you say anything to your friends or anybody I'll have you nicked.' Maxine's defence lawyer pointed out that Myra Hindley was a woman who could persuade those about her that she was a reformed character.

'She has persuaded some of the highest in the land that she is a reformed character who merits special consideration. Such is the woman who brought Croft into her thrall.'

It was revealed in court that over a three-month period, Myra had written seventy-four notes to Cairns, who had replied with fifty-one.

It was Pat Cairns' defence lawyer who objected to the Judge, Mr Justice Melford Stevenson, describing the relationship as 'a close lesbian association'. Mr Aubrey Myerson, Pat's defence counsel, said, 'The relationship was not physical in any sense whatever. It was a bond based on mutual respect and admiration for the Roman Catholic religion they shared. It had developed because they found there was an affinity which emerged from matters of mutual interest, in that they came from the same area of Manchester, had the same kind of upbringing and both felt exceedingly strongly about their religion.'

In her statement to police Pat Cairns had said it was due to her influence that Myra had made a confession to the prison chaplain, and had regularly taken communion.

'I tried to be a source of consolation and encouragement to her. Just being Myra Hindley is penance enough without the long years and rigours in prison.' She said she had become distressed seeing how prison was becoming too much for Myra, and had promised to do all in her power to help her. She said she was only aware of 'the ends and not the means' of the escape plot. 'Our emotions are sometimes too strong for our judgment,' she said.

She also said that she thought Myra's case was 'a political hot potato', and that no government would risk the criticism they would get for releasing her.

'I believe suffering can be atoned for and purified in the crucible of suffering.' The crucible of suffering is one of Myra's favourite themes: it crops up repeatedly in her correspondence.

Lord Longford gave evidence on Myra's behalf, denying that he was in her thrall by pointing out that he had seen her only four times a year in the past five years, with the Governor present each time, and that her letters to him had passed through the prison censor, 'I offer my own strong opinion that she is not a bad woman, but a woman with much good in her, making a determined effort to make amends for her past and to do good in the future.

'Only the Almighty can tell us whether to try to escape when there is no hope of being let out is a sin, although it is illegal and wrong. This woman has suffered, and she is anxious to do what she can to atone.'

Maxine Croft was sentenced to eighteen months' imprisonment, the Judge saying, 'You were undoubtedly the victim of a very wicked woman who practised upon you blackmail, and took advantage of her position to make you do things I do not think you would have done left on your own.

'A little courage would have got you out of your difficulties.'

She was sent not to Holloway but to another prison, and within three weeks of the trial her appeal was heard. Evidence about how Mrs Pat Ali had been treated when trying to inform about Myra and Pat was heard, and Maxine was freed immediately. She had served six months, waiting for the trial and the appeal.

But her dealings with Myra Hindley were not over. The following New Year's Eve, in the Black Cat pub, a hangout for gays in Camden Town, Maxine had the misfortune to run into two of Myra's old friends from Holloway. They took her into the toilets and beat her up.

Pat Cairns was given a six-year jail sentence. Sentencing her, the Judge said, 'The most sinister feature of this case is that you exercised pressure of a sinister kind on an inmate of the prison. I can find no extenuating circumstances to explain your conduct. You have not improved your position by putting forward a façade of piety which proved to be very brittle.'

She was sent to Durham Jail, and later transferred to Styal, in Cheshire. Myra arranged for a note to be smuggled to her in Durham within a few weeks of her arriving there, but, just as separation broke the spell that Ian Brady had over Myra, so it had broken the spell she held Pat Cairns under. The letter was handed in to the prison authorities unopened.

The prison officer turned prisoner did not have an easy time in jail. Other officers believed she had damaged their collective reputations, and she paid for it. At Styal she served much of her time in the punishment block, Bleak House, in rigorous conditions. When jobs were meted out, hers were always the worst. But she survived, and found herself another close girlfriend.

When she finished her sentence – she got full remission – she moved back to the Manchester area, where her family lived. They had stood by her and remained close to her through her time in jail. She found a job as a bus driver for Manchester City Council, and she lives with another woman just a couple of hundred yards from the cemetery where John Kilbride is buried. She kept the pictures she had of Myra: years later some of them were published in a German magazine, sold to them by a woman friend of Pat's.

Pat herself has always refused to talk about her years with Myra Hindley. There have been times when she has had newsmen camped on her doorstep, but she has remained stoically – though politely – silent. One particularly persistent reporter remembers: 'I waited outside her house until she came out, and she politely told me she had nothing to say. I was convinced I could persuade her, so I walked down the road with her to the bus stop, talking to her all the time. The bus came, we got on. I sat next to her, still talking. We travelled a few miles and then changed buses, me being my most persuasive. We got off the second bus and walked a few hundred yards to the bus depot where she worked. She said, 'I'm sorry, but this is private property and if you come any further I'll have to call someone to throw you out.' Those were the only words she spoke in the entire forty minutes we were together, except for saying she had nothing to say at the beginning. It took some doing to remain so calm and so polite – and so silent.'

The Judge sentenced Myra to an extra twelve months, to be served consecutively to her other sentences. He said, 'You are already the subject of a life sentence and very properly so subject. This is a temperate sentence in regard to the gravity of the conspiracy. I pass it with the intention and hope that if in the future – and I think it should be a remote event – parole should ever be considered then the activities which led to this case will be recorded and re-membered.'

She went back to Holloway. Her former Governor, Mrs Dorothy Wing, said, 'I feel sorry for Myra. She has lost everything. I feel a lot of it is my fault. If I hadn't taken her for that walk in the park, I don't think escape would have entered her mind. I feel very sad and sorry about it now. What was meant to be a kindly act and what she regarded as a kindly act resulted in her being crucified by a public outcry. When all that criticism came, she realised just how much hatred was left for her after all her years in prison.

'She will never have the chance of walking out in the park again. She's lost all that and everything else too. I feel bitter about that.'

She continued to believe that the affair between Myra and Pat Cairns was not physical, and described it as like a schoolgirl crush.

'People think it must have been a strong affair both

emotionally and physically. This is not true, and would have been very difficult as Miss Cairns was working in a different wing from the one Myra inhabits. I feel sorry for all the officers who served under me. It makes Holloway Prison out to be a glorified haven for lesbians. This is not true.'

But the Home Office rejected Mrs Wing's version of the Myra–Pat affair later that year by making a compensation award of £1,500 to Mrs Pat Ali for her lost remission.

Much later on, Mrs Wing conceded that perhaps she had been 'naive' about Myra. She confided to a friend, 'I still wish her well. But I do wonder with hindsight how well I knew or understood her.' Today she wants to forget all about the Myra Hindley episode in her life. 'It was a long time ago and I don't wish to remember it,' she says.

The month after the court case, Myra wrote about it to Lord Longford saying that the prevailing opinion among the prison authorities was that she was not to be trusted an inch. She said she accepted the judgement because she had betrayed the Governor's trust.

But she argued that there were extenuating circumstances, the most acute being her realisation that she might never be released. She pointed out that the authorities treated every decision about her with fear of the public reaction – and she cited as an example her application to study with the Open University.

The application had caused some controversy when it was made public six months earlier. But despite her protestations that it was treated with fear of public reaction, she had been given permission to go ahead, at the time the only woman among forty-six prisoners to start degree courses with the OU. She wrote to Lord Longford when she was in her fourth month of her first-year foundation course in the humanities with the university, her £25 registration fees having been paid for her by the authorities, and she was given one day a week off work for her studies. She was also allowed a portable black and white television in her cell, and a typewriter.

Although she complained to Lord Longford that she wasn't trusted an inch, Myra's privileges and freedom within Holloway were not affected by the court case. Even when, six months after the case, she smuggled a letter out of prison, she was not punished, only reprimanded.

The letter was to Kenneth Norman, a trustee of the Portia Trust, a charity which helps women offenders. Mr Norman had written four times to Myra, and had been told by the Home Office that she did not wish to reply to him. But she smuggled a letter out with a girl who was leaving – and claimed that she had not been allowed to reply to him legally, through the censored prison mail. Mr Norman took up her case by writing to Dr Edith Summerskill, Minister of State at the Home Office, in confidence. But Dr Summerskill took the view that she could not regard a breach of prison rules as confidential, and an investigation into how the letter got out was started.

The contents of the letter showed that Myra was still very much in love with Pat Cairns.

She told Mr Norman that she had made a statement to the Parole Board saying she did not wish to be considered for parole. (Her case would come up for automatic review the following month, October 1974, because by then she would have served nine years in custody from the date of the arrest.)

The letter was full of contrition, not for the escape plot but for having involved Pat Cairns in it. She claimed she had wanted to ask for her sentence to be lengthened in return for a year being knocked off Pat Cairns' imprisonment. She said she was turning down the chance of being considered for parole. 'As you will imagine, I feel absolutely wretched about Patricia, and find the burden of guilt almost unendurable, although she has no regrets whatsoever.'

Her rejection of consideration for parole was no more than window-dressing: Mr Justice Melford Stevenson's rider to her token sentence ('If in the future – and I think it should be a remote event – parole should ever be considered, then the activities which led to this case will be recorded and remembered') had underlined to Myra the hopelessness of her pursuit of parole. By surrendering any chance of it, she was not giving anything away.

But she did have something more tangible to lose towards the end of 1974: her comfortable berth in Holloway. A former top security wing at Durham Jail, reputedly the toughest prison in England, had been converted to house female prisoners. It was designed to take no more than forty, under high security conditions. There were closed circuit television cameras everywhere, and electronically controlled locks on cell doors.

Because Holloway was being rebuilt gradually, as old wings were knocked down conditions in existing wings became even more cramped. The conversion at Durham was designed to relieve pressure by removing from Holloway some of the long-term prisoners: Myra was sure that her name would be on the list to go, and she dreaded it.

She was now firmly established in cell number 1 on F Wing (the old maximum security wing, E Wing, was one of the first to be knocked down in the rebuilding programme and after a time on D Wing, Myra was transferred to F). She had floral curtains, a matching bedspread, a sheepskin rug on the floor, and a bookcase full of books. She had enough cushions to place them all around her bed, so that during the day it looked like a settee. When friends visited her cell the cushions would be strewn on the floor for them to sit on. The walls of the cell were covered with art posters and photographs of her family.

'She practically covered the walls. If she got a box of chocolates she'd cut the picture off the lid and stick it up,' said an officer who worked on the wing. 'Her cell was always spotless. She woke very early in the mornings, and that's when she cleaned it. Opposite her cell was the dormitory where the kitchen girls slept, and they had to be unlocked at five o'clock in the morning to start on the breakfasts. Myra was always awake at that time – she'd shout "Good morning" to us. Yet she never went to sleep until the early hours. We used to check her cell every half hour, and she'd be reclining on the bed, writing or listening to the radio. She always had very elegant dressing gowns: long and silky, one pink, one blue, and both with a huge rose embroidered on the back. She slept with her light on always. Her cell door was difficult to open, and she was always having to give new officers instructions about how to do it.

'Her hair always looked nice. One of the girls on the wing was a hairdresser, and she did everybody's hair. The prisoners weren't allowed hair rollers, but they got around that by using Tampax tubes. It was amazing the number of Tampax they got through. She was first in the queue at stores every week for clean sheets, and she was very picky about which she would have: she'd inspect them for stains or discoloration, or if she thought they were too stiff.

'If the weather was fine Myra would spend all her exercise period lying on the grass soaking up the sun. But even if it was wet she wanted to go out: she said she was allowed so little fresh air she wasn't going to waste any of it.'

Her weight had continued to drop, and she was by now down to a skeletal seven stone. She bought biscuits with her wages, and had her extra pint of milk every day. But she ate little of the prison food. She was practically vegetarian, although she did eat chicken. Every six weeks about half of the women on the wing would club together and cook themselves a meal, all buying ingredients and pooling them. Myra joined in and enjoyed that meal. And once a week a plump West Indian woman would cook her a meal, for which she paid with cigarettes.

She did not join in wing activities like discos, but she was singing in the church choir and took part every year in the church Christmas production. In 1974 she played Mary in the Nativity Play – and an entire wing, the remand wing, got up and walked out. Because they were all on remand they had none of them been in the prison long, so they had not had time to be won over to Myra's side.

But other women were still being won over. Myra continued to make friends – and continued to seek out 'la crème de la crap'. Anna Mendleson and Hilary Creek were two members of the terrorist group The Angry Brigade who were each sentenced to ten years in 1972 for their part in a bombing campaign. They were both educated and from wealthy families. Myra became friends with of them.

Hilary Creek worked in the garden and was allowed to bring flowers in for Myra's cell. Anna Mendleson taught other prisoners in the education classes at the prison. It was she who persuaded Myra to apply for the Open University course. She also found Myra another job: contributing a satirical agony column to a magazine she got permission to edit. Only a few issues of the magazine, called *Behind the Times*, appeared. It was closed down by the Governor because of its heavily lesbian content.

Myra's problem page, published under the pen name Betty Busybody (none of the prisoners were allowed to have their names on their articles) certainly contributed to the lesbian overload:

Dear BB: I'm tall, slim and good-looking in a masculine sort of way. This causes me great embarrassment, as everyone thinks I'm butch. What can I do? – Worried

Dear Worried: Give me your cell number. I think I can help

you with this problem. I'm tall, slim and good-looking in a feminine sort of way.

Dear BB: My problem is finding a lover. I think I am on a desert island, as in my dream no man appears. Can you help me? – Misguided

Dear Misguided: Learn to swim. Remember, we're all in the same boat.

Dear BB: My problem is that I think I have become frigid. What can I do? – Iceberg

Dear Iceberg: Think yourself lucky. Being frigid solves a lot of problems.

Dear BB: I have a peculiar problem. I think I am in love with myself. What can I do? – Narcissus

Dear Narcissus: Apply to stores for a full-length mirror. You must get yourself in perspective.

Dear BB: I have a problem with my girlfriend. Wherever we go, she seems to know everybody. Is it right for me to be jealous? – Puzzled

Dear Puzzled: As your girlfriend is a tobacco baron I don't think you need to be jealous.

Dear BB: I have fallen in love with the AG [Assistant Governor]. Is this natural under the circumstances? Do you think you could feel the same way? – Bashful

Dear Bashful: I think it's natural under any circumstances: she is rather dishy. However, she censors this magazine. Would you please write and inform your relatives of your immediate transfer to Dead-End Labour Camp, Siberia.

Dear BB: Someone is queering my pitch! I've heard that they are in love with the AG. Well, I am too, and I'm most annoyed at their idea of a joke! – Jealous

Dear Jealous: It's no joke: you and Bashful must learn to get along with each other. You're going to Siberia, too.

It was the failure of the Assistant Governor who was censoring the magazine to curb its lesbian content, and stop Betty Busybody (alias Myra Hindley) flirting with her so blatantly in print, that caused the magazine to be closed, and the Assistant Governor concerned was moved to another prison.

Myra also contributed macabre jokes to *Beyond The Times*, for example: What do you call a cannibal who eats his mother and father? Answer: an orphan. She wrote book reviews and helped select the other articles and poems which appeared in the magazine.

Anna Mendleson and Hilary Creek weren't the only women in Myra's coterie. Another close friend – though, again, not lover – was Chris Ryder, who was serving two years for travellers' cheque frauds.

Myra called her 'one of the jewels on the necklace of my life'.

'She held my head above the waterline when I almost drowned in grief, despair and everything else after they busted the escape conspiracy.'

Chris Ryder, too, was more intelligent than most of the prisoners in Holloway. After she left prison she married and later divorced a man named Tchaikovsky, and under the name Chris Tchaikovsky she is very involved in running the charity, Women in Prison. She, too, has remained a close and loyal friend to Myra, and still visits her regularly.

But for at least a year after the escape plot trial, she was badly depressed. She wrote to John Trevelyan, 'I lie down and close my eyes, but it is worse still. The thought of the mechanical succession of day following day ad infinitum is one of the things that makes my heart palpitate, the real approach of madness. The terrible bondage of the tik-tak of time, this twitching hand of the clock, this endless repetition of hours and days and years. Oh God, it's too awful to contemplate. But there is no escape. No escape.'

As well as to Lord Longford and John Trevelyan, Myra was writing long agonised letters to actor and writer Robert Speaight, who was also visiting her. She was very upset when he died suddenly in November 1976.

Her suicidal letters to her friends on the other side of

the wall could be cynically regarded as attempts to win more sympathy. But her depression stretched beyond the written page.

'For the first time I heard her scream and shout,' said a prison officer who had known her in Holloway for some years. 'She didn't have public tantrums, but in the privacy of her own cell she'd weep and wail loudly, getting quite hysterical. The theme was always: I'm never going to be let out, they're going to leave me to rot in here till I die. And if any girl came back with a gate arrest, there would always be trouble from Myra. She'd have black days, when she'd book to see the doctor in the morning for tranquillisers and then stay in her cell all day, not going to her tapestry work or even doing any of her precious studying.'

But there was one thing that could be guaranteed to rouse her: a love affair. Vicky and her mother were sentenced together for taking part in a conspiracy to import drugs. Vicky was young and pretty, recently married and determined not to become involved with the Holloway lesbian scene. Both she and her mother were new to Holloway, and Myra went out of her way to help them with the routines of the wing.

Vicky's reaction at first was one of horror: she didn't want anything to do with Myra. But she was gradually won over.

'She made the first move, but not for a couple of weeks. That was enough to change my mind about her. We got into the habit of going back to my cell or her cell in the evenings. Then one night she bent over and kissed me. I thought it was very pleasant. We talked a lot and I gradually found I fancied her.'

Vicky said she knew what she was getting into, but fell madly, hopelessly in love with Myra. They spent every available moment together, under the bed in Myra's cell, with her bedspread draped low to the floor. A friend would keep watch on the landing and warn when any officers were approaching.

'She was the first woman who ever touched me in my whole life. She made love with her eyes, her words and all her being,' said Vicky. Myra wrote poems for Vicky, copying them on card and decorating them with drawings of butterflies and flowers.

But after three and a half months together, the authorities got wind of the relationship between the two, and Vicky was abruptly shipped out of Holloway to Styal. She was so desperate not to go that she persuaded two friends to dislocate her shoulder, believing that she would then have to be kept in the prison hospital at Holloway. But she was moved nonetheless.

After her initiation with Myra, Vicky has remained a lesbian. Ironically, one girl she lived with also became one of Myra's lovers, in another prison nearly ten years later.

Vicky was replaced by another celebrity prisoner, a real celebrity. Janie Jones, the pop star who was sentenced to seven years for controlling prostitutes and for her part in a BBC payola scandal, was an obvious target for Myra.

Glamorous, she swanned around the wing in her fox fur coat, big floppy hats, double layer of false eyelashes and blonde wig. Everyone liked her, prisoners and officers alike. She was funny and tough and determined to make the best of her sentence. She was not ashamed of her crime, and delighted in telling the other women about the 'special' parties she had thrown, with girls of every shape and size and age available to suit the tastes of the clientele. She called it 'a public service'.

When her fur coat vanished one day she threatened to sue the prison service for compensation. The coat had been taken to the kitchens, cut up and pieces of it smuggled back to all the wings. For weeks it kept appearing as fur trim on slippers, fur earrings, and an entire hatmaking class used bits of it to trim their creations. JJ, as they called her, was furious.

Janie was a lesbian long before she passed through the portals of Holloway. Her affair with Myra was predicted by the officers as soon as she arrived, with some of them even jokingly talking about running a book on how long it would be before Myra seduced her. But Janie was too forceful a personality to be turned into one of Myra's sex slaves, and it was an on-off affair.

It was a note with a poem on it that was Myra's first approach to Janie:

> 'The life that I have
> Is all that I have
> And the life that I have is yours.
>
> The love that I have
> And the life that I have
> Are yours and yours and yours.

Many letters passed between the two. Janie became completely taken in by Myra's protestations of innocence.

'I began to see that she was no longer the impressionable, infatuated teenager that Brady once knew. She was a sad woman haunted by the past and filled with genuine remorse.'

Janie was one of only two prisoners to witness the most savage attack ever made on Myra during her prison years. It happened on a Sunday afternoon, and the prisoner who carried out the attack, Josie O'Dwyer, who was only nineteen at the time, has since claimed that she was 'set up' for it by prison officers.

The *News of the World* published a feature about the Moors Murders on the tenth anniversary of the trial, recapping on the full horror of the crimes. Myra, knowing that it was going to appear, petitioned to the Deputy Governor for the newspaper to be kept off the wing that day. Her request was granted.

'It made our lives easier if papers with stories about her didn't get to the other prisoners,' said an officer. 'We were always having to keep an eye on her, especially at times like Christmas or a heatwave, when everyone feels more emotional and tempers get frayed.'

But a copy of the *News of the World* was seen by Josie O'Dwyer, a tough girl who had been in and out of custody since the age of fourteen. She claims it was shown to her by two prison officers who were winding her up, looking for trouble.

Trouble is what they got. After she'd read the article she was, in her own words, 'shaking and trembling with horror' and the officers took her for a walk to calm her down. When she returned she went to the lavatory. The other prisoners had all been locked in – except for Myra and her friend Janie. Just as Josie was washing her hands Myra came up the staircase and across the bridge until she was at the same recess as Josie.

'I just couldn't handle the horror of what I'd just read so I went for her,' said Josie.

She was wearing jeans and Doc Martens boots. It took only a few seconds to knock Myra to the ground, and then she kicked her senseless. When Janie heard the commotion she ran to the scene.

'There was blood everywhere and I rushed to try to stop the girl. Yet there was not a sound from Myra.'

Another prisoner, who was locked in but could witness the whole attack because it happened just opposite her cell and she could see it from the spyhole, said, 'The alarm bells were sounding but no officers came. Josie was kicking Myra full in the face. There was blood everywhere. Then she picked her up and seemed to be trying to throw her over the rail. Myra did not scream or cry out, but she clung limply to the rail.'

Josie described the attack as 'like hitting a dead animal. She didn't struggle, she didn't cry out, not until I tried to hoist her over the rail. Then she just clung on. She was afraid of dying, but not afraid of being beaten up'.

Josie O'Dwyer enjoyed being the hero of the prison for a few weeks. She was put into solitary confinement and lost 110 days remission, but the prison officers gave her tobacco, sugar, a radio and other 'perks'. It was only when she recollected the emotion in tranquillity that she realised that she was the loser: she would serve extra time but Myra's sentence was unaffected.

Myra's face was certainly affected, though – and for her this was the silver lining to the cloud. Her nose was broken, and she had to be·taken out of Holloway to have it reset in hospital. Again, the fact that no one recognised her encouraged her. She was sure her re-modelled nose would also help to conceal her identity, and she was very disappointed when the bandages were removed and revealed that she looked very much as she had done before. Her lip and ear had also been split in the attack, both her eyes were blackened, her front teeth were loosened and she could only eat liquid food through a straw for six weeks. The attack had also damaged the cartilage in one of her knees, and this, too, had to be operated on.

She has told friends that immediately after the attack she asked for clemency for her attacker, on the grounds that it was her religious principle to turn the other cheek. Perhaps she did turn on her unctuously religious persona for the authorities: to others she was swearing vengeance. As recently as 1983, seven years after the attack, she was asking Carole Callaghan and a friend of hers to 'find that cow and break her arms and legs'. Eventually, after several other prison terms, Josie O'Dwyer straightened out her life. For a time she worked full time for the charity Women in Prison, helping to find jobs for women finishing their sentences.

A few months after the attack, something much nicer happened to Myra. She won a prison song competition with three songs she had written and sung herself, accompanying herself on the guitar. Janie Jones, a pro-fessional singer, landed a runners-up prize. The songs were played as background music at the annual pris-oners' art competition, and had Myra been less of a celebrated case she would have been taken out of

Holloway to hear them. As it was, she had to be content with the £10 first prize; Janie picked up £4.

The judge, who picked Myra's three songs, 'Prison Trilogy', 'Don't Make Promises', and 'Love Song to a Stranger', out of 100 entries, did not know the identity of the competitors. He said that Myra's songs were 'gentle with a strange beauty'.

Myra and Janie continued to be close until Myra left Holloway, after which Janie embarked on a passionate affair with a prison officer. The officer was sacked on the spot as soon as the affair was discovered: the authorities were not risking a repetition of the Pat Cairns scandal. But she and Janie remained faithful to each other, and she was waiting at the gate of Holloway when Janie was released. They set up home together in Janie's comfortable house in a fashionable area of North London.

Janie remained a friend to Myra, speaking up in her defence on a television chat show shortly after her release. But today she wants no connection with her, and plans that she had to write a book about Myra have been shelved.

12

Durham

It was five o'clock in the morning of Saturday, 25 January 1977 when a helicopter appeared in the sky over Holloway Prison. Shortly afterwards Myra Hindley was woken up, her belongings were packed for her, and she was escorted through the prison to the frosty yard where a yellow unofficial-looking van was waiting. She was on her way to Durham Jail.

She had been given no warning that she was being moved, although prisoners are usually told a couple of days before a move. But because of the security operation involved, only the Governor and a few senior officers knew what was happening. Myra was distraught. She dreaded Durham. Word travels fast round the prison circuit, and she knew that the regime in Durham was tough.

Designed to hold between thirty and forty women, at the time Myra arrived there were thirty-eight women on H Wing, the women's maximum security wing. It was a part of the prison that had temporarily closed down in 1972, when conditions were said to be too inhumane for top security male inmates. It had been reopened for Category A women prisoners, especially those convicted of IRA bombings, but many of the women held there had not committed crimes that merited maximum security: they were only there to make up numbers. All of them were serving sentences of two years or more.

Durham came as a great shock to Myra. Every

movement she made was watched. Television cameras
monitored every corridor. Prisoners were expected to
keep quiet, and could be told off just for laughing. The
wing was very cramped with little scope to move about.
Only three women were allowed to talk together at one
time, and never behind closed doors. The electronically
locked cells could not be opened by anyone except the
Governor or his Deputy, so if a woman was ill in the night
it had to be very serious before the officers were prepared
to wake the Governor and have her unlocked. Every half
an hour an officer would look through the spyhole into
each cell.

H Wing, which is in the heart of the men's prison, is
built on four floors, with iron staircases connecting the
landings. On the ground floor – known as 'the flat' – there
is a glass observation box from where male officers watch
everything that goes on. On that floor the women prisoners eat their meals, just outside the 'strip' cell where
prisoners are punished by being deprived of clothing (except for a linen dress) and furniture (except for a
mattress). Women in the strip cell are usually noisy –
screaming and crying – and often do what in prison is
called 'a dirty act' – they smear the wall with their own
faeces. The stench at mealtimes is appalling.

On each of the landings there is a sluice room for
slopping out the buckets the women have in their cells to
relieve themselves overnight. The sluices are open, and
contribute even more to the stench at breakfast time,
when the prisoners have twenty minutes to empty their
buckets before eating. The lavatories on each floor have
half doors, so there is little privacy.

Strip searches were carried out almost as a routine: all
the women would be ordered back to their cells, made to
remove all their clothing, and the cell systematically
searched.

Myra was allowed to continue with her Open University
degree studies but the number of books she was allowed in

her cell was cut to those essential for her work. The library of books she had amassed over her years in Holloway – she used to give visitors lists of the books that she wanted – had to be dispersed to her friends. There were several other women at Durham doing OU degress, but the only other education classes provided were remedial. One lifer, with a degree from Oxford, was able to help Myra and the others with their university assignments.

There were many rules that seemed petty after Holloway. Only three women were allowed to have visits on the same day, so they had to be booked in advance, which took more organising than she was used to. This, coupled with the inaccessibility of Durham compared with London, cut down on the number of visits she received. John Trevelyan, elderly by now, never made the journey to the north east. Visitors who did go felt they, too, were treated worse at Durham than anywhere else: they were photographed and searched before they were allowed in. The number of letters prisoners could receive was also limited.

Myra described the rules at Durham later as 'cretinous and strangulating'. She said, 'I hated that place. The corrosion of the bitterness and all the other negative feelings seeped into my whole system and nearly destroyed me.' On another occasion she referred to it as 'a living tomb'.

She also hated the weather in the north east, complaining about the bitter gales she had to endure during exercise. Prisoners were allowed an hour's exercise in a concrete yard, with male officers with guard dogs patrolling beyond the fence and security cameras trained on the prisoners. There was no grass or trees in sight. The yard was overlooked by the male prison, so the women were subjected to a battery of obscenities, usually accusing them all of being 'child killers' or deriding them for being lesbians. There were two benches in the yard, and usually a scramble to sit on them. It was only after

Myra had been in Durham for a couple of years that the rules were changed, permitting prisoners to stay inside if the weather was very bad.

There was little opportunity for sunbathing here, and if any woman unbuttoned the top of her blouse or hitched her skirt up she was soon in trouble with the officers. Myra's skin soon assumed the grey look that lack of fresh air brings, and that all the Durham women prisoners had. The hour's exercise each day was crucial, because it was the only daylight the prisoners saw. The windows in their cells were small and high up, with mesh across them. The whole wing was lit by fluorescent lighting, which did not help Myra's failing eyesight. She had needed glasses since her Holloway days: Durham increased the problem.

But the worst aspect of Durham was the food. It was cooked for the women's wing in the men's prison, and then left outside the door of the wing. Because the men hated the women (Myra in particular) the food was tampered with. One woman prisoner said, 'If it was anything fluid, like custard, it was always foaming when we got it. Someone had peed in it. And we knew that the men spat in it. So we didn't eat it. Even if it had not been messed with, it was horrible food. The meat was all gristle. Even if you weren't vegetarian when you went there, most women pretty soon said they were: that way you got more boiled eggs. We didn't reckon they could tamper with boiled eggs.'

The food was left in the open air, going cold, covered only with a cloth. After a prisoner claimed she had seen a rat feeding on it the prisoners went on hunger strike, and after an investigation by the Home Office sealed containers were provided for it – but the quality of the food did not improve.

Most women, including Myra, put on weight at Durham, but not because they were enjoying the food. One reason was the medication: Myra and most of the others swallowed tranquillisers, sleeping draughts and anti-depressants whenever they were available, which was three times a day.

'You could tell the ones who were on it: they looked like zombies. Myra looked like a zombie almost all her time in Durham,' said another prisoner.

But another reason she and so many others put on weight was because they did not eat the prison food, but subsisted on biscuits, crispbreads and jam bought from their canteen money (their wages). Myra successfully petitioned the Home Office for permission to buy tea and coffee out of the £12 a month prisoners were allowed to have from friends and family to spend – previously it had had to be paid for out of their weekly canteen money.

After many applications to the prison Governor, the women were allowed to have a toaster (provided by the Roman Catholic priest attached to the prison) and their bread ration was sent over from the men's prison untoasted.

The misery the prisoners endured over food was exacerbated by the fact the officers on H Wing had their own small kitchen, where they cooked their own food: the smell of steaks cooking did nothing to improve morale.

There was no exquisite tapestry work for Myra to do either. She was in the 'grotty' workroom every day with the other women, making coarse denim dungarees on industrial sewing machines. She hated it. Only one prisoner was allowed to leave the room to go to the toilet at any one time, because of the risk of lesbian encounters. The blue of the fabric rubbed off on to her clothes, so that it became practical to wear dark colours all the time. And in the evenings there was nothing to get dressed up for; for the first time since she had been in prison she became careless about her appearance. She dressed in kaftans in the evening and jeans all day, and only bothered to change for church or a visit.

She was allowed three changes of clothing plus a kaftan or dressing gown, but unlike Holloway (and later

Cookham Wood) she wasn't allowed to exchange one outfit for another whenever she wanted to. Every six months the prisoners were permitted to change their three winter outfits for three summer ones, but that was all. With her books limited, knitting became her main relaxation, but even the amount of wool she was allowed was rationed.

There were only two types of work at Durham, scrubbing or the workroom, and of the two the workroom was preferred because it paid better: Myra could earn £3.50 a week. But she had taken to smoking again, so the money did not go far.

Another reason she had been dreading going to Durham was the company she knew she would be keeping. Bernadette, the woman she had fought with over her lover Norma in the maximum security wing of Holloway, was there, and Myra was not looking forward to having to cope with her. As it turned out, Bernadette was still hysterical, but her vitriol was not aimed at Myra, and the two managed to co-exist relatively peacefully, although Myra complained that Bernadette was a 'constant moaner'.

The severity of the regime crippled Myra's sex life. It was much more difficult to find a time and place for her illegal lesbian activities. But it was not impossible, and it was in Durham that Myra fell deeply in love again, almost as deeply as she had been with Pat Cairns.

The object of her affection this time was a prisoner called Dorothy, a pretty Scottish woman, married with children. It was a grand passion for Myra: when Dorothy left Durham Myra had a deep depression that lasted for six weeks. More than two years after they separated she was still desperately trying to track down Dorothy, who had been moved to Styal Prison and then released. Myra called her 'my butterfly lady' and had friends trailing to different addresses around North London trying to locate her.

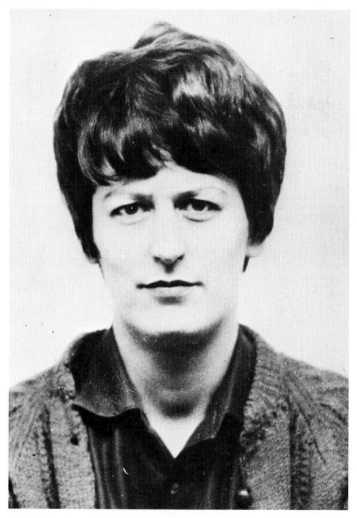

The Hindley image continued to change: now at Cookham Wood prisoner 964055 is a short-haired brunette

Above: At Maureen Scott's funeral Patrick Kilbride, father of victim John, falls to the ground after trying to attack a blonde-haired woman he thought was Myra

Left: Ann West, mother of Lesley Ann Downey, reads the letter from Myra Hindley which claimed her daughter had not been physically tortured

Above: Pauline Reade, finally laid to rest in August 1987 – her mother Joan sprinkles earth on the coffin, supported by her husband Amos and son Paul (Photo: Press Association)

Right: A recent photograph of David Smith, whose terrified phone call to the police triggered one of the most notorious trials of the twentieth century

Mrs Hettie Moulton, whose daughter's crimes have forced into the life of a recluse

Mrs Winnie Johnson, mother of Keith Bennett, watches as police search Saddleworth Moor for the body of her son

The Rev. Peter Timms, the Methodist minister and former prison governor to whom Myra finally confessed

Above: In July 1987, after the discovery of Pauline Reade's body, Brady (in dark glasses) was allowed out on the moors as police searched for Keith Bennett (Peter Topping is on his left)

Right: Boiler-suited Detective Chief Superintendent Peter Topping holds an impromptu press conference on the moors

16 Wardle Brook Avenue, scene of the killing of Edward Evans, shortly before it was demolished (Photo: Press Association)

'Tell her, Lady Butterfly, I have no net, I would never use one, but I do have a posy of jasmine and honeysuckle for a butterfly to alight on if the fragrance is to its taste,' she pleaded.

But 'La Papillon', as she referred to Dorothy, was an elusive butterfly. Myra's friends never found her to deliver Myra's messages or the birthday present of a tapestry work purse.

It was Myra's affair with Dorothy that caused the introduction of the rule about prisoners never closing their cell doors when another prisoner was in there. They were caught together, and it was shortly afterwards that Dorothy – or Dill as Myra also called her – was moved to Styal.

But her overweening love for Dorothy did not stop Myra dallying with other women. She had an affair with another married woman, who was only in Durham for a few months, and who left and later remarried, had a baby, and asked Myra to be godmother to the child. Myra also had a relationship with a Nigerian girl called Kate, another lifer. She and her girlfriends would be seen together holding hands and kissing, and they shared showers.

'Many of the screws were bent, so they didn't say much about what was going on,' said a prisoner.

She had other friends, though, who were not lovers. They were known to other prisoners as 'Myra's minions', women who basked in the reflected notoriety of being close to her. They cleaned her cell, filled her flask for her.

She also made another loyal and longstanding friend, a woman called Jenny Hicks, who had been sentenced to five years for her part in a quarter of a million pound fraud. Jenny shared a year in Durham with Myra, and has visited her regularly ever since. Like Chris Tchaikovsky ('Chike') she became active in the Women in Prison charity, and also helped to set up Clean Break, a theatre company for female ex-prisoners.

The Roman Catholic chaplain at Durham, Father Algy Shearwater, was a seminal influence on Myra's spiritual life. He is a Jesuit who had worked at Risley before coming to Durham, so he was experienced at handling the problems of prisoners. Some of the women at Durham complained that the help he offered was too ethereal. But he was a practical man, too: he not only supplied the toaster but also a music centre for the wing, and the year he cooked two 15 lb turkeys for Christmas lunch was the first time any of the women had tasted real turkey since they arrived at Durham (they were normally given tinned turkey for their Christmas lunch).

But it was not his cooking that endeared Father Algy to Myra. She did not complain that his approach to religion was too unworldly. She liked their long, spiritual discussions, and she was very interested when he told her about a system of praying and reflecting about the Bible that is outlined in a little black book published by the Jesuits. He explained that the system, called The Spiritual Exercises, had helped other prisoners cope with the tensions of long-term confinement. He acquired a copy of the exercises for her, and under his direction, Myra started them.

Soon after she arrived in Durham, Myra Hindley started work on a remarkable document: a 21,000 word plea for parole. She had been in prison for more than eleven years, and she and Brady were two of only three prisoners serving more than ten years who had never been considered for parole. The average time served by a lifer is ten years.

It took her eighteen months to write the document – thirty-six closely written pages of her cramped handwriting – which was then sent in 1979 to the Home Secretary in the Labour government, Merlyn Rees. It told the story of a wronged, innocent young girl being savagely punished for crimes that had little to do with her. It was the same story she had told endlessly to psychiatrists, to Lord Longford, to Rachel Pinney, the one which she had spent hours rehearsing with all the other prisoners. She had convinced them, she had almost convinced herself, she was sure she could now convince the highest powers in the land – even though the chairman of the Parole Board, Sir Louis Petch, had said that·public opinion was a key factor in deciding whether to release a prisoner, and that in her case that made a recommendation for release unlikely.

Myra wrote, 'To me they [the Moors] have represented nothing more and nothing less than a beautiful and peaceful solitude which I cherish. Of the bodies and graves I know nothing.'

Her version of the murders was a rerun of the defence case at the trial, except that now she was acknowledging Brady's guilt: she knew nothing about John Kilbride's disappearance and death; she was present when Lesley Ann Downey was being photographed but the child left the house alive, it was only a handkerchief that she was telling the child to keep in her mouth; and when Edward Evans was killed she was in the kitchen where she claimed she had hidden because Brady and Evans were fighting. She made no reference to any other killings, and she renewed her assertions that Brady's partner in crime was David Smith, not her.

Much of the document concerned her love for Brady, which she wrote about in her typically overblown, emotional style.

'Although it may sound trite and dramatic, I fell hopelessly in love with Ian Brady practically from setting eyes upon him. . . . I feel it is crucially important that the whole essence of such feelings and emotions is understood and appreciated fully for what it was, for it is this that is at the heart of the whole tragic case in which everything that transpired had its roots, and that these roots began their growth in virginal, vulnerable soil nourished, as it were, by unassuaged grief and despair and the hopeless yearning of a young and inexperienced heart which was almost overwhelmed by the strength and fierceness of hitherto unknown emotions.

'Within months he had convinced me that there was no God at all (he could have told me that the earth was flat, the moon made of green cheese, that the sun rose in the west and I would have believed him). He became my god, my idol, my object of worship and I worshipped him blindly, more blindly than the congenitally blind.'

She wrote on and on, streams of words justifying the minimal involvement in the crimes to which she admitted. She stressed the horrors of her punishment, not admitting to any of the compensations she had found to sustain her in jail.

'If I take one average or typical day in prison, then I take the whole of my life for the past 13 years; thousands upon thousands of days, each one exactly like the other; boring variations upon a stagnant theme.'

And there was arrogance, too, about her right to lead a different life. 'Society owes me a living,' she wrote.

She explained that if she was released she had a new name and a new life to assume, and would 'not be any kind of burden on society as such'.

Perhaps the most staggering statement, in view of the tissue of lies the document was based on, came at the end of a passage when she was again discussing Brady: 'I had placed Ian Brady on a pedestal where he had always been, aloof and out of reach, and I had loved him blindly. . . . Flaubert said we should never touch our idols, for the gilt always rubbed off on our fingers. One day I gained the courage to reach up and touch, and the gilt did rub off. He crashed from his pedestal, and the dust and ashes of a dead love flaked around my feet.

'But it was unbearably painful, *it always is when one is prepared to face reality squarely*' [my italics].

She ended her statement with a plea: 'The light in the

tunnel has never been very bright, but with no hope of release I can only see it diminishing until nothing remains but a bottomless pit of black despair. Are you prepared to consign me to this fate? Hope springs eternal, but I'm afraid the spring is drying up.'

Merlyn Rees was prepared to consign her to at least another three years of imprisonment. On the recommendation of a joint Home Office–Parole Board committee he announced that her case for parole should not be considered for three years.

A copy of Myra's statement was leaked to a newspaper. Myra was furious. But she was even more furious when, four years later, she discovered that the *Sun* was planning to print extracts from it as part of a feature series about her. She complained to the prison welfare service (by this time she had been transferred to Cookham Wood Prison) who alerted her solicitor, and she was able to obtain a High Court injunction stopping the *Sun* from using the extracts. She was allowed legal aid to apply for the injunction.

She said in a statement to the court that publication would seriously damage her chances of winning parole. ('Continued publication is likely to cause me serious loss for which damages are not an adequate remedy.') Her barrister said that the *Sun*'s series about Myra breached the copyright laws, since she holds the copyright on anything she has written, and broke confidences because her parole plea was never intended for publication.

Despite claims by the *Sun*'s defence barrister that the document could not damage her parole chances, as it was her own words setting out her own case, the injunction was granted, and the newspaper was not allowed to print extracts from the parole plea that week. But an injunction is only a temporary action, taken rapidly to halt matters until they can be properly aired in court. Myra's lawyers then had to go ahead and sue the *Sun*.

She was confident she would win. 'It's good, n'est-ce

pas?' she wrote to a friend, 'I'm quite chuffed to be able to sue Rupert Murdoch – I think he's lowered the tone of the *Times* and the *Sunday Times* as well as profiting from a scabby bunch of scandal rags like the *News of the World* and *Sun*.'

But she never did sue them. The case was dropped because, as her own lawyer said, 'When she confessed to her involvement in the murders of Pauline Reade and Keith Bennett it was clear that the whole parole statement was basically untrue. In view of that, we decided we would probably lose the action against the *Sun*, and in public too. That wouldn't do her any good, so she agreed with me that we should quietly let it drop.'

But all that came later. In the meantime there were other matters to do with 'those damned newspapers' to preoccupy her. The *Daily Star* had tracked down and bought, from a German picture agency, the photographs taken in her cell at Holloway by Maxine Croft, six years earlier.

Myra was devastated when they were published. All her hopes of never being recognised when she finally obtained her release were dashed: the pictures were so unlike the formidable mugshot which, with artists' impressions and Brady's moorland snapshots, were the only pictures of her published until then. One of her secret delights was to stand near new prisoners and hear them ask, 'Which one's Myra Hindley?' knowing that they had no clue who she was.

She hated any reference to her appearing in print: it always stirred up trouble with the other prisoners. Ironically, Durham, the prison she hated most, caused her the least risk of physical attack: partly because of the close supervision, but also because the other prisoners were all serving long-term sentences. They, too, had committed serious crimes and many had suffered opprobrium, albeit on a lesser scale, because they had been involved in terrorism or drug dealing. They were interested in survival, not reprisal.

One prisoner she never met but disliked from afar was Mary Bell, who was jailed two years after Myra for killing two little boys when she was eleven years old. Another girl, aged thirteen, was acquitted of the killings because the court was told she was educationally subnormal and dominated by Mary. The trial caused almost as big a sensation as the Moors Murders case, and Mary's adolescence in prison attracted almost as much media attention as Myra's prison career. Myra, despite constant protestations that she abhorred publicity, resented this instance of the spotlight being on someone else.

But she took some comfort from Mary's progress through the prison system. Despite absconding from Moor Court Prison for three days in 1977, Mary had eventually been sent in 1979 to Askham Grange, an open prison for women. Here she was found a job outside the prison, and was prepared for release.

Despite all the publicity, she was released in May 1980 when she was nearly twenty-three years old. When she gave birth to a baby in 1984 she was guaranteed anonymity and the chance to build a new life when a High Court order made her daughter a ward of court.

Myra believed that she would follow the same path as Mary, and so did many staff in the prison service. An officer at Moor Court, the prison in the Midlands which closed down when Cookham Wood was opened, said, 'We were told that when Mary had successfully been released Myra would come here for a year, then a year at Askham Grange, and then out.'

But the anti-Myra publicity continued, and in 1979 when the Tories took power she became dispirited. She began describing herself as a political prisoner, one whose release was too controversial for any government – especially a Conservative one – to risk.

She finished her Open University degree course at the

end of 1979 (the academic year of the OU runs from January to December). The university operates on an adaptation of the American system of building up a degree by credits, students gaining one credit for every successful year-long course. Six credits are needed for an ordinary degree. Because students are not restricted to following one subject all the way through their university career, the degree awarded is always a BA. Myra, in fact, had studied arts subjects all the way through, with the exception of one year when she took a Social Sciences course. Among the courses she took was twentieth-century poetry, and Renaissance and Reformation culture. Her degree was presented to her at a special ceremony in the prison in January 1980, with her course tutors present.

She decided to carry on with her studies to convert her degree into an honours degree, for which she needed another two credits. She missed out 1980 'to have a break' but then took and successfully passed her next course in 1981. Her final course, Man's Religious Quest, started in 1982, but she dropped out during the year, partly because she broke a heel in the gym at Durham which caused her a lot of problems all that year. Her aim at that stage was to continue studying after the honours degree, by doing an external MA in English literature with either Durham or London universities.

But she did not believe her academic success would affect her chances of release. 'After all, what will it matter to the decision-makers that I've obtained a degree, when I wasn't sent to prison because I was illiterate? The public are only concerned with the myth they've been saturated in.'

Although she had been given time off prison work for her studies, she complained that the noise in the prison meant she had to study at night, the only time it was quiet enough. (All prisons are noisy, mainly because there are so many disturbed hysterical prisoners. But Durham has particularly bad acoustics, with noise reverberating around the well of the wing.)

It is also notoriously cold and damp, and just after taking her final degree examination, she had become ill with pleurisy, and had been moved to a warmer cell on the wing.

In 1981 she had some good news. The Home Office published Standing Order 5, which brought Britain in line with EEC countries by allowing ex-prisoners to write and visit prisoners still in jail. Myra received a flood of letters from the faithful Rachel Pinney, and visits too. Chris Tchaikovsky, Jenny Hicks and others followed.

Myra still pined for the fun of Carole Callaghan's companionship, and she asked Rachel Pinney to try to track Carole down. Rachel did this, and Carole, too, began to correspond with and visit Myra. Myra was astonished to find that her friend was married again and running a café in North London. Their friendship was immediately close again and Myra wrote long letters in her usual fulsome style, punctuating them with tiny drawings of smiling faces, and the odd phrase or word in French.

'It's just struck me how natural it feels to be writing to you after over twelve years have passed, and to be able to pick up the thread with no effort at all. But we knew it would be like that, didn't we, when we used to talk about being in touch just by being in touch,' Myra wrote.

Although Carole had talked to journalists about Myra on more than one occasion, she had confined her comments to how much Myra had changed, how religious she now was, and other propaganda that tied in with Myra's own perception of herself. Carole, after all, had been convinced of Myra's innocence in those long deep conversations they had shared on E Wing in Holloway. So she was forgiven.

The year 1981 was a momentous one for Myra for another reason. It was the year that Michael Fisher became her lawyer. Fisher, then aged thirty-four, was a keen, left-wing criminal lawyer, with good credentials and a penchant for difficult cases. He was introduced to Myra by Sarah Trevelyan, a prison psychologist daughter of John Trevelyan, who was visiting her regularly in Durham.

Myra had had two other solicitors since the unfortunate Charles Fitzpatrick who had walked unsuspectingly into the biggest case of his life at Hyde Police Station in 1965. There had been relatively little for her solicitors to do for the ensuing sixteen years, but Michael Fisher took a more active interest in the case than any of his predecessors.

He's engaging and, by his own admission, slightly naive. He met Myra in Durham and was impressed by her: he also needed no convincing that the conditions in which she (and the other prisoners) were being held were inhumane. It is unlikely that he fell hook, line and sinker for Myra's version of the crimes, but he perceived her role in events to have been very much secondary to Brady's, and he was sure that she had not had a fair chance either at the trial (through her own choice) or since, because of the constant media attention. He was, as so many other people have been, bowled over by the apparent normality and niceness of the woman portrayed as a monster.

He may have been following instinct, or it may have been a carefully calculated campaign. Whichever it was, Michael Fisher introduced a policy of *glasnost* into Myra Hindley's affairs. He felt if only the world could see more of the Myra that he and others close to her saw, then society would be prepared to accept her rehabilitation.

One of the first moves he made on her behalf, though, backfired – at least in the eyes of the Myra camp. When two journalists from the *Sunday Times*, Linda Melvern and Peter Gillman, approached him and various other friends of hers with a proposal to write a couple of long, serious articles about her, they decided to collaborate. For the first and only time, Myra asked her mother, her friends like Rachel Pinney, Honor Butlin and Carole Callaghan, to see the journalists. Myra even met Linda Melvern, who visited her in Durham.

'We thought because it was the *Sunday Times* it would be OK,' said Rachel Pinney. 'We were duped.' What she means is that they thought they would get a lengthy parade of Myra's story, yet another run-through of the parole statement. In fact, when the journalists submitted questions to Myra about the content of the statement, she wrote another 6,000 words answering them.

But the features, when they appeared in April 1982, were headlined 'The Woman Who Cannot Face The Truth'. They were a fair and realistic reappraisal of the case – highlighting flaws in the parole statement – and they made much of Myra's ability to manipulate her friends and allies.

The Myra camp, including Michael Fisher, was horrified. Instead of helping Myra's case, the *Sunday Times* articles positively hindered it. The assumption that an intelligent and reasoned reassessment of the case would find in Myra's favour had been implicit in all their dealings with the two journalists. In fact, because the articles were lengthy, well argued, and appeared in a 'serious' newspaper their anti-Myra tone was far more damaging than any 'Evil Myra' or 'Moors Monster' headline from the popular press.

To this day, Myra has never trusted another journalist or writer. 'Remember Linda,' she writes to her friends, when they broach the subject of talking to journalists.

The new rule allowing ex-prisoners to visit meant that in 1982 Myra could have another visitor: Jimmy Boyle. Boyle, then thirty-seven, had just been released from Glasgow's Barlinnie Jail, where he served fifteen years for a gangland killing, and where assaults inside the prison contributed to his reputation as Scotland's most feared villain. But Boyle, like Myra, had discovered education while in prison. He had also met and fallen in love with the prison psychologist, Sarah Trevelyan. He and Sarah were married in the prison in 1980.

So naturally, when her husband was released in 1982,

Sarah took him to meet Myra. Jimmy and Sarah Boyle are now both members of Myra's group of supporters, and they visit her whenever they can. When their daughter Susannah was born it was rumoured that Myra would be godmother by proxy, a rumour they denied. (Myra is godmother to at least three children, one born to a black woman who was in Holloway with her, another the child of one of her Durham lovers, and the third the child of a friend from Cookham Wood, a baby born in 1987.)

In February 1982, Myra petitioned to go back to Holloway. Getting out of Durham was now even more of an obsession for her than getting parole. She did not want to go back to the prison she had left five years before, but anything was preferable to Durham. She was told she could not go then, but might be moved back at the end of the year when another section of the new Holloway was opened up.

Home Secretary William Whitelaw had announced that she would not be considered for parole for another three years, and the prospect of spending that time in Durham appalled her.

In the summer of that year there was very worrying news for her: Brady was asking to see the police. There were rumours that he was going to start talking about the killings of Pauline Reade and Keith Bennett. Myra was stung into writing a letter to a journalist stressing that she knew nothing about these deaths. 'If I could help I would – and would have done so a long time ago,' she wrote. It transpired that it was a false alarm: Brady wanted to see the local police to make a complaint against the Senior Medical Officer in Parkhurst, part of a campaign he was waging to get himself transferred from prison to a secure hospital.

By November, despite the fact that the new section was not open, she petitioned again, saying she'd be happy to go back into the old Holloway and wait. This time there was no reply from the prison authorities, so in desperation, early in 1983, she started a hunger strike. She went without food for three weeks, and was severely depressed. Being ill in Durham is not easy: anyone who is ill loses all their canteen money. It is a system designed to prevent malingering, and it works. For Myra to have remained 'sick' for so long meant that she really was clinically depressed.

Then, at Easter, the good news came. Again she was given no warning that she was being moved. Again, there was a helicopter in the sky above the jail. Again the van that she was escorted to was unmarked and inconspicuously painted.

It left Durham in the afternoon of 30 March 1983 and headed south. But Myra was not going back to Holloway. She was going somewhere much better: she was on her way to Cookham Wood, Britain's show place jail for women prisoners.

13

Cookham Wood

Cookham Wood Prison opened in 1978, a modern red-brick building in the grounds of the original borstal, in Kent. It had been intended to build a remand home for boys, but the crisis of accommodation in women's prisons had forced a change in plans, and the building was converted to a prison, sharing a large open site with the boys' borstal. It was everything the new Holloway had been supposed to be but had fallen short of: well designed, roomy, every cell with its own flush lavatory.

Cookham Wood houses 120 prisoners, divided into two wings: North and South. Most of the prisoners are Category C, serving short sentences, but there are a few LTIs (long-term inmates) and three or four lifers at any one time. Many of the staff were recruited from Holloway, and are old friends of Myra's.

Myra could not believe her luck when she arrived at Cookham. She said it was 'as different to Durham in every respect as a Matabele Zulu warrior is to yer average Wall Street executive'. She wrote to a friend that, after seventeen and a half years in prison, she finally had her own toilet, washbasin, and a light switch inside her cell. 'Too much, just like real living! It's one helluva place – a good one.'

Another prisoner who also arrived at Cookham from Durham said, 'It was like going on holiday to Butlins. You hear prisoners complaining about Cookham but they're the ones who have never done time in any other prison:

what they're complaining about is prison. Anyone who has been in Risley, Durham, Styal or Holloway doesn't complain: they can't believe their luck when they get to Cookham.'

Myra was housed on South Wing, and the other three lifers who were there when she arrived were on North. Everyone else on Myra's wing was a short-term prisoner. Although they were all locked in their cells during the afternoon, Myra and the other lifers were not locked in at all, from eight o'clock in the morning until, officially, eight o'clock at night (for prisoners like Myra who took sleeping medication) or nine o'clock for all the others. But even this rule was relaxed for lifers.

On the evening of Myra's arrival at Cookham Wood the rest of the prisoners had been locked in since lunchtime. News of the new prisoner's identity had already leaked out, and the officers were expecting trouble. For two days after her arrival Myra did not leave her cell. The rest of the prisoners were warned by officers: attack her and you lose parole. But there were still plenty who were prepared to plot violence against her.

'We were all dying to see her,' said one woman who was serving nine months for shoplifting. 'Lots of girls were talking about what they were going to do to her. When we did see her it was a bit of an anticlimax: she didn't look a bit like everyone had expected.'

Myra was forty when she reached Cookham, but looked much younger – in contrast to the way she had looked forty when she was twenty. Her hair was rinsed an auburn colour, cut short. She wore very light make-up. Although she had put on weight at Durham she was still slim, and held herself straight. 'She could have passed for twenty-seven,' one prisoner said.

Although she was delighted to be at Cookham, experience told her that the first few months are the most dangerous. With an ever-changing prison population she runs a much greater risk of attack at all times than she did at Durham, but she was most vulnerable in the first few months when her presence was a novelty, and before she had had time to surround herself with friends and protectors.

The loud whispers behind her back started again, and the taunts. There was an attempt to pour boiling water over her, which was foiled by some of the other prisoners who did not want trouble. Many of the others took vows never to speak to her. Her food was tampered with again, and her bed linen was soaked with urine. On one occasion there was a scuffle in the prison chapel, when several prisoners pushed her on to the floor and kicked her. And on another occasion she was attacked in her cell by one other prisoner who scratched and punched her.

'I need my wits about me in here until the initial impact of my arrival wears off,' she wrote, 'But I'm so goddamned mind and bone weary, I can't see straight let alone think straight.'

But on the whole, life was much better than it had been for six years. The 'hostile reaction' she described in her first letter from the prison died down, just as she had predicted it would. 'People are getting used to the idea of me (tough for them if they don't),' she wrote.

The lack of rules overwhelmed her. Soon after she arrived she was summoned to an office for a meeting. When she didn't turn up a prison officer went to investigate and found her waiting patiently outside her cell. She was waiting for an escort of prison officers, and could not believe it when she was told that she could move around the prison freely and on her own. At Durham prisoners were always accompanied by two officers.

'I feel almost as free as a bird,' she wrote.

In her cell she was allowed curtains, a bedspread, her own bed linen, a rug, her own plate, cup and saucer, plants and flowers, pictures, a radio, a record player, paint brushes, a hair dryer, a battery shaver, curling tongs or hot brushes – and as many books as she wanted. Within weeks of arriving she was writing to all her friends, round-ing up the books she had been forced to scatter around them while in Durham, and asking for her records to be returned too. Her taste in music continued to be catholic: Wagner was a favourite, but she also liked Joan Baez and Elkie Brooks. She is widely read, and has a large col-lection of feminist books including everything written by Rita Mae Brown, the author of *Rubyfruit Jungle* who was once Martina Navratilova's lover.

When she arrived Myra was put on 'full time' education, which meant that she was allowed to study her Open University courses every afternoon, and only had to do prison work in the mornings. She was delighted that her first prison job was in the garden, which, unlike Holloway's garden, is not surrounded by a high wall. She could enjoy grass and trees and flowers for the first time for six years. She could see cars and traffic on the nearby road, passers-by walking their dogs, mothers pushing prams, children on bicycles. It was a contact with the real world that excited her and made up for any aggravation she might suffer from the other prisoners.

When one day she was able to stroke a prison officer's dog she rushed inside to tell her friends, she was so thrilled. The last dog she had handled had been Dorothy Wing's cairn terrier during her ill-fated walk on Hampstead Heath eleven years previously.

One of her friends made her some shorts to wear in the garden, by cutting down and fraying some jeans. The first time she wore them she ripped them on the lawn-mower brake handle, and had to go back to wearing dungarees until they were patched. But she took advantage of her open-air job to soak up as much sunshine as she could, and by her forty-first birthday, just four months after arriving at Cookham Wood, she was looking brown and healthy. She even applied to have her working hours switched, so that she could study in the morning and enjoy the garden in the afternoon, but that request was turned down.

It didn't take her long to find friends and protectors. When a plump middle-aged West Indian woman came into the prison on a shoplifting sentence, officers realised she was an old friend of Myra's from Holloway days.

'They asked me if I would help them take the heat off Myra. They said most of the trouble was coming from black girls, and that these girls would lose their parole if they did anything rash. They were girls with children themselves – that's why they felt so strongly about Myra. But I knew how stupid they would be if they lost parole over her, just like Josie had done in Holloway. The officers asked me to look after my own people. So after I'd been there a day or two and settled in, got my bearings, I went down to Myra's cell for a chat. Some of the other girls said, "You talk with her?" And I said, "Sure I do. What people did outside prison I worry about when I'm outside. Inside I worry about how they goes about getting on with everybody else, and Myra never makes trouble for anyone else." So after that, they all eased up on her a lot. And if the officers thought somebody was heading for trouble, they'd send her to me to straighten her out.'

Five months after she arrived at Cookham, her legal battle with the *Sun* began. She complained about how much of her time it took up – she was often up all night writing letters and keeping up with her OU course work. One of the allegations made in the *Sun* was that she was allowed to make phone calls to friends and family, with staff turning a blind eye. Although it had never happened regularly, it had happened. More usually, she could ask her welfare officer to make a call on her behalf. But the publicity caused a clampdown even on that, which angered her.

Other claims made about special privileges did not worry her: it was revealed that when she went for dental treatment to the surgery at the boys' borstal she was taken on her own by car, whereas other women went in groups, on foot. The Home Office replied that Myra's special arrangements were for security reasons. She herself, craving all the fresh air she could get, would have preferred to be allowed to walk.

The *Sun* also published an official photograph of her, taken in 1977, and showing her with short dark hair. It had been smuggled from the prison, and its publication triggered a police investigation into staff at the prison, which resulted in everyone who had access to Myra's file being fingerprinted. There was a backlash against Myra from the officers and other prisoners, who resented the fact that her very presence made life more difficult for them. Many officers were outraged at the implication of dishonesty, and some even took legal advice as to whether or not they had to be fingerprinted. Myra herself was angry at the publication of the picture, for the same reasons that she had been distraught when Pat Cairns' snaps of her were published: convinced that she would eventually be released, she was banking on not being recognisable. The move to Cookham Wood was, she felt, the first stage in a preparation for parole, which she feared the publicity would jeopardise.

But in other ways she was very happy. Her friend and lover from Durham, the black girl Kate, was transferred to Cookham Wood for a month to allow her to have visits from her family and friends. She became very friendly with a German woman, which allowed her to practise her German. And she was gradually establishing herself with the officers and the other prisoners. Although some officers (particularly the older ones) wanted nothing more to do with her than necessary, others, just as in Holloway, were prepared to spend time talking to her and listening to her.

Myra had already discovered that Cookham Wood was an easy place to carry on lesbian relationships: almost as easy as Holloway. And because so many of the prisoners were in for short sentences, Myra embarked on a series of equally short relationships. She became involved with a girl called Terry, and another called Lou, both junkies, and both of whom showered her with letters and presents when they were released. And there were others, often more than one at any time. Myra usually lost interest in them as soon as they left prison, describing them as 'just ships that pass in the night'.

But when she met a girl called Sandra she fell, once again, deeply in love. Sandra had been living with Myra's old Holloway girlfriend, Vicky, before she went into prison. She and Myra then had a passionate affair which lasted for many months after Sandra left Cookham Wood and moved back to share a cottage with Vicky, not far from the prison. Myra referred to her glowingly in her letters, and said that when she was released Sandra would be sharing a great deal of her life. She even arranged for Sandra to visit her mother, although she said she would not tell her family they were anything more than friends.

The freedom to visit each other's cells means that relationships can thrive in Cookham, but the staff are not involved, in the way that they were in Holloway in Myra's time there.

'In Holloway you know every one of the staff who is lesbian, they make no secret of it. And you get affairs between them and the prisoners from time to time. But that doesn't go on at Cookham, the officers keep their private lives much more to themselves. We heard about one parole officer, a married woman, who had an affair with a girl and we were all amazed: it just doesn't go on at Cookham. Some of the officers are known to be bent, but they keep quiet about it,' said one ex-prisoner, who has spent time in Holloway, Styal and Cookham Wood.

Her Open University work suffered without the help she had had at Durham from the Oxford graduate, and for the first time since she started her studies, she failed to get a good enough grade in her examination at the end of 1983 to give her the honours degree she'd been working for. She started another course in 1984, but dropped out halfway through, after a tidal wave of depression confined her to the prison hospital for eight weeks.

The trigger for the depression may have been Sandra leaving Cookham Wood on 6 July, although Myra herself said the root cause of it went back to 'the beginning of prison. Too much prison, too many hassles, too much publicity and too many brainwashed prisoners, too much noise, too many pressures.' She went into the sickbay on her forty-second birthday, 23 July, telling the doctor that she felt she was on the verge of a breakdown – a contrast with the previous year, when she had entertained friends and family on her birthday looking relaxed and tanned.

It was almost as though the new and less rigid regime of Cookham Wood was harder for her to take, mentally, than the austerity of Durham. It is not an uncommon phenomenon for prisoners to ask to be sent back to high security conditions when they have graduated to softer regimes, simply because they find it harder to endure captivity in conditions that are comfortable enough to mock their lack of freedom. Myra never considered asking to go back, but the strain of long-term imprisonment started to show more than it ever had before. She had taken tranquillisers (medicine, not pills) in Durham, and although she tried to cut down on them in Cookham, she did not succeed.

Her inability to sleep (she seldom slept for more than three or four hours) and the bags that formed under her eyes earned her the nickname The Robot in the hospital wing. Another prisoner who was in there at the same time as Myra said, 'I was sick and I had to keep getting up in the night. Every time I put my light on, Myra was awake, watching me. She never put her light out, she never seemed to sleep. She told me how she tried to get really tired in the day, so that she would sleep at night, but it just didn't seem to work.'

One thing did help her sleep, though, and it was something she could get easily in Cookham Wood: cannabis.

'It is easier to get a smoke in there than it is to get a day's parole,' said one ex-prisoner. 'Myra told me the only time she got a good night's sleep was if she had a smoke. Then she would sleep for six, maybe seven hours: for her that's a long time.'

She had first tried cannabis in Holloway, but it had not been very plentiful there. At one time it was being smuggled into Holloway stitched inside dead pigeons, which were thrown over the wall into the garden, and the drugs removed by prisoners on garden work. At Durham, contraband of any sort was practically non-existent, and there were certainly no drugs available. At Cookham it was far more easily come by, smuggled in by visitors.

Like everyone else, Myra would know who had the drugs. Sometimes her old friend Carole Callaghan would smuggle some in to her, but most of the time she would buy it on the prison black market, or she would earn it by doing favours for other prisoners. Occasionally there has been so much dope being smoked that the smell has drifted down the corridors.

'Once when the screws asked what the smell was we told them we'd been smoking tea bags,' said one prisoner, 'They know what's going on, but dope calms people down and makes them easy to deal with: the officers turn a blind eye, as long as it is kept discreet.'

She had learned to 'buy' friendship early in her prison life, and at Cookham Wood she was in a better position to make herself useful to others than ever before. The lifers had much more freedom within the prison than the other prisoners, so Myra could carry drugs and messages around for others. Her closeness with two or three of the officers – old friends from Holloway – meant that she often had early warnings of 'spins'. A 'spin' is prison slang for a search of cells by officers looking for illegal substances, weapons, anything else. Myra and the other lifers would often be excluded from these searches, so she'd hide drugs or drink that had been smuggled in for prisoners.

She could also get away with less serious breaches of the prison rules, like having too many clothes in her cupboard. Each prisoner is supposed to have only three outfits of clothing, with any extra clothes they possess held in the prison stores. But the lifers were allowed more leeway than the others, and Myra often has five or six outfits in her cell. When 'spins' were on she would look after extra clothes for other prisoners, and extra pillows (each cell is only supposed to have one).

'If officers are looking for drugs and they can't find them, they'll often nick a girl for having an extra jumper, then they'll fine her 50p: which, when you are only earning £3 a week, is depressing. I've heard girls screaming, "What about Myra? She's got this and that" but the screws just say, "Never mind about Myra." It causes a lot of resentment: that's why Myra has to make it up to everybody by looking after their things.'

After her spell working in the gardens she worked in the library and later on reception, handling the property of newly arrived prisoners and organising the weekly purchases for all the prisoners. She also worked preparing teas for senior officers. It was this job that put her in a position to do more favours. She could find out when prisoners were going to be transferred or paroled, and she could warn others that they were going. Prisoners, who have so little money and so few goods at their disposal, are very sensitive about debts: one source of great bitterness and fighting is that some prisoners are transferred or leave without settling their debts. Myra's information service prevented that.

On reception, too, she was able to help the new prisoners. Many of them come straight to Cookham Wood after two or three days of assessment at Holloway, during which they are unable to work and earn any wages. On arrival at Cookham they are given an advance of 80p and they are given one letter with stamp. But most of them want to buy another stamp, as they have at least two urgent letters to write. The prison takes 3p a week out of everyone's wages (1p for television repairs, 1p for television licence and 1p for upkeep of library books). So for her first week a prisoner is left with less than the price of half a packet of cigarettes, and has to make do with the issued soap and tooth powder (which they all hate).

This is where Myra steps in. Often before a prisoner knows who she is they will be in her debt: she hands over cigarettes, shampoo, toothpaste to help them through that first difficult week. Because she herself only smokes occasionally – she cut down her smoking again when she got to Cookham – she always has spare cigarettes. Because she has more than one job she is better paid than other prisoners, and has built up supplies of toiletries which she can afford to lend.

The only job she has not enjoyed since arriving at Cookham was working in the kitchens. She complained that the hours were long, and that she got greasy and dirty and needed to wash her hair more often.

Like the other lifers, Myra can have 'special orders'. This means that because she is in for a long time the prison is prepared to send out for the shampoo and cosmetics that she wants: in Myra's case she buys Vidal Sassoon shampoo. Other prisoners, even after they have enough wages to buy goods, are limited in their choice: they can buy Boots shampoos, Palmolive or Lux soap and, if they get a doctor's note saying they need it for a skin condition, Cuticura or Simple soap. The only make-up available to them is a cheap brand, and they are only allowed to buy clear nail varnish, diluted to stop it being used by sniffers to get high. Myra has coloured nail polish, and she paints the nails of other prisoners as a favour when they are having visits from husbands, boyfriends or girlfriends.

She can also have special orders of knitting wool, unlike the others who have to order once a month from a catalogue. Myra's letters to friends are peppered with requests for specific types and colours of wool (she even names shops where it can be bought). Knitting has become her main pastime since she abandoned her Open University studies, and she knits for the babies and small children of other prisoners. One prisoner whose very pregnant daughter visited her in Cookham Wood was surprised when she got home to receive a parcel of baby clothes from Myra, for her grandchild.

Another way in which she can help other prisoners is in the preparation of parole pleas. Each prisoner has to write her own application for parole. Myra's education and her barrack-room lawyer knowledge of the system means that she acts as consultant to women who are having trouble framing the application.

'She helped me write mine, and it was so good I got my parole OK,' said the black woman who acted as her protector. 'When I was leaving she asked me if I was going to sell a story about her to the newspapers, like so many other prisoners did. She said she didn't mind, as long as it was something she would tell me to say. Then she said I could split the money with her, and send her some nice clothes in. She even knew which newspapers paid the most money for stories about her. But I wouldn't do it. She said she knew I could do with some money, and it was one way she could repay me for keeping other girls off her back.'

Her interest in clothes and her looks – which she had neglected in Durham – returned. She was thrilled to receive two tracksuits from Carole Callaghan, a grey one and a red one. 'I feel a proper mod con,' she wrote, explaining how she was determined to lose 'some bulges' before wearing the red one. She also started wearing short skirts again, after Honor Butlin sent one in to her, and she received compliments about her legs: she had dressed in nothing but trousers and kaftans for many years.

Again, Myra was 'buying' friendship, sharing her skills and privileges not out of Christian charity, but as a means of having enough supporters to ensure her protection.

When her time working in the garden ended, she kept

up her suntan by using the sunbed in the doctor's surgery. The bed is provided for women with skin complaints, but rarely gets used. Myra is able to use it when the other prisoners are locked in, and she has an all-year-round healthy tan.

'The first time I saw her walking on her own along a corridor I thought she was a prison visitor, or maybe one of the tutors from the education room. She doesn't look like a prisoner. She looks refined and elegant, like a schoolteacher with a bit of money. She wears good quality blouses and smart skirts, and she has crocheted shawls which she puts around her shoulders when its chilly.

'She talks quietly without a trace of a Manchester accent. And she uses long words, so you know she's a cut above everybody else,' said one ex-prisoner.

Prisoners at Cookham Wood are allowed to take newspapers, and Myra gets the *Guardian*. She borrows other newspapers to read, and she watches news on television at lunchtime and again in the early evening, both times when other prisoners (apart from lifers) are locked in their cells. Unlike her time at Holloway, when she deliberately cut herself off from news of the outside world, she now relishes it.

But she rarely watches television at any other time, unless it is to see Wimbledon. She loves tennis, and every year tries to make sure that she watches her idol, Martina Navratilova. She watches with the other lifers, and she's been lucky in Cookham Wood because she has been able to get on reasonably well with the two or three others who have been in there with her.

Lifers are known to other prisoners as 'a funny lot', jealous and distrustful of each other, often squabbling among themselves. Prison for them is home, whereas for the others it is a temporary staging post. One of the lifers in Cookham when Myra arrived was a woman called Lizzie, whom she knew from Durham and with whom she became very close. They smoked cannabis together in

Myra's cell. Another, an older woman called Rose, she had known from Holloway and Durham, and although they did not particularly like each other Rose was as intent on avoiding trouble as Myra.

Their comparative freedom throws them on to each other's company. At Christmas and New Year, when the others are locked in early because of the shortage of staff on duty, the lifers have parties with the officers, and Myra drinks her favourite Tia Maria. On their birthdays, too, lifers are usually allowed out of their cells late for a quiet celebration.

'We reckon they are out lots of evenings. Myra always seemed to have seen films that were on television too late for the rest of us to see,' said one ex-prisoner. 'If you asked her how she knew about them she would never tell you, just smile secretly to herself. She goes to great lengths to avoid trouble: she'll never pass on any gossip, even though she knows it, and she never grasses anybody up to the screws. When Lord Longford came in once a girl yelled abuse at him and then lifted her skirt and flashed at him. Myra discussed with me whether she should grass her up, but said she didn't see what good it would do.'

The comparative freedom that lifers have, and the small number of them in Cookham at any one time, resulted in a crop of news stories describing Myra as 'Queen of the Nick', which contrasted with others describing how she walked around the jail in fear, never knowing when the next attack would come.

The truth lies somewhere between the two. She is certainly not the queen of the prison, and what privileges she enjoys are also shared by the other lifers. As, for a long time, she was the only lifer on her wing, it is perhaps easy to understand why other short-term prisoners on that wing thought she was being accorded special treatment. Because of her name, she has a higher profile than the other lifers anyway: she'd prefer it if that were not so. But the high profile does result in her getting more attention from some of the officers.

There have been claims that she has been allowed out of Cookham Wood to go shopping in nearby Chatham and Rochester. The claims, made by a local publican who has been inside Cookham Wood to entertain prisoners (he's a fire-eater and sword-walker in his spare time) are untrue: all the details the publican gave, including the description of 'Myra' with long hair, are inaccurate. He has seen a prisoner out shopping: just as Dorothy Wing in Holloway allowed certain prisoners to go on expeditions outside, so the authorities at Cookham Wood have allowed at least one prisoner out under escort. But that prisoner is not Myra Hindley.

She has been out once though – to have a barium meal test at a local hospital. She was not found to be suffering from any serious complaint.

And she has had some contact with the outside world. She recalled with glee the occasion when a group of firemen visited the prison, 'Guess what? I had to make tea today for twenty-two firemen!' she wrote, 'Good grief, I've only seen a handful of men in donkey's years. I got someone to help me carry the urn in and told 'em to help themselves 'cos I wasn't playing mother. Just then the aggro bell went and the officer rushed out saying "Hold the fort, Harry" (I've been christened Harry because it goes with Hindley). She told me later that one of the firemen said, "You've got Myra Hindley in here, haven't you?" She said yes and the guy asked if they'd seen me this afternoon. She didn't say where, but she said they had. Ha! Chief said it would help to break me in, seeing all those men. Well, I don't wanna be that broken in! Twenty-two is a whole heap!'

As for her walking the jail in terror, she is constantly aware of the threat to her safety, because of the ever-changing prison population. She treats new arrivals with great caution, following the precept she explained to

Rachel Pinney many years before of never talking to anyone first, always waiting until they approach her. And perhaps her greatest protection is her coterie of friends, some of whom fit the description given to them in Durham, 'Myra's minions', women who just enjoy the notoriety of being associated with her. Others are women who, ignoring the crimes she is in prison for, find her more refined company than most of the other prisoners.

She follows politics closely, supporting the Labour party because she has told her friends that she knows she has no hope of parole while the Tories are in power.

But despite her *Guardian*-reading left-wing views, she hated it when protesters from Greenham Common were sent on sentence to Cookham Wood. Their arrival caused temporary congestion in the prison, with some inmates having to share cells. Myra was not, of course, affected by that. But she described the Greenham women as 'dirty' and wanted nothing to do with them.

Other prisoners deduced that she felt threatened by them, because many of the Greenham women were better educated and more articulate than her.

Like all prisoners, she makes the most of diversions like horoscopes, and other fortune-telling devices like the I Ching. Her birthday, 23 July, is on the cusp of Cancer and Leo, but she always tells people she is a Leo. She does not like the meek, home-loving, gentle characteristics of Cancer subjects, but prefers to see herself as a dominant, proud, strong Leo, despite the fact that this is at odds with the 'official' image she was still fostering as the wronged victim of terrible circumstances. And within the walls of her cell she demonstrates the Cancerian influences by covering every available surface with little crocheted mats, by making a cover for the prison chair, and covering her bed with patchwork cushions. When Sarah Trevelyan bought her pink curtains and a matching bedspread she wrote to Carole Callaghan complaining that she wanted a new rug, because hers was black and yellow, which didn't match. When one of her ex-lovers bought her a pink rug she complained that she wanted a burgundy-coloured one.

She became interested in 'auras', the belief that people give off a coloured aura which betrays the attributes of their personality. She decided that her own aura was green.

She was fascinated to receive in 1983 a letter from a clairvoyant and spiritualist, who claimed to be getting messages from 'the other side' from someone who had known Myra well and was very fond of her. But Myra was too canny to reply directly, sensing that she might be walking into a publicity trap, and commenting cynically on the spiritualist's prediction that the next few years held a lot of change for her, 'I doubt that she needs to be clairvoyant to assume that'. She asked her friend Carole Callaghan to find out more, but Carole didn't have time.

'I was going through the break-up of my marriage, and still managing to write and visit Myra, buying her clothes and batteries and anything else she needed,' said Carole. 'She had me running all over London looking for one of her lovers, and she saddled me with looking after a junkie friend of hers who came out of Cookham. I couldn't fit in any spiritualist!'

During the break-up of Carole's second marriage, Myra acted as counsellor and advisor, writing long emotional letters to her friend about her problems. Her religious beliefs run through them like a thread: she makes frequent references to Carole being 'purified in the crucible of suffering'.

'Ah, it's so painful, it's the Via Dolorosa – you've been there before, we trod the Via Dolorosa together, hand in hand, hearts in our mouths, fear clutching at us like the hands of the crowd trying to clutch the Son of Man as he laboured his way through them, carrying, dragging, the weighty cross of their sins – Father forgive them for they know not what they do,' she wrote.

The analogy of herself to Christ is a recurrent theme. In

one letter she wrote that she had told her priest 'the weight of her cross was too much to bear.' The priest said, "Jesus fell under his, three times." I told him with all respect to Jesus I think I've broken His record. The priest said, "He was crucified too, remember." I just stretched my arms back and told him I think I've been there too.'

But often the succour she offered her friend Carole was not religious: 'Sit quietly, relax, be peaceful, feel me moving slowly around you – I'm weaving a green and gold web of mystical, magical strands, I'm spinning a calming cocoon of quiet sanity, an oasis of tranqility [*sic*] in the desert of near-nervous breakdown madness in which we've both been stumbling for too long now. Rest your poor, almost mind-blown head against my breast, and feel gently towards me as my heart feels kindly towards you, and there shall be the soft, soft tremour [*sic*] as of unheard bells between us.'

At the height of Carole's problems, she was receiving a letter a week full of such outpourings. Throughout 1983 and for much of 1984, Carole was Myra's closest friend, receiving more letters and paying her more visits than anyone outside her family. But the closeness of the relationship could not survive: in February 1985 Carole Callaghan, desperate for money after the break-up of her marriage, sold her letters from Myra and the story of their prison years together to the *Daily Star*. At the time Carole was living with a woman who had been her lover in Holloway years before, and to whom she had remained close ever since, and who corroborated her story.

Myra was furious. She was anxiously awaiting news of whether she would be considered for parole, and was convinced the scandal – the articles gave details about her lesbian relationship with Pat Cairns – would jeopardise her chances, as well as upset her family. When Carole wrote to her she replied in acerbic terms, accusing her friend of having 'syphilis of the brain'.

'I can't forgive you at the moment, I hope I can in time

because I try always to forgive because I can't expect God to forgive me if I don't forgive others,' she wrote, adding that although she felt the articles had done irreparable damage 'I think deep in my heart I kissed Freedom Street goodbye some time ago'.

Her affection for Pat Cairns was still evident from the letter, as she referred to 'Tricia's' suffering, especially as she lived in Manchester. 'The Mancunians in particular are rooted in the myth right up to their heads; they're narrow-minded, conventional people who believe everything they read or see or hear – and they're vengeful.'

It was the last letter Myra wrote to her 'cariad', because although she signed it with love Carole knew that it was the end of their closeness, that she was no longer one of the jewels on the necklace of Myra Hindley's life.

Today, remarried, Carole Callaghan has grown to hate Myra.

'Even when I did those articles about her, I still stressed to the reporter that I believed she was innocent of the crimes she is in prison for. I honestly thought I was helping her in some way, I didn't intend to damage her. But when she confessed to two more murders, I realised that I had been conned for twenty years. I had been preaching about her to everyone I met, because I believed in her innocence. I had travelled hundreds of miles to visit her in Durham, I had spent money on her and her family.

'When the original trial took place I was living in South Africa, so I only ever heard her version of it. And I believed her. Now I know that I have given a lot of my life to defending lies. It hurts, especially when I think of the families of Pauline Reade and Keith Bennett.'

But Myra's distress at the *Star* articles soon abated when, two months later, she heard with delight that a Prison Review Committee had recommended her for parole. It was the first big breakthrough in nineteen years of imprisonment, and she was ecstatic. The committee, made up of the Cookham Wood Governor or his representative, a senior probation officer, a member of the Board of Prison Visitors and two local people, recommended her as suitable for release on licence. Their findings were sent to the Parole Board, who were due to consider her case as, under new rulings, parole reviews had become automatic and not a matter for the Home Secretary's discretion.

Myra, who had talked so recently about having kissed Freedom Street goodbye, now began to live on hope. With a firm recommendation from the local committee, she was sure that the Parole Board would have to rule in her favour. She told herself – and others – that her preparation for release would probably take years, but at least she was confident of being 'given a date' – the most prized possession of any prisoner.

The news that the committee had found in her favour prompted a rash of anti-Myra stories in all the popular newspapers, and relatives of the victims recited threats of what they would do to her if she was ever released. Danny Kilbride, brother of John Kilbride, was photographed holding a butcher's knife with a six-inch blade.

The publicity should have prepared her, but didn't. She was taken completely by surprise when, in May 1985, the Home Secretary Leon Brittan announced in the House of Commons the decision of the Parole Board that she should stay behind bars for at least another five years before her case for parole was heard again. Privately, Leon Brittan was reported as saying that he believed she must serve at least another fifteen years in prison.

She was shattered.

14

Family

'She thinks it's tough in prison – she should try living out here with this millstone round your neck all these years. It's been hell.'

'That is how one of Myra's relatives described having to cope with the permanent stigma of being part of the family of the Moors Murderer. The victims of Ian Brady and Myra Hindley were not just buried on the moors. They live all over the Manchester area: some of them grieving lost children, others grieving a simple, normal way of life that ended the day their names were catapulted into the headlines.

For Maureen Smith, Myra's precious Moby, a life sentence of suffering began before her sister was committed to prison. While the trial was still on in 1966 she was attacked in the lift at the block of flats where she and her husband David lived. She was eight months pregnant at the time. Her home was daubed with paint. Every post brought hate mail: 'Don't let the children play outside – we are going to take them away and bury them on the Moors' was the usual sort of thing.

'I'd open them and scream with horror. Can you imagine any other mother in England getting letters like that through her own front door?' Maureen said shortly before her death.

'I couldn't let my children out of my sight when they were little. They were too young to tell them why they had to stay in, to explain why they couldn't go out to play like all the other children.'

Within three years of the end of the trial, Maureen and David Smith had three sons: Paul, David and John.

In 1969 David Smith was sentenced to three years in jail for knifing a man in a brawl, a brawl he claims was triggered by the abuse and attacks he has suffered ever since the trial. His arrest signalled the end of his short and violent marriage to Maureen. They had known very little happiness together.

Maureen, frail and frightened and left alone with her young sons to take care of, was still only twenty-three. Terrified and broke, she asked the Social Services of her local council to take the children into care, and she moved from the flat where everyone knew who she was into a one-bedroom place.

'She wanted to get a job, earn some money, and get a bigger place so she could have the boys back,' said Bill Scott, the man who would later become Maureen's second husband.

She found work in a department store. Nobody was openly cruel, but she knew that all her workmates knew who she was. . . .

'And the whispering didn't stop at work,' she said. 'A petition came round the estate where I lived asking people to sign it to get me out. They couldn't bear to think they lived near Hindley's sister. They would all talk behind my back when I went shopping. They were only ordinary people like you or me.

'I learned to stick my nose in the air and close my ears to them. You've got to make up your mind that you are going to stay firm, no matter what you feel inside. You must act hard on the outside and say, "Look, I don't care what you say, I'm not budging."'

There was no comfort for Maureen from her family. At the trial, her mother had supported Myra and turned against her, saying that it 'could be' because of David Smith that Myra was in the dock, and contradicting Maureen's evidence that Myra shopped regularly at Ashton market (where John Kilbride was abducted).

Maureen had not seen her mother since the trial, and her father had dropped out of her life a few months earlier. He had left his wife after discovering she was having an affair with another man, Bill Moulton. He blamed both of his daughters for not letting him know it was going on, and while Myra was under arrest and waiting for trial he told her he would have nothing more to do with her: not because of her crimes but because she had covered up for her mother.

After serving two years of his sentence, David Smith was released from jail. He already knew Mary, the girl who became his second wife, and moved in with her straightaway. He applied immediately for custody of the children. Maureen, who had been visiting them regularly, was distraught. She, too, applied for custody. But her living arrangements were inadequate, and the three boys went to live with David and Mary.

Maureen was completely alone.

But out of the blue came a phone call from one of her aunts. Her mother wanted to see her. Would she agree?

Maureen was delighted: 'It was just as if we'd never been parted. After all, your mum's your mum! We talked about everything.' She moved in to live with her mother Hettie, who was by now married to Bill Moulton and had a modern council maisonette in Gorton, only a few hundred yards from where Maureen had been brought up.

And within a few months came the best thing ever to happen to Maureen. She was waiting for her mother in the Hyde Road Hotel, a short walk from the house. The social life of the Hindleys had always revolved around enjoying a few drinks together, and Hettie and her daughter Maureen were now drinking companions.

At the bar was a lorry driver who tried to chat Maureen up and buy her a drink. She refused. 'She was such a skinny, frightened little toad, all on her own,' says Bill Scott now. 'But she wouldn't have a drink so I called her a silly cow and carried on talking to the guvnor of the pub.'

Bill was a most unlikely saviour.

Twenty-two years older than Maureen, a married man, and a southerner. But he had a couple of very important things in his favour. First of all, he was persistent. He asked her to have a drink on the next three or four occasions that he saw her in the Hyde, and eventually she said yes.

And secondly, Bill must have been one of the few people in Britain who had never heard the names of Brady and Hindley. He did not know who the Moors Murderers were.

'I only ever read the sports pages in the papers,' he says today. 'Headlines didn't mean a thing to me.'

Bill made a regular lorry run from London to Manchester, sometimes being in the northern city for three or four nights a week. 'There was a crowd of us lorry drivers, maybe as many as thirty or forty, and we all had digs around the Hyde Road area. We'd meet up down the Hyde Road Hotel for a few bevvies.'

It was early in 1972 that Bill persuaded Maureen to go out with him for an evening. Their first date was a meal in a steakhouse in the centre of Manchester, followed by a few drinks at a nightclub.

'Then we got in a cab and went to my digs, where I kissed her on the cheek and paid the cabby to take her home, after arranging to see her in the Hyde the next time I was in Manchester. . . . I don't think she could believe that I didn't want anything else from her!'

'We'd had some good fun and a few laughs, and she told me later it was the first time she'd laughed since 1965. All I wanted to do was stop her being as miserable as sin.'

Bill stayed with his wife for a few more months, seeing Maureen whenever he was in Manchester. 'My marriage had been on the blink for years, but I'd never messed around. I didn't believe in it. My five kids were all grown up, so in the end I left my missus and found a flat in

Manchester, which was a good idea because the digs were all being knocked down.'

This was towards the end of 1972. Within a few weeks of Bill moving in, Maureen came to live with him. 'My sole aim in life was to make her happy. She'd suffered so much, and she hadn't committed any crimes. People should have been grateful to her for forcing David Smith to go to the police and shop Brady and her sister. But instead she got nothing but bother.

'I wanted to help her get over that. She told me who she was straightaway, she never mucked about. She told me later she had to screw up her courage to say, "I'm Myra Hindley's sister." And then all I said was, "Who?" It didn't mean a thing. The Moors Murders wasn't so big down south as they was in Manchester, especially as I only ever read the sports results in the papers.'

Bill soon came to realise just how much those few words 'I'm Myra Hindley's sister' really meant.

'I saw the way people treated her. She used to get jostled and pushed in the street, pushed to the back of bus queues. When we lived together we'd get things written outside the flat "Myra Hindley's sister lives here". It was written in letters a foot high on a blank wall near where we lived in red paint. Maureen got up and scrubbed at it with white spirit, because the paint was still wet. But you could still see it.

'So we made a game of it. I used to say to her: it wasn't you, you didn't do anything wrong. I haven't done anything wrong: it's you I'm going out with, not your sister. So it's the other buggers who are making something of it who are barmy, not us.'

Maureen became very dependent on Bill very quickly. She travelled the country with him in the cab of his lorry.

'She started to enjoy life. We had something special that they couldn't spoil. Often, people would try to start rumours that I was seeing someone else down south, just to hurt Maur. What they didn't know was that she was with me when I went down there!'

Maureen's three sons visited her and Bill a few times.

'She'd buy lots of presents for them before they came, and then break her heart again when they went away again.'

Then in 1975, Maureen's newfound happiness was completed. She had another baby, a daughter called Sharon. 'She was over the moon. It was like a seal on our togetherness,' says Bill.

'Something else happened too. Her mother told her that Myra wanted to see her.

'They hadn't had any contact for ten years, so it came out of the blue. Maureen still felt ripped apart by guilt that she'd shopped her sister. So she was pleased that Myra wanted to see her, and we said we'd go down with her mum.'

Bill, Maureen and six-week-old baby Sharon went the following month to see Myra in Holloway. It was the first of many visits.

'They hugged just like two sisters who hadn't seen each other for a while, and they both cried a bit. Myra said it was like old times, as if nothing had happened. They talked about Manchester and people they knew: I just had a cigarette and kept out of it.

'It did a lot to ease tension inside Maur. She felt much better, and after that she and Myra wrote letters to each other. Myra always addressed them to "Mo" or "Moby", which is what she called Maur as a kid. She cramped her writing up really small because she only gets a certain amount of paper, and she'd try to get as much in as possible.

'They were long chatty letters, all about what had happened, who she'd seen, what had been in the papers, Lord Longford. Mo got one most months, although sometimes she'd be fed up because Myra hadn't bothered to write.'

Bill says he has destroyed the letters, but they were doubtless as heavily emotional as all the letters Myra writes from prison. She had worshipped Maureen – her darling 'Moby' – as a child, and now that they were reunited her sister was an obvious target for her over-stated affections.

Maureen herself described her visits to Myra, in an interview with *Woman's World* magazine in 1979: 'I was really nervous the first time. I think, honestly, in the back of my mind, I still had a repulsion for what she'd done, what she'd got herself involved in . . . I didn't know whether I would be able to act normally.

'I went in and there she was. She was nothing like she was when she first went in. Actually, at first I didn't realise it was her. She'd really changed.'

The visits continued. Hettie, Bill, Maureen and Sharon visited Myra every three months in Holloway, and later in Durham.

Myra adored her tiny niece, and decorated her cell with photographs of Sharon. She called her 'Queen' and 'my little ray of sunshine'. And every year, at Christmas and her birthday, there would be presents for Sharon from Auntie Myra.

'Usually they are stuffed toys. Sharon still gets them, even now she's twelve. I expect Myra arranges with one of her friends outside to send them,' says Bill.

Maureen and Bill's happy life together continued, too. Baby Sharon travelled with them in the lorry from the age of six weeks, until she started to go to nursery school at the age of three and a half, and so did Maureen's mongrel dog, Rusty. Gradually, Maureen was getting back the relationships she had lost with all her family. Another one was to come.

Shortly after meeting Myra for the first time in ten years, Maureen also found her father, Bob Hindley. She had had no contact with him since he left her mother, before the trial. She had tried to trace him, but without much success. Until one day a friend of a friend gave her an address in Hopedale Close, Beswick – about a quarter of a mile from her mother's home.

'Maur wrote and asked him if he'd like to see her and his granddaughter. His home help wrote back and said yes.

'We went round there together,' says Bill, 'Maur was nervous, but the old man was really pleased to see us. He had had seven strokes and so he was confined to bed. He was living alone in a council maisonette, but his brother and sister-in-law looked after him.

'He could hardly talk after all those strokes but he and Maur got on like a house on fire, and we went to see him regular after that.'

Eighteen months after Sharon was born, Bill and Maureen were married.

But three years after that, tragedy struck.

Bill and Maureen were having an evening out in the Golden Tavern pub, near to where they were living on Rochdale Road, Manchester, when Maureen complained of a headache.

'I said we would go home but she said she was all right,' says Bill. 'The next morning when I woke up she was spewing her heart out. I called the doctor and he said it was probably just 'flu. But when he came he took one look at her and had her rushed into Monsall Hospital.'

Maureen was transferred that same day to Crumpsall Hospital, where a brain haemorrhage was diagnosed. She was operated on, and started to recover well, so well that she was due to come home from hospital.

'But I got a phone call saying she'd had a relapse. So I rushed down there and stayed with her. She was in a coma and the doctors were rushing around with lots of gadgets. They switched her life support machine off at 11 a.m. the next day.'

Myra was distraught when she heard of her darling sister's illness. The Home Office gave permission for her to be rushed from the top security women's wing at Durham Jail to the hospital. But she arrived just one hour too late.

'When I gently kissed my love, my dove, my beautiful one on her forehead, a feather-light touch of my lips, she seemed to sigh, as much as to say, "I've been waiting for you, you're here now and I can go now."'

That's how Myra described it in a letter to a friend. Bill was present, and so was a neighbour, Mrs Babs Murray, who had spent hours sitting at Maureen's bedside. Bill asked Myra to say hello to Babs, and thank her for everything she'd done.

She wrote that Mrs Murray burst into tears and wept because she had arrived too late for Maureen to know. Myra told her that Maureen did know she was there.

Three years after Maureen's death, Myra described the pain of her sister's death as almost unbearable.

And five and a half years later she made the most bizarre comment to a reporter who visited her in Cookham Wood Prison. She said she saw Maureen's body in the hospital chapel: 'It was the first time I had ever seen a dead person.'

Myra did not attend Maureen's funeral. But because press reports suggested she might, it became an unpleasant affair. Patrick Kilbride, father of John, was there, and so too was Lesley Ann Downey's mother, Anne West.

When Bill Scott's daughter, Mrs Ann Wallace, arrived at her stepmother's funeral, she was greeted with fury. Because she is roughly the same height as Myra and blonde, Patrick Kilbride rushed at her – and was knocked to the ground by one of the other mourners. Anne West started to scream, and police reinforcements had to be called to deal with the scuffle between the mourners and the victims' families and friends.

'You would have thought she could have had a decent funeral. After all, as I keep saying, it wasn't as though she did anything wrong,' says Bill.

All the time, Myra was 200 miles away in her cell at

Durham. But she sent a wreath of carnations and chrysanthemums to the funeral, at Blackley Crematorium, north Manchester. The message on the card read, 'There are no words to express how I miss you. I love you – Myra.'

Seven years after Maureen's death, Bill Scott is still visibly upset. 'There's not a day goes by without me missing her. She was my world. I was with my first wife twenty-five years and with Maur for nine, yet those nine mean more to me than the rest of my life. She was a good kid.'

The year 1980 was a grim one for Bill. A few months before Maureen's death he had been made redundant from his driving job, after more than twenty years with the same firm. He was fifty-six and there was little prospect of another job.

What's more, his health had begun to break down.

He suffers from an unusual medical condition in which the top and base of his spine have started to erode. There is no cure, just a daily diet of painkillers. And he is unable to sit in one place for long, or walk very far. He uses a walking stick.

'It was as though while I was working everything kept going, and when I packed up my body packed up too. Maur and I used to talk about death, but we both thought it would be me that would go first.'

It was Bill's job to break the news of Maureen's death to Bob Hindley: the shock hit the sixty-seven-year-old hard, and his health deteriorated rapidly. 'Mo and I had made promises to each other that whichever of us died first, the other would keep in touch with their family,' said Bill. 'So I still went round to see the old man, regular. I was with him the day before he died. I put him to bed that night. The next day when I went down there, I found he'd died.

'It was the best thing. He couldn't move about and he could hardly talk. And where he lived he was always being broken into – the kids round about knew he couldn't do nothing to stop them. Some of them knew he was Myra's dad, so they used that as an excuse for doing it. He was better off out of it.'

The cause of death was recorded as a heart attack, persistent vomiting, general debility and several previous strokes.

Myra, who had had no contact with him, did not send flowers to this funeral.

Before her death, Maureen had spoken of her hopes that her sister would be released one day, and said that the door of her home would always be open to Myra. Because of that, and his promise to Maureen to keep in touch with her family, Bill Scott continued to visit Myra, taking Sharon with him. She wrote to him. But Bill, who finds reading difficult and writing even harder, was not always able to reply.

'I made the effort once, though. It wasn't long after Maur's death and she was writing to me about how hard it was inside. I wrote back and told her, "It's just as bleeding hard out here." It's a living hell. I've been bothered ever since Maur's death, whether the worry of it all contributed to her illness. I'll never know.'

But Bill did not blame Myra.

He became close to Myra's network of friends, meeting Rachel Pinney and relying on Carole Callaghan for lifts from Euston Station in London to Cookham Wood. He even became the centre of an extraordinary plan to marry him off to Myra.

The plan was to arrange a wedding, in the hope that the promise of a stable married home outside prison would help Myra's parole bid.

Today, Bill denies he ever agreed to it, or even contemplated it. But in 1983 Myra was writing about it in a letter from Cookham Wood to her friend Carole Callaghan, who was the go-between in the bizarre plot.

'Forget the bridesmaid, matron of honour or best man or anything bit, I ain't marrying no one unless it's on my own terms and I don't think they'd be acceptable to Bill.'

She said that although she loved him it was as a brother and not as a potential husband. She said he had misinterpreted her looks of 'loving affection and compassion'.

'I seem to have a trait that results in some people picking up what I'm not putting out, a wrong interpretation of the vibes. Apparently I also give the impression that I'm putting out when it's news to me that I am.'

According to Carole Callaghan, Bill was willing enough at the time, and what went wrong with the plan was Myra falling head over heels in love with another prisoner.

But Bill says, 'It never happened. I can remember it being suggested, and just laughing. Since Maur died I haven't wanted to marry again, although it might have been a good idea for Sharon's sake. But not to marry Myra – that would have been a packet of trouble.'

Until she was eleven, Sharon visited Auntie Myra regularly, with her father and her grandmother, Hettie.

Before Maureen's death, she and Bill had discussed how one day they would have to tell Sharon the truth about her aunt. 'When she is old enough for it to sink in and intelligent enough for her to understand,' said Maureen at the time, 'I will take her to the newspaper section of the library and let her read all about it for herself. She will then have to make up her own mind about it.'

With his wife dead and a daughter to bring up on his own, the burden of deciding when to tell the child about Auntie Myra has fallen on to Bill. 'We thought that eleven would be the right sort of age to tell her, but it came earlier than that. She was about nine when she really understood. Before that, I think she realised we were visiting prisons. But she'd done it from birth, she was used to spending one day every few months travelling all day to spend a couple of hours with her auntie.

'I told her in little bits and pieces, so as not to overload her. I told her Auntie Myra had done some bad things when she was much younger and didn't know what she was doing. I told her how everybody does some bad things – and then gradually I told her more. She didn't really ask questions. She seemed to take it all in her stride, finding out about it gradually.

'But now she's a bit older she makes it clear she doesn't like it. She knows she's the same age as Lesley Ann Downey was. She's found it hard to believe that Myra did that. She's trying to take it in. You can't force it.

'Some of the kids at her school know who she is, and they say things. But there is one thing Maur and I learned, and that's how to cope with all that. I've brought Sharon up to cope in the same way, by treating it as a game.

'I'm hoping that the nastiness will die out – after all, her name isn't Hindley. By the time she's leaving school and trying to make her own way, I hope everybody will have forgotten who she is.

'It's tough enough having lost her mother. A mother is always top pin in a kid's life, a father can never quite take a mother's place. I've done my best, but it's not been easy.'

Myra partly blames the near-breakdown she had in the summer of 1984 on the problem of telling Sharon about her past.

'Too much prison and too many hassles, too much publicity and too many brainwashed prisoners; too much noise; too many pressures – and a problem about the necessity of telling Sharon I'm in prison, a problem as yet unresolved, though not for the want of trying,' is how she described her need for three months in the Cookham Wood sick bay.

From inside, Myra has mobilised her forces to help Bill, arranging for clothes to be bought for Sharon. Her letters are preoccupied with organising lifts to get them and her mother to the prison. 'Sharon is simply beautiful and it was lovely to see her and hold her,' she wrote in a letter, 'I really enjoyed her last visit with all of us together, and this place ceased to exist for the duration of the visit.'

In another she wrote, 'I'm looking forward to seeing my little ray of sunshine again.'

But Myra has not seen her 'queen' now since 1986. 'We've stopped going,' says Bill, 'Ever since she confessed to the other two killings. Maur had asked Myra outright twice about those two kids. She was especially worried about Pauline Reade, because she and Myra knew the family when they were kids.

'Myra denied knowing anything. She said she would never have left that poor woman Mrs Reade suffering all these years. Maur believed her. Now she's admitted she was lying, so I reckon that lets me out of my promise to Maur that I would carry on visiting her. Also, I think it's wrong for Sharon now. She doesn't want to go, she doesn't want anything to do with Myra.

'You see, young as she is, she knows how it has spoiled all the lives of those around Myra. And she dreads it when something appears in the paper. "Oh, not again," she says, because all the bad feeling is stirred up.'

Sharon is the only one of her four grandchildren Hettie Moulton sees. But when newspaper headlines are full of Myra, Hettie refuses to leave her home, even to visit Bill and Sharon. At all times, the curtains are drawn across the windows, upstairs and downstairs.

'She sits in there in darkness, rocking backwards and forwards in a chair. She has the telly on but she doesn't watch it,' says Bill.

'Sharon normally goes there for the weekend, but she can't since it has all been in the news again. We wouldn't risk it. People always turn on the old woman for what Myra did. So when Sharon sees anything in the papers or on telly, she knows it means she won't see her Nan for a while. She hasn't got much family – all my lot live down south – so her Nan means a lot to her. They sit and talk together, watch telly, or they go out and do a bit of shopping.

'Normally at Christmas her Nan takes her down to town

to see the lights and do some Christmas shopping, but not when Myra is in the news. So Sharon misses out. At Christmas in 1986, when they'd just started digging on the moors again just before Myra's confession, she didn't see her Nan at all.

'Funny how it all seems to blow up over the papers around Bank Holiday times. Me and Sharon have had a lot of holidays spoiled by it, because we've had to stay indoors.

'I'm happy-go-lucky normally, but I can't afford to be careless for Sharon's sake. There are always people after her, trying to find out about her.'

Carole Callaghan, in one of her financial liaisons with a newspaper, turned up at Bill's flat with a reporter in tow, introducing him as her new husband. Once inside he said who he was and tried to persuade Bill to give him a photograph of Sharon. Bill learned from that that he must never leave any photos out on display.

'Sharon knows her life is different from her mates'. One day I should think she may resent that. Or she may grow up and want to go and see Myra – I'll leave it until she's older and let her make up her own mind.

'I'm finished with Myra now.'

But Bill's promise to Maureen keeps him in touch with Hettie.

'I've never really seen eye to eye with the old lady, but I won't have anyone hurting her. She's been hurt enough already. She's only the mother, but people try to make out it was all her fault. Lots of people have tried to persuade me to move down south, after all I'm a Londoner, and nobody would know me and Sharon there. But if we left, what would there be in life for Hettie?'

Hettie has now given up work, but until police started searching the moors again for Pauline Reade and Keith Bennett she had been working in the early morning as an office cleaner.

'Then when the newspapers started following her to

work she gave up, and she has hardly been out of the house since,' says Bill.

Hettie and her second husband, Bill Moulton, do no more than co-exist. He no longer travels with her to visit Myra, although he did in the early days of her imprisonment.

'When she got life, so did we,' he says. 'We shall suffer for ever. Our lives are in tatters. We just want to be left alone to forget the past.' He says that if she was ever released she could not live with them.

'I do not want to see her or talk to her again. Myra is on her own. Her mother's health is going down fast. How do you think she feels when she reads these dreadful stories about her daughter? She is a broken woman. Stories about Myra being a beast and evil obviously upset her, because in her heart she loves her.'

Bill's retired, and spends as much time as he can afford away from the house in one of the several local pubs he visits. Hettie rarely goes with him. And while the pressure of publicity is on, he does all the shopping for her.

Myra does not approve of him. In a letter to a friend written in July 1983 she bemoans the fact that her mother was having to do three different cleaning jobs.

'She really misses Maureen – she's got used to me not being there, yet her eyes still fill with tears when she has to go. But Maureen used to go round and hassle her out of any rut she was in, and make her get changed and go out for a drink with them, and she always enjoyed herself in spite of being reluctant at first.'

She blamed her stepfather for her mother working too hard, and said that if either Maureen were alive or she were free they would be able to take care of their mother properly.

Hettie has coped with even more abuse over the long years than Maureen did. And she's coped by isolating herself from everyone around her. She doesn't speak to her neighbours.

When she goes out, she scurries along the pavement, with her face turned away from passers-by.

But like Maureen, and Bill Scott and, until recently, David Smith, she's refused to move away from the area and start a new life in a different part of the country, where her connection with Myra would not be known.

'We've talked about it,' says Bill Scott, 'and the old lady feels like the rest of us. This is where she's from. Why should she move? But it's a living death for her.

'She got through all those years by never believing her Myra did anything. She hates Ian Brady and thinks it's all down to him. But she feels a shame from it all, and that's why she locks herself away.

'When Myra confessed to being involved in the other two, that hit her really hard. I still think she hasn't taken it in. She's still somehow convincing herself that Myra's innocent. I don't know how she stays sane.'

So, at the age of sixty-eight, when most women are settling down to a contented old age with their knitting and their grandchildren, Hettie Moulton's life is empty and blighted.

The only time she has ever spoken in public about Myra is when she told a *Sun* journalist in June 1985 that her daughter would be better off dying in prison.

'It's better she dies there than comes out of prison and gets killed out here. Myra's been in prison all these years now, so what difference does it make if she stays there forever? If Myra came out she couldn't come here. I don't know where she would go. People wouldn't let her alone. She might as well die in prison.

'Poor Myra. Life means life for Myra. For others it means just a few years. When they call her a beast or a devil, they don't know what they are talking about. They don't know her. She is still my daughter. I love her just like I always have done. Something like that does not change.'

Hettie has turned down offers of hundreds of thousands of pounds to tell her story, although she lives in near poverty.

'We would rather be poor than cash in on Myra's misfortune,' she says, looking as bewildered today as she did in the witness box at Chester Assizes, when she answered a question about her two daughters with the reply, 'I have always done my best for both of them.'

David Smith's life, too, has been permanently blighted by his involvement in the case. Ian Brady and Myra Hindley had tried to drag him into their crimes at the trial. While the public agreed with the jury that their protestations of innocence were false, at the same time it has never quite accepted David Smith's innocence. Mud sticks: and in Manchester it has stuck hard to David Smith. He has lost jobs, been banned from pubs, his children have been taunted at school and attacked in the street, and finally he has been forced to leave the area.

His second wife, Mary, was only fifteen when he moved in with her family after coming out of prison and finding his marriage to Maureen a write-off. A year later she was pregnant with David's daughter, Jodie, now a pretty teenager. Before they could marry, David faced court again: this time accused of murder for the mercy killing of his father, who had terminal cancer. The court freed him.

Today he lives in Lincolnshire with his three sons, Paul, David and John, now strapping young men, Mary and Jodie. The family experienced a short-lived relief when after her confession Myra stated that there was no third person involved in their crimes: it seemed to the Smiths that at last David had been exonerated, and they might be allowed to get on with leading a normal life.

But shortly afterwards Geoffrey Dickens, the Tory MP whose constituency includes Saddleworth, announced that there *was* a third man involved in the killings, and that he was expecting the police to make an arrest. The finger pointed immediately at David Smith again, and in no time the press had tracked him down to his new home.

David Smith hates Myra more than he hates Brady. 'She is the worst. At least he had the decency to go mental. How could she smile at the children, knowing all the time that Brady was going to squeeze the last drop of breath from them?' And he adds that the years of silence have been as wicked and cold-hearted as the original murders.

Like all the other victims of the Moors Murderers, David Smith no longer expects to be free of the scourge that has blighted his life since, as a young and impressionable teenager, he tagged along with Ian Brady's schemes. He knows that he, too, is serving a life sentence.

15

Confession

Where was Ian Brady all the long years that Myra was hoping and praying for parole? He, too, was being moved from one prison to another. But he had found life on the other side of the wall a very different proposition from Myra's. There were no love affairs for him, no escape plots to while away the years, no long tête-à-têtes with the prisoners or prison staff, no Open University degree.

Prisoner 602217 was in solitary confinement, his only diversions books and the radio, his Braille work (he translates books into Braille for the blind), the occasional visitors, including Lord Longford – and a mental game of chess he was playing with 'the girl', Myra Hindley. He felt her rejection of him acutely, and from the moment that she broke off contact with him he channelled his mental energies into regaining some of his old power over her.

It had never deserted him: while there were still two bodies unaccounted for, two children still officially listed as missing, he knew that 'Hess' could never afford to turn her back on her 'Neddie' completely. Every so often, he found ways of reminding her just how dangerous he was.

When Lord Longford appealed for her release in 1977, Brady sent out a letter which was published in the *Daily Mirror*, saying that Lord Longford did not represent his views on the subject of parole, and that he had stopped seeing him as a result of his constant fight on behalf of Myra.

'I have always accepted that the weight of the crimes

both Myra and I were convicted of justifies permanent imprisonment, regardless of expressed personal remorse and verifiable change.'

Myra clung lamely to the fact that he said 'convicted of', not 'guilty of'. When William Whitelaw announced that Myra would not be considered for parole until 1985, Brady again wrote a letter rejecting consideration. 'I shall not require the parole board's consideration, in 1985 or even 2005.'

After the *Sunday Times* articles appeared, Lord Longford wrote to Brady claiming he had been 'conned' by the journalists: Brady promptly wrote to the *Sunday Times*, again reiterating, 'The weight of the crimes both Myra and I were convicted of justifies permanent imprisonment.' He added that Lord Longford was right in saying he had been conned – but not by the *Sunday Times*.

Again, in April 1985, one month before Leon Brittan was due to make his announcement about Myra's parole, Brady had another letter delivered to a journalist, this time at the BBC. It was the same theme: he did not want any part in any 'political farce' of parole consideration. As ever, the timing was impeccable. Not only did it pre-empt the Home Secretary's announcement, but each time that Brady published his views it prompted newspapers to run opinion polls on whether he and Myra should be released. The results were always the same, the British public gave a decisive thumbs-down to any suggestion of parole for the pair. It did not matter which newspaper conducted the survey: the *Times* found 83 per cent against their release, the *Sun* found 86 per cent.

Ian Brady, lonely, and increasingly psychotic, was still able to pull the strings and manipulate Myra. And in the summer of 1985 he determined to show just how much power he retained.

Brady allowed a journalist, Fred Harrison from the *Sunday People*, to visit him several times in Gartree Prison, Leicestershire. Harrison claims that during their meetings Brady confessed to several more killings, most notably those of Pauline Reade and Keith Bennett.

The information he claims Brady gave him is largely inaccurate. The details of Pauline Reade's death do not square up with what Brady and Myra subsequently told the police, and Harrison claimed that Brady confessed to the murder of Philip Deare (police are satisfied that Deare was not one of Brady's victims), as well as other murders that it has been impossible to substantiate.

However, the detail didn't matter. The impact on Myra was enormous. She had been in a severe depression since the announcement that she would not be considered for parole for another five years, which had coincided with another close girlfriend, Shirley, being released from Cookham. A pair of scissors vanished from the prison kitchen, and a massive search by staff was launched, because there was a real fear that Myra was intent on committing suicide. All the prisoners were locked in their cells for two days until the scissors were found, in another part of the prison, where they could have been hidden by Myra.

She was so depressed that, for one of the few times in her years in prison, she did not take another lover. Her succession of girlfriends had continued, with often more than one at a time (one threesome she was involved in was nicknamed The Pervert Sandwich by other prisoners). But after the rejection of her parole bid she lost interest in everything, and lived in the prison hospital swallowing tranquillisers. Her solicitor Mike Fisher was taking her case for parole to the European Court of Human Rights but that didn't afford her much consolation.

When the news of Brady's confession broke, she was already precariously unbalanced. But she reacted with venom, angrily denying it and telling those around her that it was just Brady's way of hurting her. She even told another prisoner that she would not have left 'that poor woman' Joan Reade, the mother of Pauline Reade and a woman Myra knew, in suspense for so long.

She said, 'God, I really want to scream this prison down, but I have to think of 118 women in here who are just waiting for me to crack. I have to repress everything, every facial expression, when all I want to do is throw myself on the floor and scream.'

She wanted to scream even more when, a few months later, Fred Harrison hit her for six again. By this time he was working for *Today*. The headlines screamed, 'Hindley Confesses: We Killed Another Child.' The 'confession' was based on claims from a woman who said Myra had admitted to her involvement in the death of Pauline Reade. The woman, a nurse at Holloway, claimed she had heard Myra screaming about Pauline's death in the maximum security wing at Holloway nearly twenty years earlier. The only other witness to the outburst, she said, was the spy Ethel Gee, who had recently died.

It did not matter that once again the version of events did not tally with Myra's own knowledge – or Ian Brady's. What mattered was that Myra could see that the question of the other murders would never go away. There would always be Fred Harrisons raking over them. And what's more, if Brady was giving interviews – however garbled – to journalists, how long before he decided to talk to the police? After the publication of his 'confessions' he had been visited by Manchester police, though he had refused to co-operate with them – but he could always change his mind about that.

Ian Brady had achieved his own personal end with his 'confessions' to Harrison. The publicity, coupled with increasing pressure from the prison medical service, had resulted in him being transferred from prison to a secure mental hospital, Park Lane, in Liverpool, where conditions were easier for him, and where at last he was able to receive treatment for his deteriorating mental health.

Cynics have suggested that Brady pretended to be psychotic to 'work his ticket' to the softer regime of the hospital. They claim that he was sane whenever he wanted to be, mad when it suited him. But all those who had close dealings with him were in no doubt that he needed hospital treatment. Years of solitary confinement, with no more than minimal contact with prison staff, had crumbled his mind. His occasional lucidity was mingled with bouts of acute paranoia and deep depressions.

Immediately before his transfer to Park Lane Hospital Brady was in Gartree Prison, where he lived in the hospital wing. He mixed only with the other prisoners in the hospital, preferring to spend his time alone in his cell. He was hallucinating: imagining that he could hear voices asking him questions about his crimes, coming from the radiators, the radio and his tape recorder. He slept little, and at night could be heard cursing the judge, the prosecution lawyers, Myra, the Home Secretary and Margaret Thatcher. He is a rabid left-winger, and in his lucid moments used to harangue other prisoners about politics.

Much of the time he needed to be sedated, and the drugs left him slow and muddled. He is a compulsive eater, with a taste for anything excessively sweet. At Gartree he would spend his money on packets of icing sugar, custard powder, dried fruit and sweets, and at mealtimes he would eat huge portions. But he remained skeletally thin until a problem with water retention caused him to swell up and made his gaunt features bloated.

At night he refused to sleep on his bed, preferring to huddle over his radiator in a chair, clutching plastic bottles filled with hot water. Some nights he would fall asleep and burn his legs, chest and even his face on the radiator. He was too well protected for other prisoners to wreak vengeance, although one ex-prisoner has claimed that his water retention problem was caused by ground glass (from a light bulb) being put into his food.

His physical health has improved since his transfer to Park Lane, and he enjoys the improvement in his surroundings. His fascination with tape recorders has never left him, and he was astonished to see a video recorder. But his mental health is undoubtedly precarious. He is dogged by the same hallucinations. He still needs large amounts of sedatives, which leave him shuffling and zombie-like, and he talks regularly about suicide.

Since he arrived at the hospital his mother, Peggy, now a widow in her late seventies, has started visiting him again. In prison he refused to allow her to visit because he felt it would cause problems for her, both in travelling to see him and in reprisals from other prisoners' relatives. But he has written to her regularly, and because Park Lane is only thirty miles from her home she is able to visit.

He has also been visited by two young girls, both of whom appear to be fascinated by him. One, who was put in touch with him by Lord Longford while she was a student at Edinburgh University, had a long correspondence with him about philosophy and Russian literature. The other, from Manchester, wrote to him and visited him, eventually making the astonishing – and improbable – claim that she believes Brady is her father. There are other regular correspondents, the majority of them attracted by a ghoulish obsession with him and his crimes: the same sort of inexplicable obsession that led to Wardle Brook Avenue becoming a regular sightseeing spot for day-trippers. When the house was pulled down in 1987 (the council found it impossible to get any tenants to stay there) bricks and other bits of rubble from the demolition were taken away as souvenirs.

Psychopaths, as one forensic psychiatrist said, often have very compelling personalities, and the power that Brady had wielded over Myra does not appear to have entirely deserted him.

Hospital strengthened him, and with strength came a willingness to re-examine his life before jail. Ill though he was, he reached the situation of being able to look back at the truth of the crimes he and Myra had committed long before she was able to. She had built around herself the defence of her own version of events, a version in which she was near-innocent. It was a dream-package that probably saved her sanity during her years in Holloway and Durham – and saved her physically, too, because it was the sincerity of her protestations of innocence that persuaded others to believe her and protect her. She had come to believe her own lies.

It is a common psychological trick: at a much lesser level most people distort some aspect of their own behaviour to present themselves in a more favourable light to themselves.

Brady, whose version of events even at the trial was nearer to echoing his true involvement than Myra's, had since 1977 (and possibly earlier) been accepting responsibility for the crimes for which he had been convicted. To admit to the others was not a repudiation of the fabric of his life as it was for Myra.

Early in 1986 he formed an unusual alliance: he started corresponding with Mrs Ann West, the mother of Lesley Ann Downey. Just as Brady's words and actions had dogged Myra's prison years, so too had Ann West's. How any mother will react to the loss of a child in brutal circumstances is impossible to gauge. Mrs West and her husband Alan have become obsessed. They had dedicated their lives to the pursuit of the Moors Murderers – particularly Myra Hindley.

'I don't just hate her once a day, once a week, once a month. Hindley is inside my brain all the time,' she said. Ann West has become an expert at handling the media. She knows who to phone with each new development in her story. She has cried on television, pleaded on radio, poured out her heart in print. When Myra was moved to Cookham, Ann West camped outside the prison for a few days. On another occasion she tried to buy a gun. Twice she had to fight sick attempts by pop groups to cash in on the Moors story. Her husband at one stage tried to get a job in the prison service in the hope that he would get near to Ian Brady.

Just as Joan Reade coped with her tragedy by retreating into an impenetrable shell, and Winnie Johnson survived the years on a diet of tranquillisers and the support of her large extended family, and the mothers of John Kilbride and Edward Evans preferred to nurse their grief away from the spotlight, so Ann West coped by seeking attention, parading her agony in public. Myra grew to hate her name, because with it would come a new wave of hostility.

In February 1986, Mrs West announced that she would like to visit Ian Brady and wrote to him, asking if he would see her. For the next few months they corresponded, and he said that he was willing to meet her. But the Home Office vetoed the plan for her to visit him.

'I can assure you personally of the remorse I feel, but I prefer actions to words,' he wrote, 'I have spent the last eighteen years doing Braille work. I know I can't balance the past, of course, but at least I can do something positive and useful.'

He told her that it took him weeks to reply to her first letter 'because I couldn't find the words to cover pain and further distress. I only knew that I had to answer'.

Their subsequent correspondence covered the weather, his mother's 'flu, her family problems, and his constant theme of hatred for the press.

While this surprisingly cosy relationship was developing, Myra's routine life in prison continued. She took part in the national Sport Aid charity run, clocking up six miles round the prison grounds with seventy other prisoners. She was given permission by the Home Office to start work on her own autobiography, encouraged as ever by Lord Longford. But despite gaining official permission, she has not yet started work on the book.

In July she learned that her case had been rejected by the European Court of Human Rights as 'inadmissible'. In her application, her lawyers had argued that her treatment in Britain's prisons had been 'degrading' and that as a normal life sentence is fourteen years (in fact, the average time served by lifers is ten and a half years), she, who had been in jail for more than twenty years, had been discriminated against. But she had not pinned too many hopes on the European court, and was not as profoundly depressed by the news of the rejection as she had been a year earlier, when she learned she had not been granted parole.

Throughout this time she was seeing the Reverend Peter Timms, a Methodist minister and ex-Governor of Maidstone Prison. Mr Timms first visited her in September 1983, at the invitation of the Roman Catholic chaplain at Cookham Wood, who had worked with him in the prison service. The priest knew that Mr Timms was used to dealing with prisoners, particularly counselling long-term prisoners, and that he lived near Cookham Wood. He was an ideal support for the priest, and was allowed as much access to Myra as if he was her spiritual advisor (clergymen, priests and other spiritual advisors are allowed free access to prisoners).

'He is a committed Christian, and yet a man with so much experience of prisoners that he is not duped by them. You don't get anything past Peter Timms. Yet at the same time he knows there is good in everybody and he looks for it,' said an ex-colleague of his.

When he first met her, Peter Timms brought with him David Astor, ex-editor of the *Observer*, and a personal friend. Astor became another of Myra's supporters.

She was continuing with the spiritual exercises she had started under Father Shearwater at Durham. She had found friends among the staff at the prison, and was still enjoying the comparative luxury of Cookham Wood.

But there was a growing disquiet about the past, either caused by her conscience or by the fear that Ian Brady was on the verge of a full confession. This fear was compounded when, in November 1986, his correspondence with Mrs West was made public, in a newspaper, Mrs

West stressing that she had only entered this unholy alliance to try to get information about the missing bodies.

In the same month, and almost simultaneously, two things happened to Myra Hindley. First, she received a letter from Mrs Winnie Johnson, the mother of Keith Bennett.

'For years I thought everybody had forgotten about Keith. Occasionally someone would bring the subject up in the newspapers. Once a man came to the door and said he had information about Keith being buried in a scrapyard, but the police came and after a bit they told me to take no notice of the man, he was a crank,' said Winnie.

'But then it all started to come up again. It was in the news all the time. I'd managed to get by, trying not to think about it. But then I decided I had to try to find out what happened to my boy. So although I hate and detest Myra Hindley, I knew I'd got to hold a light to the candle. I had tried writing to Ian Brady, and I never even got a reply. My letter lay unopened on his desk, the doctors told me, because he was too frightened of its contents to even slit it open.'

The idea of actually writing to Myra came from Winnie, but a journalist helped her compose the letter: 'Dear Miss Hindley, I am sure I am one of the last people you would have ever expected to receive a letter from. I am the mother of Keith Bennett, who went missing no-one knows where on June 16 1964. As a woman I am sure you can envisage the nightmare I have lived with day and night, 24 hours a day since then.

'Not knowing whether my son is alive or dead, whether he ran away or was taken away is literally a living hell, something which you no doubt have experienced during your many, many years locked in prison. My letter to you is written out of desperation and faint hope, desperation because I know that for so many years neither you nor Ian Brady has ever admitted knowing anything about my son's disappearance, and hope that Christianity has softened your soul so much that you would never any longer knowingly condemn someone to permanent purgatory.

'Please, I beg of you, tell me what happened to Keith. My heart tells me you know and I am on bended knees begging you to end this torture and finally put my mind at rest. Besides asking for your pity the only other thing that I can say is that by helping me you will doubtless help yourself because all those people who have harboured so much hate against you and prevented your being released a long time ago would have no reason left to harbour their hate. By telling me what happened to Keith you would be announcing loudly to the world that you really *have* turned into the caring warm person that Lord Longford speaks of.

'I am a simple woman, I work in the kitchens of Christie's Hospital. It has taken me five weeks labour to write this letter because it is so important to me that it is understood by you for what it is, a plea for help.

'Please, Miss Hindley, help me.'

The letter profoundly affected Myra. It was the first time she had had any direct contact with the family of one of her victims, and it reinforced her feeling that the time was approaching when she would have to speak out. Cynically, she knew the crescendo of publicity that was building up was not going to die down. But she appeared also, to those around her, to be genuinely moved by Winnie's letter. She showed it to Peter Timms, and she and he were working on a reply to it when the second important development happened. Myra had a visitor.

Detective Chief Superintendent Peter Topping, head of Greater Manchester CID, had been a uniformed bobby when young Pauline Reade and Keith Bennett had gone missing. He remembered Pauline's case well: Gorton was the area of Manchester where he pounded the beat, he knew the streets where Myra played as a child, he bought hot pies from the same baker's shop that Myra used to run to for a loaf for her Gran.

Ever since he became the head of CID, he had been studying all the old case notes, talking to the policemen involved in the original investigation. He had two unsolved murders on his books, and, however long ago they had happened, he wanted to clear them up. A married man with two young daughters, he understood as well as anyone just how deeply the Moors Murder case had eaten into the soul of a whole city. But the futile visit to Ian Brady had demonstrated to him that he had to handle the two murderers with care if he wanted any co-operation.

He had a reputation for toughness and determination. Before his promotion he had led a three-year investigation into corruption in the Manchester force, which concluded with the 'bent coppers' being brought to trial. He was well aware that results take time.

When he arrived at Cookham Wood he was not expecting instant success. Remarkably, he got a bigger breakthrough than he had anticipated. Winnie's letter had convinced Myra that she should help the police, whether out of genuine pity or self-interest, and although she was not prepared to admit any involvement in the killings, she told the detective she was prepared to look at old photographs and maps to locate spots she had visited with Brady. As Topping had by this time probably made his decision to reopen the search regardless of whether or not she helped, she was again adroitly manipulating an existing situation to best advantage.

Peter Topping's personality had a lot to do with his initial success. He belied Myra's memories of policemen: he was quiet, polite, considerate. She had only experienced the tough adversarial role of the detective, bent on breaking her down before the trial over twenty years before. Now she experienced a different approach. Peter Topping was shrewd enough to know that a woman who had not broken in over twenty-one years in custody, a woman who had survived the rigours of prison relatively unscathed, was not going to crack under browbeating. She would talk if she wanted to: otherwise she would continue to parrot her protestations of innocence. He played his hand right: Myra liked him, Myra talked.

In a statement made through her solicitor, Michael Fisher, Myra said, 'I received a letter, the first ever, from the mother of one of the missing children, and this has caused me enormous distress. I have agreed to help Manchester Police in any way possible, and have today identified from photographs and maps places that I know were of particular interest to Ian Brady, some of which I visited with him. In spite of a 22 year passage of time, I have searched my heart and my memory and given whatever help I can to the police. I'm glad at long last to have been given this opportunity and I will continue to do all I can. I hope that one day people will be able to forgive the wrong I have done, and know the truth of what I have and have not done.

'But for now I want the police to be able to conclude their inquiries, so ending public speculation and the private anguish of those directly involved.'

The statement again implied her innocence, and laid all blame at Ian Brady's feet. From his hospital room in Liverpool he struck back: he revealed that he had love letters written by Myra during their early prison years, and he implied that these could prove she was not an innocent dupe under his evil influence at the time of the killings. The correspondence was given to his solicitor, Benedict Birnberg, who said, 'He is annoyed with Myra Hindley, stung by what she has told the police. He was very concerned that she should be made aware that letters she wrote to him over a long period of years when they were first in prison are still in existence.'

Myra's response came via her solicitor. She was not, Michael Fisher said, deterred by anything Ian Brady might say or do. 'She is determined to give the police every help in resolving these mysteries.'

Topping's team started digging on the moors at the

worst possible time of year, November. It was raining
sideways up on Saddleworth, and it continued to do so
until the rain turned to snow, which in turn was washed
away by heavy rain. Police dogs helped the search, despite
the fact that the trail was twenty-two years cold. RAF
spotter planes were called in to take new photographs,
which were shown to Myra. Experts scoffed at the chances
of finding anythiang in the shifting terrain of the peaty
moorland, and MPs started to clamour about the expense
and waste of manpower.

There was an air of déjà vu on the moor itself. The cars
looked more streamlined, and now the reporters and
photographers fiddled with their push-button in-car telephones instead of having to drive off down the road to
queue at a public phone box. But the card games they
played behind the misted windows of their vehicles were
the same as another generation of newsmen played
twenty-one years earlier. And the misty, aching cold of
the moorland had not changed for centuries.

Meanwhile Winnie Johnson wrote to Myra again, this
time asking to meet her. Her request was widely
publicised, including quotes from Winnie referring to
Myra as 'that monster', and photographs of her outside
Cookham Wood. After consultation with Michael Fisher
and Peter Timms, Myra turned down the meeting. Her
solicitor said it would be 'enormously distressing' for both
sides.

Against a background of immense media speculation
about whether Myra would be taken to Saddleworth to
help with the search, Peter Topping approached the
Home Office for permission to do just that. There were
tremendous security implications: the fresh interest in the
case had rekindled all the old hatreds, and there were
threats that if she went up to the moors she would not
return alive. Only Paul Reade, brother of Pauline, was
singing a different tune: let her live, he said. 'I've always
hoped in my heart no harm would come to Myra. She and

Brady are the only two people on earth who can bring our family some peace of mind.'

The Home Secretary, Douglas Hurd, agreed with Topping that it was worth the risk. He gave permission for Myra to go. 'Time will tell if she knows something,' he said.

Just after half past four on the bitterly cold morning of Tuesday, 16 December, a convoy of four police cars left Cookham Wood Prison in Kent. At roughly the same time, police were sealing off all roads to Saddleworth Moor. Two hundred policemen, forty of them armed, were driven up to the moor. An hour later, Myra and her solicitor Michael Fisher boarded a helicopter at an airfield near Maidstone for the 250-mile flight. It touched down just after 8.30 a.m.

Myra, who left Cookham Wood with a headscarf round her head, was issued with a donkey jacket and balaclava (the same as her police guards were wearing) to keep out the biting wind, and to protect her from being identified by the hordes of press photographers, none of whom got close enough to get a recognisable picture of her through their telephoto lenses. Three journalists who did stray inside the police lines were made to lie face down on the sodden ground and were searched for weapons.

By 3 p.m., after she had been driven and had walked around the area, she was taken back to the helicopter, and whisked back south. She returned to Cookham Wood at quarter past seven, driven through the crowds of pressmen in a blacked-out van.

Michael Fisher explained how Myra felt about the day: 'She said it was strange, that she had lost her bearings in all that open space after so many years in prison,' he said. 'It took her a few hours to recognise the place. She was confused and frightened. She was particularly worried about the helicopters overhead. She was asking, "Who are they?" The idea was obviously in her mind that someone could be trying to take a pot-shot at her. At one point about six helicopters were hovering above and she broke down in tears. To Myra they were incredibly threatening, very noisy and she didn't know who was in them. It was all too much for her.'

The British public reeled at the presumption of such fine sensibilities from a woman who, as the press constantly reminded them, had killed children.

Myra wasn't the only one it was too much for. Flak flew from all sides, most of it aimed at Peter Topping. The day on the moors was described as a 'fiasco', a 'publicity stunt', a 'mindless waste of public money'. There were no immediate results, no bodies discovered. Topping became everybody's favourite target.

He was driven to defend himself publicly. He said he had been taken aback to find Myra willing to help. 'That dimension eventually fuelled an enormous fire. We realised it was not possible to keep such a visit secret. It was bound to leak out that we were either about to speak to her or had spoken to her.

'We had taken the view that we needed a thorough systematic search of the moor which would be recorded in grid form. It would never have been possible to carry out such a search in private.'

He said that Myra's visit to the moor had helped a lot. The sceptics remained unconvinced.

Throughout that winter, when the search had to be called off because of the appalling weather, Peter Topping continued to visit Myra Hindley. So, too, did Peter Timms and of course Michael Fisher. It took two and a half months, but eventually Myra was ready to confess. She made the decision herself, although both Timms and Fisher were pushing her towards it.

Michael Fisher's policy of openness was quite startling to journalists working on the long-running story. He spoke to them pleasantly, answered questions, persuaded his client to put out statements. It was less of a formulated policy, more a derivative of his personality and his instinctive feeling that any rehabilitation of Myra would have to come through the people who had, in part at least, been responsible for perpetuating her imprisonment: the media. He wanted her to be completely frank about her role in the crimes, partly because he cared for her as a person, and partly because he felt that was his best way forward as her lawyer.

After his divorce from his schoolteacher wife, Myra's role in his life had become increasingly dominant as the case commandeered the headlines. He admitted 'my last relationship broke up when I was accused of being in love with Myra Hindley'. He works for her unpaid, except for the legal aid she was granted while suing the *Sun*, and at this stage being Myra's lawyer was almost a full-time job.

'But I am a criminal lawyer, and this has got to be one of the best cases ever. I have made less money than I would have done otherwise, but that doesn't matter.'

His concern for Myra is genuine. Before she made her confession to Peter Topping in February, Myra's various advisors held a meeting to decide how she should proceed. David Astor arranged for them to meet Lord Goodman, perhaps Britain's most celebrated solicitor, for him to adjudicate whether it best served Myra's interests to confess. It was really a meeting to test Fisher's fitness to continue in the job: if Lord Goodman had ruled that the young solicitor's tactics were wrong, her friends (notably Lord Longford, who was not at the meeting, but who advocated a policy of silence) would have tried to persuade her to change him. Fisher argued his case for confession to Lord Goodman. Peter Timms, who supported him, listened intently. Eventually, Lord Goodman gave his opinion: Myra Hindley's freedom was not the immediate concern, because there was no foreseeable chance of that. The press would never let the story go: she should confess.

Fisher and Timms were relieved, because they knew that Myra had already made up her mind to do it, but was finding it hard because of the warring factions of her advisors. Now, with confirmation that it was not only her best road forward morally but also legally, the path would be smoother.

Months later, when the meeting was presented in a newspaper as a conspiracy to 'break Myra Hindley', Fisher and Timms were both angered.

'We did not conspire to break her. We did not need to, she had already decided to see Peter Topping and make a full confession. We simply wanted reassurance that we were handling the case correctly,' said Michael Fisher. 'Any attempts to present those of us around her as heroes who conspired to "break" her is ridiculous. The heroine in this story is my client. She has been very very brave.'

The bravery of Myra Hindley is something that the public finds hard to appreciate. Nonetheless, it would be wrong to dismiss entirely the personal courage that was needed for her to admit her part in the crimes that she had, for nearly twenty-three years, been denying. She did not risk the loss of her liberty, but she risked the loss of many friends and family who had swallowed her pro-testations of innocence whole. Her mother had survived by clinging to her belief in her daughter; her brother-in-law was bringing her niece up to reject all the popular conceptions about her aunt; there were endless other people like Rachel Pinney and Honor Butlin who had supported her in the belief that she was the victim of terrible and cruel circumstances. There would be, she knew, a massive wave of renewed hatred outside the prison. And inside, the risk of physical attack would be greatly increased.

Myra confessed in February 1987. She spent four days with Peter Topping. Because there was a clampdown on publicity by Topping, Michael Fisher and anyone else in on the confession, the news did not break until over a month later.

In the meantime, Myra had received another letter from

Winnie Johnson, sent privately. It again pleaded with her to help the police find the body of her son Keith: 'The trouble is that a lot of people as I am sure you know have said that your visit to the moors was pointless because you never intended to help the police, just enjoy a day out and string everybody along. I do not believe that and I cannot believe that because it is the only thin thread that I have to hang my hopes on.' She went on to beg Myra to give more help to the police, or to agree to see her.

This time Myra replied, thanking Winnie for both of her letters and explaining that she had not answered the first one because of the publicity surrounding it.

It is an astonishing letter in which Myra claims that if Mrs Johnson had written to her fourteen years earlier (after she had broken with Brady) she would have been as willing to confess and help the police find the missing bodies as she is today. It is an unlikely assertion: fourteen years ago she was just getting into her stride with her 'poor wronged innocent Myra' act.

Also in the letter she paid tribute to Peter Topping, describing him as very different from the original police officers handling the case. She thanked Mrs Johnson for believing in her sincerity, and told her that she prayed regularly for her and the other victims' families.

She said she hoped that one day the rest of the British public would be influenced by Mrs Johnson's Christian attitude into forgiving her a little. She promised to write another, longer letter in the future. Her letter was delivered to Winnie Johnson with a covering note from Peter Timms.

The search of the moors had resumed, and Myra was taken there again, this time with considerably more secrecy than on her first visit. She stayed in Manchester overnight, in the flat of the police chief in charge of the Greater Manchester Police Training School at Sedgley Park, Prestwich, and went up on to Saddleworth twice.

After her visit, police started searching with metal detectors. They were trying to locate a metal box that Myra had told them about, which they believed contained photographs and other evidence. They also adopted a new system of searching, carefully on their hands and knees removing all the topsoil, a technique taught to them by archaeologists. Peter Topping, dressed in a boiler suit and armed with a small trowel, a field telephone by his side, joined his small team of nine on his knees in the stinking, soft peat.

In April Myra's confession became public. It received all the attention she knew it would, leading the television and radio news bulletins and being splashed across every national newspaper. Mrs Winnie Johnson was photographed up on the moors. Mrs Ann West said how relieved she was for the other families, with whom she had suffered, she said, for so many years. Lawyers argued in print the pros and cons of another trial.

Lord Longford weighed in with a plea that she should eventually be released, 'It isn't right to keep her in prison just to satisfy mob emotion. Myra was a nice girl before she met Ian Brady and she is a nice girl now. To say she is an evil fiend is completely wrong. With a possible inquest and trial coming up, I'm not seriously suggesting she should be released immediately. But with a saner appreciation of her character, it should be possible in the future.'

Michael Fisher's telephone line was permanently engaged and he was besieged by reporters every time he visited Myra. He said, 'I have warned her that she could be walking into a murder charge. She accepted that. She wants to put an end to the case and at the same time do her public duty.'

Because of the intense media interest, he persuaded Myra to put out a statement, 'When I was arrested, tried and convicted I was still obsessed and infatuated with Ian Brady. I could not bring myself to admit the truth about our crimes.

'Between 1966 and 1977 I served my sentence in Holloway Prison. There I did what I could to hide the truth from myself and from others, believing this was the only way I could survive the ordeal of a very long prison sentence.

'From 1977 to 1983 I served my sentence in Durham, where I became completely ostracised from the outside world, living a totally unreal life with thirty or so life and long-term women prisoners.

'I was aware that public hostility towards me was if anything increasing and I reacted by withdrawing more and more into myself.

'In 1983 I was transferred to Cookham Wood prison. This move was interpreted by some as a first step towards my eventual release but I knew this was simply an alternative prison for me. Since I have been here I have received considerable help and encouragement which has strengthened my resolve and I began to become more confident that I could be open and frank about my case.

'Throughout my sentence I have been haunted by the continued suffering of the relatives of the two children who were missing at the time of my arrest, and until recently I have been utterly overwhelmed by the numerous difficulties of revealing the truth.

'I have had to consider the consequences for my family who have suffered far more than I have and I have been fearful of the effect that facing up to the truth would have on me and my existence in prison, which has always been a tremendous ordeal.

'In 1985, under the personal direction of a Jesuit, I continued the Ignatian Spiritual exercises which I began in Durham prison with the Jesuit chaplain. These spiritual exercises lasted over a year and gave me great strength and brought me closer to God than I have ever been before. It was then I realised I could no longer live a lie.

'The former prison governor Peter Timms, now a Methodist minister, agreed to help me with the task ahead. His experience of dealing with life sentence prisoners and their cases has been invaluable.

'On 31 October I received a letter from Mrs Johnson begging for help. This was the first such letter I had ever received and on 18 November I resolved to assist the Greater Manchester police who had reopened the case of the two missing children.

'I felt able to co-operate with the officer leading that inquiry, Det Chief Supt Topping, whose approach to me was professional but kind and sympathic.

'I was taken to the moors a few weeks later and did what I could to identify the places where I believed the children were buried. However, this trip was frustrated by the enormous press interest and by the weather.

'It was to Peter Timms that I first was able to make a full admission of guilt and immediately afterwards I instructed my solicitor to contact Det Chief Supt Topping who attended at the prison with his assistant, Det Insp Knopfer to hear my voluntary statement on 19, 20, 23 and 24 February.

'In this statement I admitted my role in these awful events and said that I considered myself to be as guilty as my former lover, Ian Brady, although our roles were different.

'Later I was taken to the moors secretly and out of the glare of publicity I was able to be far more specific about the location of the graves and I now believe that I have done all that I can in helping the police in this respect.

'I know that the parents of the missing children may never be able to forgive me and that words of mine can NEVER express the remorse I now feel for what I did and my refusal for so long to admit to the crimes.

'I hope that my action now in making my confession to the police will speak louder than any words. I want nothing more than to help the police find the bodies so that their poor relatives can at last have the comfort of giving them a Christian burial.

'To those who believe that I am seeking some narrow advantage I would stress that I am in my 24th year of imprisonment, that my next parole review is not due until 1990 by which time I will have served 26 years.

'I have informed the Home Office that I do not wish to be considered for release on parole in 1990 and for as far ahead as I can see I know I will be kept in prison.'

The Reverend Peter Timms immediately became the focus of media attention but he, like Michael Fisher, relinquished any heroic role, insisting that Myra had reached the decision to confess alone. He was more temperate in his praise of Myra.

'I can't say I admire her – that word has the wrong connotation – but I respect her courage. She has done the right thing. I'm very pleased at the outcome of the turmoil she has been through. She could have kept silent. She has nothing to gain from speaking now, except perhaps some peace.'

He asked the parishioners at his church in Gillingham to pray that some good came out of Myra's revelations, and although he admitted that his role in the affair, and the attendant publicity, had brought some abusive telephone calls he said that most people had been understanding.

The debate about whether Ian Brady and Myra Hindley ought to stand trial again continued, with the balance of informed opinion being that it would be a pointless waste of money, and that Brady would probably be deemed unfit to plead. There were calls for a new trial from Peter Bruinvels (then a Conservative MP) and others, including some relatives of the victims. Myra herself said she was prepared to stand trial, although it would be an ordeal for her mother as well as for herself. She stressed that, contrary to some rumours, she had never asked for immunity from prosecution in return for her confession.

'I feel as if I have been on trial for 22 years, and whatever sentence a court can pass it will not exceed my expectation of life imprisonment,' she said.

She exonerated her ex-brother-in-law David Smith from any part in any of the murders apart from Edward Evans, and she even wrote for the first time in many years to Ian Brady, asking him to help police in their search for the missing bodies, and telling him that if he did not it would be because 'for your own selfish and morbid gratification, you do not want this whole ghastly nightmare to end'. She sent the letter via the BBC, thus publicising her rather dubious claim to the high moral ground. Brady did not reply directly, but told his solicitor he regarded Myra's plea as a public relations stunt.

The search of the moors was continuing, but experts were still criticising the project as an impossible task and a waste of resources. Topping countered them with 'God help us when we come to the day when we don't investigate murder'. But his name was becoming a byword for hopeless causes: in the force they joked that 'They'll be putting him on the Glenn Miller case next'. The number of reporters and photographers up on Saddleworth watching the painstakingly slow progress of the small task force had dwindled, and so had the stream of sightseers. Snoopy's Café, the mobile tea caravan from Huddersfield – which sells hot drinks and snacks from the isolated car park close to Hollin Brow Knoll on the Lancashire–Yorkshire border all year round, search or no search – was reporting business more or less as usual, after selling out of bacon sandwiches day after day to hungry newsmen and macabre tourists.

Then on 1 July 1987, after more than 100 days of digging, they found a body, lying in a three-feet-deep grave just 100 yards away from the spot where Lesley Ann Downey had been found nearly twenty-two years earlier. The discovery was made towards the end of the afternoon, but it was another two hours before four men from Topping's team, translated into stretcher bearers, carried the remains of Pauline Reade from the grave where she had lain for twenty-four years. Had she lived, she would have been a mature woman of forty.

There was the same mixture of elation and sadness that another team of policemen had felt on that same spot. But Peter Topping's feelings, which he kept well-hidden, must have included a large measure of relief. At last, the critics would be silenced.

The news that Pauline's body had been discovered came too late for Mrs Reade, living in a psychiatric hospital. 'All the years of torment and agony have got to her,' said her husband Amos. 'She's in a world of her own. She doesn't even talk about the moors now.'

Pauline's brother Paul, now with two children of his own, was just one of the people to renew the clamour for a trial – and to bring up, again, the accusation against a 'third person'. Geoffrey Dickens, the Tory MP for the area, went on television to say that he had evidence of a third person's involvement. David Smith was forced once again to deny any role in the deaths of the children found buried on the moors – and if he had experienced any relief at Myra's exoneration, he knew now that the minds of the people of Manchester were indelibly dyed with a belief in his guilt.

Myra heard that the body had been found from a newspaper report. According to Michael Fisher, she was upset and relieved. 'She shed tears, but she is relieved that after all this time something has happened,' he said.

For Winnie Johnson, the discovery of Pauline's body was a difficult development. She of all people did not begrudge the Reade family what relief it gave them, but it intensified her own feeling of loss and isolation. Bereavement counsellors do not underestimate the need for the tangible focus of grief that a body and a grave provide. Mothers of stillborn babies are today encouraged to hold their infants for a few moments, and to take photographs of them, so that in the agonising weeks and months ahead of them they will be able to channel their sorrow into mourning, and recover from it. When the dead child was removed before the mother had time to see it – which hospital staff did in the misplaced belief that it was better for the mother – the healing process took much longer.

And so it is for Winnie Johnson, and for countless others who have lost close relatives in unexplained circumstances. Winnie began to see a psychiatrist regularly, to help her prepare for what was ahead: the discovery of Keith's body would be traumatic, but for it not to be found would be worse.

After the body was found, Brady made a formal confession to Peter Topping. He had been co-operating with the police for some time before the body was discovered – Topping was with Brady when Pauline was found. Now there was a rerun of Myra's first visit to the moors, only this time the star of the massive media show was Ian Brady.

The visit was a fiasco. Brady's mental state had degenerated so much that he was unable to get his bearings or contribute any useful information. There is the possibility that he was deliberately withholding help because of some tortured perception of himself still holding the trump cards in a macabre game he had been playing with the police and with Myra for years. But even that bears testimony to his derangement: it is unlikely that he could have survived being taken into the open vastness of the moors after nearly twenty-two years in close confinement without mental trauma.

But the fact that Peter Topping had risked taking him there underlined a fact that was becoming increasingly apparent: Myra had only been able to help with detailed information about one grave.

Myra's relationship with Peter Topping was going through a difficult phase: she resented Topping having any contact with Brady. She was possessive about her nice policeman, she didn't want to share him. She was enjoying her role as the one who had done the decent thing: she didn't want to share that moral ground with Brady.

'She has a childlike capacity to throw her complete trust into people. She did it with Peter Topping. Then she was terribly hurt when he didn't ring her, didn't come to see her as often as he had been doing,' said Michael Fisher.

'And she was annoyed with him that he took so long finding Pauline Reade's body. She gave him very good information about how to find it. On the other body, she gave him a clue that he thought he could crack – information about something, not a body, buried on the moors. He preferred to go after that first, and he failed to find it. We believe he would have been better going for Pauline Reade's body first.'

But after Brady's failure to contribute anything useful, she felt redeemed. And her relationship with her nice policeman was strengthened again after a bizarre letter from Brady to the BBC, claiming responsibility for five more killings. The letter was a reprisal from Brady for Topping's refusal to allow him to visit the moors again: 'I keep repeating that I need a second chance at it, but with no success.'

He then went on to throw at Topping the accusation that he had given the policeman details of five more killings (or 'happenings' as Brady refers to them). 'He does not seem interested in them. For example, a man on a piece of waste-land near Piccadilly [Piccadilly Manchester, not London], a woman in a canal, a man in Glasgow and another on the slopes of Loch Long etc. The latter two were shot at close range. There's another on the opposite side of the Moor road. One had a rag tied on a wooden post as a marker. But unknown to me all the wooden posts had been changed to plastic.'

Topping's reply to the public reprimand from Brady was to say that inquiries had been started into his allegations. Myra's reply was that she knew nothing of any of these killings, and Topping believed her.

The inquest on Pauline Reade opened, hearing touching evidence of identification from her father, who recognised the pink party dress his daughter had worn for the dance the night she had disappeared. The funeral followed. Mrs Reade, pumped full of tranquillisers, attended with two nurses from the mental hospital that is now her home. It was August, but Manchester was rainswept and cold as the coffin was lowered into the ground of Gorton Cemetery under the unremitting gaze of the national press. The burial followed a Requiem Mass at the Monastery of St Francis, where Myra had attended the funeral of Michael Higgins many years before, and had started her conversion to Roman Catholicism.

Mrs Ann West, Mrs Winnie Johnson, Patrick Kilbride, father of John Kilbride, and two of John's brothers were at the funeral, and among the wreaths there was one from Peter Topping's team.

It made moving copy in the newspapers next day, and Myra knew what to expect. She was attacked twice by other prisoners, but she was not seriously hurt.

'The officers were expecting it too,' said one ex-prisoner, 'She was never out of their sight long enough to take a real hammering. But it was enough to let her know how people felt about her.'

After her confession, the Home Office had withdrawn from the Reverend Peter Timms the right to visit Myra freely, reneging on a previous commitment they had made to him that he would be able to help her for as long as she needed. He still sees her, but has to go on a VO, the regulation permission to visit that prisoners send out to their friends and families.

'That hit her very hard indeed,' said Michael Fisher, 'She needed all the support she could get, and the Home Office withdrew it. But she is surviving all right. She has a great measure of support from certain members of the staff at the prison, and they have helped her through. She has weathered the storms with other prisoners, and she feels reasonably secure.'

It was, perhaps, a false sense of security and a belief

that she was to some extent rehabilitated that prompted Myra to write to Ann West. It was a long, detailed letter expressing her remorse, once again exonerating David Smith from involvement in any killing other than that of Edward Evans, and attempting to offer some comfort to Mrs West. It contained adjectives and similes that Myra must have absorbed from popular press coverage of the case: she wrote of 'heinous crimes' and described herself as 'an utter disgrace to womankind'.

But there was one sentence that destined the letter for the sensational treatment it was given, splashed across the *Sun* and the *Daily Mirror* (who paid Mrs West a substantial sum for the right to publish it, and her reply to it). The sentence read, 'I now want to say to you, and I implore you to believe me, because it is the truth, that your child was not physically tortured as is widely believed'.

Although the word 'physically' was included, from which, if she is telling the truth, we can deduce that Lesley Ann Downey was not sexually assaulted (and that belies the evidence of a sexual element in all the other killings) it was the denial of torture that etched itself into the public consciousness.

Even taking the evidence at face value, Lesley Ann was stripped, made to pose for photographs, bullied, and her suffering tape recorded. She was then killed. To any right thinking person, that constitutes torture.

It was a very odd assertion to make. And it was even odder that Myra and Michael Fisher both flung up their hands in horror when the letter was published, claiming that it had been a private letter written for Mrs West's eyes alone. They knew, or should have known, from experience that the letters Ann West had received from Ian Brady had found their way into print, that the letter Myra had written to Winnie Johnson and that many other letters written by her over the years have been made available to journalists.

Why did she write it? One interpretation has got to be that she is, once again, building an image of herself to herself. She has abandoned her 'I am an innocent and much wronged woman' stance. She faces many more years – if not a lifetime – in prison. Is she now building herself another survival kit? Caring Myra, the woman who did not torture children, but only killed them?

Time, and how she handles the inevitable further developments, will tell.

16
The Future

Myra Hindley is Britain's longest-serving woman prisoner. She has been in prison for more than twice the length of an average life sentence. The year 1988 marks a mid-point in her life: twenty-three years of freedom before her arrest, twenty-three years of imprisonment.

The vast majority of people in Britain believe she should stay in prison. She herself apparently now accepts that her future will be spent behind bars, and has given up her sustained campaign for parole, although it is possible that by publicly espousing an attitude of guilt and humility she is working towards a long-term goal of freedom.

Should she, could she ever be freed? It is a question that has taxed successive Home Secretaries, all of whom have come to the conclusion that she cannot be released – at least, not during their term of office. Myra has described herself as a political prisoner, implying that she is unjustly trapped by the reluctance of any Home Secretary or Prime Minister to grasp the hot potato of her release.

There are many different reasons proffered for why, as a society, we incarcerate those who offend against our laws and mores, and what we expect that incarceration to achieve. There's the deterrent model: we hope to prevent others emulating the behaviour of criminals by demonstrating that the consequences of that behaviour are unpleasant and unrewarding. For crimes like Brady's and Hindley's it is difficult to talk about deterrents: they were mad crimes inspired and committed by a psychopath who, under the definition of psychopathy, had no thought for the conseqences of his actions. Brady could never have been deterred by threat of punishment: indeed, when the crimes were committed the death penalty was in force. He was almost as obsessed by punishment as he was by murder (he dwelt on the Marquis de Sade's theories of punishment, and he revelled in Dostoevsky's *Crime and Punishment*). Myra Hindley, too, whose mental condition at the time of the crime is much more difficult to gauge, was nonetheless obviously beyond reason, and shared Brady's mad tenet of invincibility. Similarly, other mad men who embark on indiscriminate multiple murders will not be deterred by the long sentences Brady and Hindley have served.

Then there is the rehabilitation model: the belief that we put people in prison to train and educate and treat them, so that when they emerge they will not be driven back into a life of crime. This model has been largely abandoned, although its theories were current in the 1960s when Brady and Hindley were jailed. By 1977, in an official review of the prison service, it was accepted that 'research findings give little support to the view that imprisonment can directly alter the long-term behaviour of prisoners', and in 1979 the May Report into the prison services proclaimed 'we think that the rhetoric of "treatment and training" has had its day and should be replaced', in other words, if a prisoner does turn his back on crime after a prison sentence, it will be because of some external impetus, not because he has gained deep insights into himself and his behaviour through the treatment he has received from the experts available to him in prison.

Myra Hindley's followers, though, would argue that she is the exception that proves the rule. They believe that she has changed and developed in prison, and that this is, in some measure at least, due to the facilities that have been made available to her (access to her religion, to education, to the attention of committed visitors like Lord Longford and Sarah Trevelyan), facilities which were not so easily available on the backstreets of Gorton.

It is unarguable that she has changed on the surface: the tough, smug, rather common young woman has matured into a quietly spoken, well-educated woman in her forties (the 'schoolteacher with a bit of money'). It is also unarguable that, should she be released, she would not revert to crime, and certainly not to the appalling crime of murdering children. Whether it was prison or the removal of Ian Brady from her life that 'cured' her *is* arguable, but the result is the same: she would desist from murder either because of a now-genuine abhorrence or because she has simply 'learned the lesson' that such socially unacceptable crime does not pay. If prison is seen to be there to 'cure' criminals, the end result is all-important, and she would by that criterion be deemed to be cured.

Another reason that society imprisons its offenders is for protection: to protect the innocent in our ranks from the violation of their persons or property by the criminal. Although this model does not have the same high-flown idealistic motivations as the rehabilitation model, the measure of its success must be the same: if the criminal will not reoffend we no longer need to be protected from him or her.

But then we come to the retribution model. This means, in essence, that prison is there to punish the criminal: and it is for retribution that more than 80 per cent of the British public consistently vote for the continued imprisonment of Myra Hindley. There are faults in the overall application of the retribution model to crime and imprisonment (the American system of drawing up a league table of punishments and applying them to the crimes, not the criminals, was found to be fundamentally faulty because it did not take account of mitigating circumstances or the differing degrees of pain offenders would feel at the same punishment).

However, if there were such a system of laid-down

punishments here in Britain Myra Hindley's crimes would be off the scale. There are some things that can never be punished enough: and that's the public view on Myra Hindley's offences.

All the protestations of piety, all the demonstrations of change, all the arguments about the inhumanity of her indeterminate sentence are outweighed by the fact that for two and a half years she lived a life of such unremitting moral degeneracy that she has put herself beyond the pale, outside the normal considerations of efficacy of sentence. The bottom line is that she participated in the sexual torture and killing of children: from that there can be no return.

There is yet another reason why Myra Hindley is held in prison, a reason appreciated by even her staunchest supporter, her mother Mrs Hettie Moulton. 'My Myra must die in prison,' she said, the only words she has ever uttered publicly on her daughter's predicament. She recognises that, in Manchester, feelings run so high that Myra Hindley is being held in custody for her own protection – and to protect the relatives and family friends of the victims from the consequences of their own actions. If she were ever released, there would be a race between the Kilbrides and the Wests to see who could get to her first. Nothing save her death will assuage their hatred.

They, and many others, believe that, of the Brady–Hindley partnership, she is the more evil. The evidence belies this: Brady was the general and she was the lieutenant. But, as Mrs Ann West points out, Brady has 'had the decency to go mad'. The world can accept, now that he is demonstrably unbalanced, that he was perhaps never responsible for his own actions. Insanity does not excuse evil, but it makes it more comprehensible.

Myra, on the other hand, is seen as quite sane. What's more, she is clever, manipulative and she has friends and allies: all these things make her a more suitable focus for anger and hatred than an isolated, lonely, sick man.

And she is also, and this is the most vital consideration, a woman. Women do not commit crime on a comparable scale with men (there are 45,700 men in prison compared with 1,700 women). What's more, 75 per cent of all women offenders are found guilty of theft or handling stolen goods, and more than half of those who go to prison go for not paying fines (usually imposed for theft or prostitution offences). More than half of all women in prison have been given sentences of less than eighteen months, and 50 per cent of these are in for less than six months. Women prisoners, in other words, are petty offenders serving short sentences.

Even those who are in for long sentences (there are fewer than seventy women serving life sentences compared with 2,200 men) commit a different sort of crime from their male counterparts. Leaving aside the IRA bombers, the murders committed by women tend to be 'crimes of passion', albeit sometimes cold-bloodedly executed. The victims are usually lovers or husbands.

Women commit sexual crimes so rarely as to be statistically non-existent.

Myra Hindley is a woman who offends against all these 'norms'. She is unique. Prison officers and prisoners alike talk about another case, one that has gone into prison folklore as paralleling hers in enormity and repulsion: the case of Carole Hanson, who has been in jail since 1970. They quote the Hanson case as an example of how a woman can be committed to prison for appalling crimes and yet not attract media attention on the scale that Myra Hindley has. Yet none of them knows the details of the Hanson case: the myths that surround it have compounded it out of all recognition. It *was* a horrific crime: young children were enticed into the Hanson household to take part in 'sex games' with Carole Hanson and her husband Michael, and eventually one small girl was murdered. But if we judge horror by the death tally, then Myra Hindley's crimes are five times as odious – although the Hanson case, and that of Mary Bell, are the only two in recent history even to approach hers.

So her notoriety, and that of the whole Moors Murders case, rests upon the fact that she is a woman. Had Brady committed the offences alone, or with the aid of another man, the case would have made massive headlines at the time, but his name would have been all but forgotten by now. As for his assistant, a male who took as unequal a role in the actual killing as Myra did would have been quietly released on parole many years ago, after serving perhaps ten or fifteen years in prison (the variable that might have affected that is that prison life for a male sexual offender who preys on children is so horrific that solitary confinement becomes a necessary protection, with all the concomitant results in terms of his mental health).

We do not expect women to kill. More importantly, we never expect women to kill children. The evidence that condemned Myra Hindley to a lifetime of being hated and reviled was the evidence of the tape: a little girl pleading with a woman to help her against unimagined horrors is a very potent image, and one that no amount of 're-habilitation' can dispel.

She was, as she said herself in her letter to Lesley Ann's mother, 'an utter disgrace to womankind'. We have higher standards for women than men when it comes to comforting, protecting and succouring little children. All our deep-rooted (and biologically sound) conceptions about women come into play.

Research evidence shows that although on the whole women are treated more leniently in court than men, where their offences go 'against the grain' of the traditional ideas of femininity, women are actually treated more harshly than men by the courts. No offences ever committed have cut more deeply across the grain than those of Myra Hindley, and it is that that has led us – via the press – constantly to pick at the sore of her presence in our midst. Had she and Brady hanged, by now her name would be folklore.

Perversely, it is her singularity that has helped to protect her in prison. Her notoriety – which she deeply resents – has worked to her benefit by attracting to her women who are prepared to protect her physically. And it has made prison staff acutely aware that she is a focus for violence ('whenever there's a heatwave or it's near Christmas or any other special time, we know we've got to keep an eye out for Myra'). She has been hit and kicked and spat at countless times, but she has only received one severe beating. Other women, in prison for much lesser crimes, have had worse treatment.

It has also helped in the pursuit of her love life. Her name alone attracts attention, and she compounds this by her cultivated aloofness. She has no shortage of lovers, and many of them remain devoted to her for at least some time after they leave prison.

Is she really a lesbian, or is it what forensic psychiatrist Hugo Milne describes as 'facilitative lesbianism'? In other words, there are no men so women will do. Even animals indulge in homosexual activities when deprived of members of the opposite sex. Myra has had no physical contact with a man since Ian Brady was arrested, and he was her only male lover. She is now very experienced at female love and sex: she has had relationships that have been short-term and purely sexual and she has fallen deeply in love several times. She is immersed in feminism ('my only politics are feminist politics,' she says) and is committed to lesbianism, although she has admitted to friends that she is curious about heterosexual sex. Before she met Ian Brady her pin-up was Elvis Presley: today it is Martina Navratilova.

She has now reached a major watershed in her life. After nearly twenty-two years in prison, she finally confessed the truth about the killings, which was a psychological breakthrough for her. She was able to do it and survive it largely because Cookham Wood is a good prison, where staff, though bedevilled by shortages, do their best for the prisoners. The only women who complain about Cookham are those who have never been in Styal or Durham or Holloway for long. Myra is more comfortable, physically, than she has been throughout her sentence – although it is not accurate to describe conditions in Cookham as 'like a four star hotel', as newspapers do from time to time. The long-term loss of liberty, the noise, the lack of privacy and the inability to make any personal choices that are inevitable in prison mean that there is no need to compound imprisonment with appalling deprivation (like the women in Durham endure).

Although she may secretly believe she will one day be freed, she realistically accepts that this is long-distance planning. Perhaps just through growing older, she no longer suffers from the 'rampant gate fever' that beset her in Holloway.

'It is very difficult to see how public opinion about her will ever change,' said Michael Fisher. 'All the people who hate her so much and who stir up publicity against her are roughly the same age as her. They're not going to die away, and neither is their hatred. Myra knows this, and she sees her future as prison.

'I myself actually believe that in light of the confessions, she may eventually be released: but not for at least another ten years.'

One of the main problems Myra and her advisors now face is what to do about her confession. When the Director of Public Prosecutions has ruled that there will be no second trial, that means the only details to be released about how the children were actually killed will come out at inquests: the method of Pauline Reade's murder, and the respective parts in it played by Brady and Hindley, is known. If Keith Bennett's body is ever found, we will hear the details of his death.

But for the others, John Kilbride and Lesley Ann Downey, there is no public forum where the circumstances of their deaths can be revealed. Perhaps Detective Chief Superintendent Peter Topping will choose to tell the families what he knows: he has before him two confessions, one from Brady and one from Hindley, made independently and at a time when there was no collusion between them, and they tally very closely. The only discrepancies are those that are to be expected when two people recall events that happened a quarter of a century ago. The documents in Peter Topping's possession are undoubtedly the truth: there is an obligation on the authorities to share that information with the families.

Myra Hindley herself is toying with the notion of publishing her confession, either by writing her own book or by issuing a lengthy statement through her solicitors. The first course of action might prompt Brady into spiking her guns by issuing a statement himself. He certainly accepts that his future will be spent under lock and key, and he would lose nothing by publishing his confession.

Myra, on the other hand, might gain some narrow advantage by having the whole subject opened for discussion. The confessions will reveal that she really was the second in command, not the prime mover, in all the crimes, and that she did not take part in killing any of the victims. It will not exonerate her (as both confessions exonerate David Smith from involvement in any of the deaths except Edward Evans) but it might mean that she could anticipate parole many years hence.

'What she did in not confessing until now is reprehensible, indefensible. She will have to pay for that for a long time to come, in addition to the crimes themselves,' said Michael Fisher.

At the end, there is only one really interesting question about Myra Hindley, and it is one that will never be answered. She herself has volunteered differing answers, and her inability to be honest with herself as well as others invalidates them: Why did this plausibly normal woman commit such appalling crimes?

Dr Hugo Milne says, 'Sometimes I think we look too hard for explanations. The capacity for evil is a sliding scale, and we are all on it somewhere. Some of us are more capable of evil than others: but that doesn't mean we go out and commit crimes like these. Myra Hindley had the capacity for evil, and the impetus to commit it.'

Lord Longford's answer is that Myra was a nice girl before she met Brady and is a nice woman now – infatuation with Brady is the total explanation for her crimes.

Mrs West and Mrs Johnson both believe that she was and is a monster, an inhuman creature who cannot be discussed rationally.

Michael Fisher admits it is the one question he does not know the answer to. 'It is what we will never know: just how innately evil she was, as opposed to being under the influence of a very evil man.'

The most famous book published after the trial of Adolf Eichmann was called *The Banality of Evil*. It is the banality of Myra Hindley's personality that makes it possible for Lord Longford to use the word 'nice' about her: by nice he means ordinary. But finding that someone is ordinary for 99 per cent of their lives does not excuse them that 1 per cent of gross abnormality which, in Myra Hindley's case, allowed her to help her lover kill children.

And even if it were possible to answer Michael Fisher's question, would it make any difference? We cannot condone innate evil, but no more can we condone those who allow themselves to be influenced into evil.

The bottom line for Myra Hindley is that she committed acts that the vast majority of the population would not be capable of committing. She can never atone for what she has done but she can be – and is being – punished. It is right and fitting that her punishment should be lifelong.